The Grammar of the Machine

Edward W. Stevens, Jr.

THE GRAMMAR
OF THE MACHINE

Technical Literacy and Early Industrial
Expansion in the United States

YALE UNIVERSITY PRESS NEW HAVEN AND LONDON

Published with assistance from the foundation established in memory of Philip
Hamilton McMillan of the Class of 1894, Yale College.

Designed by Nancy Ovedovitz and set in Century Expanded type by Tseng
Information Systems, Inc. Printed in the United States of America by
Edwards Brothers, Ann Arbor, Michigan.

Library of Congress Cataloging-in-Publication Data
Stevens, Edward, 1938–
    The grammar of the machine : technical literacy and early industrial
expansion in the United States / Edward W. Stevens, Jr.
    p.   cm.
    Includes bibliographical references and index.
    ISBN 0-300-06106-4
    1. Technical education—United States—History.   I. Title.
    T73.S63   1995
    607.1'073—dc20   94-41615
                                           CIP

A catalogue record for this book is available from the British Library.

The paper in this book meets the guidelines for permanence and durability of
the Committee on Production Guidelines for Book Longevity of the Council on
Library Resources.

10 9 8 7 6 5 4 3 2 1

To Claudette

Contents

Acknowledgments

Acknowledging the sources of one's inspirations and ideas is always difficult, not because the names and influences are forgotten but because the
paths of influence are subtle and complex. Much of my motivation to continue studying the history of literacy and education can be traced to my
colleagues and their work. I will always be indebted to Daniel Resnick,
Harvey Graff, Carl Kaestle, Lee Soltow, and Bill Stephens for their enduring work in the field of literacy studies. Paul Mattingly and David Tyack
provided good advice at critical times in the preparation of this work.

There is, as is often the case, one person without whom this work would
not have taken shape. Steven Lubar of the National Museum of American
History, Smithsonian Institution, guided me through the world of technology and its history when I was a short-term fellow at NMAH in 1988
and again in 1989. For this opportunity and his assistance I am grateful.
While I was studying at NMAH he shared his insights into the world of
technology with me and introduced me to the records, documents, and literature necessary for carrying out this study. He was more than generous
with his time and with his own collection of books, and he made access to
the resources of Smithsonian easier. I cannot thank him enough.

I am also indebted to the many librarians and archivists who made my
research possible. These include those who searched and answered questions at the rare book rooms of the NMAH, the Library of Congress, and
the Hagley Museum, as well as the staffs of the National Archives in Washington, the Massachusetts Historical Society, the Cincinnati Historical
Society, the University of Cincinnati, the State Library of New York at

Albany, and Ohio University. Special thanks go to Barbara Wiley, librarian at the Emma Willard School, and to John Dojka, archivist, and Cari Palmer, assistant archivist, of the Folsom Library at Rensselaer Polytechnic Institute. They made my stays pleasant and led me to sources I had overlooked. Well-informed guides at the Hagley Museum in Wilmington, Delaware, and in Lowell, Massachusetts, gave me much-needed visual contact with the material world of technology.

I wish also to thank Alan Myers, dean of the College of Education at Ohio University, and William Rader, director of the School of Curriculum and Instruction at the university, for their willingness to arrange for my leave to study at the National Museum of American History.

Finally, I acknowledge my long personal relationship with Lawrence Corwin, who opened my eyes to the spatial world of technological thought.

To all these people I owe an enormous debt of gratitude. I am mindful, however, that while the strengths of this work can be traced to many, its weaknesses are mine alone.

THE GRAMMAR OF THE MACHINE

Introduction

Defining a New Literacy

Between 1820 and 1860 the American economy moved steadily toward a manufacturing base and greater mass production, even though most Americans made their living on farms. At the same time, common school reformers succeeded in extending the availability of public schooling to most children of elementary-school age, even though school attendance itself varied by race, ethnicity, region, urbanity, and family income. Historians have often assumed that these trends have some causal connection and that traditional literacy, a product of public schooling, also served the interests of the expanding economy.

The first hint of difficulty with this interpretation lies in the nature of the work demanded by an emergent industrial economy. Without question, much of it was low skilled, but those special skills that were indispensable to technological progress and mechanized production were not taught in most public schools. A strong argument can be made that the socializing effects of schooling reinforced mainstream Protestant values and the discipline of the factory. But this argument explains neither the sources nor the nature of the skills and knowledge needed to feed the new economic engine. Public schooling responded to changes in the organization of labor as labor became the object of the new discipline of the factory. That response, however, was ambiguous and tangential. Most curricula in public schools, in fact, ignored that knowledge immediately relevant to technological change, including *applied* mathematics and science.

In this book I argue that between 1790, when Oliver Evans invented the automated hopper grist mill (patented 1791), and 1853, the year of the New York Crystal Palace Exhibition, a new literacy emerged that was qualitatively different from (though it included) alphabetic literacy. I call this "technical literacy" to signify that it had a close relation to new technologies but shared some attributes of traditional, alphabetic literacy.

The transfer of technology and indigenous technological development, the emergence of an entrepreneurial manufacturing economy, and the launching of a democratic experiment in the United States in the late eighteenth and early nineteenth centuries set the stage for this new type of literacy, which was expressed in multiple notational systems and strongly linked by its advocates to the development of new man-machine relations in the workplaces of American manufacturing.

The relation between the material aspects of technology and technical literacy was governed largely by deictic terms that acknowledged, like literacy in general, a shared meaning. Thus the relation between technology and its expression was both experiential and symbolic. The skills and knowledge that underlay technical literacy were also metaphors for technological progress. These skills released the imagination and were the means for translating imaginative thought into practice. Democracy, in turn, unified the intellectual, practical, and moral aspects of civilized life.[1]

Technical literacy required mastery of four notational systems and their related vocabularies and grammars: alphabetic expression, scientific notation, mathematical notation, and spatial–graphic representation. Mastery of these "languages" led to cognitive growth and to acculturation into communities that determined membership by such mastery. This should not be surprising, for in many respects new technologies and the resultant organization of labor were as much cultural events as material achievements.

The literacy that accompanied new technologies was a bearer of dreams and values as well as a producer of material wealth. It was more comprehensive than the people who shaped it and the machines within which it was embedded. While it transcended the world of experience when it was expressed in mathematical and scientific notation, it remained firmly within the experiential and presentational world of those who designed and operated machines. Moreover, the expression of this world of experience required special skills of spatial representation quite different from those of alphabetic literacy.

According to Tuman, "Literacy is the inner speech of the community" through which we "constantly judge our present perceptions of the world against a verbal objectification of other possibilities of being." In reading and writing we "construct what is not always present as a means of generating such possibilities."[2] Technical literacy, like traditional alphabetic literacy, could release the imagination, resulting in technological invention and innovation and uniting materiality with ideality. Translated into textual form, it included both visual representation and alphanumeric expression. This special literacy was the heart of nineteenth-century attempts to bring the material worlds of manufacturing and workshop together with formal knowledge.

The many problems faced by educator-advocates of technical literacy included the identification of generic skills that would serve the demands of technological convergence in manufacturing. These were skills that could bridge the gap between the Baconian empiricism of shop experience and the science and mathematics that underlay new power technologies and machining. Frequently the advocates of technical learning and literacy sought to overcome provincial attitudes that obstructed innovation and invention.

Pedagogically and epistemologically, it was difficult to integrate the disciplines and notational systems of alphabetic expression, science, mathematics, and graphic representation. A new pedagogy evolved that helped to reinforce the skills of technical literacy. Concerns about utility, cognitive growth, and moral development were combined in efforts to develop a balance among pedagogy, purpose, and "useful knowledge." The creation of a technically literate class, however, encountered numerous obstacles. For example, learning mathematics was a persistent difficulty for many. This was most obvious among students of algebra, but it also was apparent in perspective geometry classes, where proportionality was an elusive concept for some. Drawing in perspective relied as much on a grasp of spatial relations as on visual acuity.

Science, when confined to the classification and compilation of observations, posed few problems for students, but science as the study of the lawful behavior of physical bodies expressed mathematically was the object of frequent complaint. The prevailing view of science as useful knowledge certainly helped to popularize its study and no doubt motivated serious students. Yet the Baconian thrust of American science pushed aside the deeper epistemological difficulties with scientific study, particularly the question of whether a geometric or an algebraic view of space and motion was more accurate.

To integrate different disciplines and notational systems under a moral umbrella supported by the ideal of progress was a formidable task. The moral dimension of technical literacy forced educators to confront two major issues: the relation of theology to science and the place of liberal studies in a curriculum for technical and scientific learning. Neither issue was new, but attempts to create a technically literate society made them more obvious. Often a compromise was worked out, as in the teaching of natural philosophy. Here the thematic (moral and religious content) of the subject was confined for the most part to elementary texts while the mathematized study of science prevailed in more advanced texts.

Achieving the proper balance between the liberal and the technical posed a more difficult problem, however. They were compatible from a pragmatic standpoint, for the education of the upwardly mobile mechanic required both. Yet together they put impossible demands on an already crowded curriculum, which included remediation in basic skills. Moreover, they required the mastery of different "languages" and often required different methods of teaching. Thus the uneasy union of hope and convenience between the liberal and the technical required constant attention.

What came to be called the liberal/vocational controversy was incipient in the emergence of technical literacy. In antebellum America liberal knowledge was seen as a moral foundation both for further intellectual advancement and for respectability and social status. Moreover, its aim was to develop enlightened citizens whose moral worth and verbal skills would make them the cultural and intellectual pillars of the new republic and whose commitment to the ideal of material progress formed the foundation for political well-being. Technical knowledge was more specifically the way to profit. Generically, it was the knowledge of technique; practically, it was the art of constructing and producing.

The goal of acquiring technical knowledge was to become technically literate, or functionally literate relative to occupational utility. Daniel Resnick summarized the functional "literacy transaction" as one that "develops when a reader uses a text to negotiate a particular, practical, here-and-now situation." He observed that "the rise of useful knowledge seems to occur whenever personal and face-to-face relationships are no longer adequate to convey cultural information of a practical kind." His insight helps us understand the task educators faced when they attempted to translate the experience of shop and field into textbooks and the formal curricula of mechanics' institutes, which offered a broad array of day and evening classes, lecture series, and exhibitions of technical know-how to apprentices and mechanics.[3]

Technical knowledge was not scientific knowledge, but science made the technical respectable while it challenged with its analytic method the entrenched verbalism of the liberal studies. Scientists sought to make their special domain of knowledge legitimate in its own right, but science was also a stepping-stone for technology's future. The "light of science," said John Craig, one of the founders of the Ohio Mechanics' Institute, should be diffused "over every department of the useful arts and manufactures."[4] As educators and political leaders attempted to secure republican institutions on the basis of popular enlightenment, science competed with technology for intellectual status while sharing center stage in the drama of nineteenth-century material progress.[5]

Debates over the purposes of liberal and technical knowledge actually were debates over the worth of knowledge and over various ways of learning. The two forms of knowledge required different but not mutually exclusive intellectual and perceptual skills. Technical learning, for example, relied heavily on the experience of shop, farm, and factory. Educators who attempted to transfer this experience to the formal curricula of mechanics' institutes and to textbooks faced the problem of how to express material culture in the abstractions of language and graphics. They sought to move students through the perceptual and visual activity of representing spatial relations (drawing and graphics) to the complex process of design (planning and synthesis of spatial relations) to the verbal and symbolic tasks of classification and inference required to master mathematical formulae. This was no easy task given the students' limited academic preparation, the infant science of pedagogy, and the basic differences in styles of thinking between natural philosophers and artist-machinists.[6]

INTEGRATING SCIENTIFIC KNOWLEDGE

The tension between the liberal and the vocational, the attempted reconciliation of experience and theory, and the efforts to merge a culture of print with a nonverbal culture of experience remained at the center of the controversy in technical education through the first half of the nineteenth century. In their attempts to join the experience of the workshop with formal learning, educators were forced to recognize that technical and scientific learning involved a dialogue between material culture and a culture of print. This recognition led them to rethink their assumptions about the transfer of technical knowledge and how its structure related to the structure of work and machines and to mathematical and scientific knowledge.

The experiential basis of practical learning and the determinism of scientific principles were philosophically incompatible, yet the Baconian thrust of American science limited theorizing, allowing the practical and the theoretical to sit side by side. Daniels has argued that the utilitarian view of science reached such extremes that research was not taken seriously unless it had useful results.[7] Rae observed that the relation between science and technology in the nineteenth century was "somewhat casual." "The man who could devise a gadget or a technique which would work was making a recognizable contribution to the growth of the country," he continued, "whether he understood the fundamental principles he was using or not."[8]

The coexistence of the liberal, scientific, and technical in the early nineteenth century was not an integration nor a synthesis. Rather, it reflected the common desire to secure the moral foundations of an emerging republic. Perceptually, conceptually, and pedagogically, the liberal, technical, and scientific had differences so great that only an overriding moral and civic context for education could tame their divergence.

The empirical, experiential bases for technical learning linked it to the world of shop and manufacturer, not academy and college. The determinism of science and the verbalism of liberal knowledge did not begin with the same perceptual base as the technical. Of the three, however, it was science that had conceptual elements in common with the other two. Its empiricism gave it an affinity with technical knowledge, and its roots in natural philosophy linked it to the traditions of liberal studies. But the abstractions of science and its foundation in mathematics separated it from the experiential basis of technical knowledge. The language of science was far different from what students encountered in the traditional liberal disciplines. Thus students experienced difficulties with notation and vocabulary at the same time that they were attempting to reconcile the analytic style of science with the synthetic style of liberal knowledge.

Of the three types of knowledge—technical, scientific, and liberal—technical knowledge was perceptually and conceptually the most separate. Its foundation in material culture and its powerful visual component made it difficult to integrate with subjects that relied on the manipulation of symbolic notation (verbal or mathematical) and propositional logic. Instructors therefore were forced to substitute hands-on, experiential learning for traditional pedagogy.

Its empirical foundations tied technical knowledge to scientific inquiry, but its concern with practice over explanation hindered the integration of the two. Only because it was important to the social and economic fortunes of mechanics did technical knowledge share a common purpose with the scientific and liberal. The nexus of moral and technical knowledge rested on the experiences of successful shopkeepers and manufacturers who had demonstrated the utility of such virtues as prudence, temperance, honesty, and initiative, and such habits as discipline, circumspection, and reflection. These were behaviors that the technical, scientific, and liberal could all claim to develop as a foundation for moral citizenship in the new republic.

EMPIRICAL FOUNDATIONS
FOR TECHNICAL LITERACY:
ECONOMIC EXPANSION,
TECHNOLOGICAL CHANGE,
AND WORK

Between the beginning of the nineteenth century and the Civil War, manufacturing underwent major structural changes in the United States. These included greater control of manufacturing by capitalists, the development of interchangeable parts, the creation of mass markets, and the use of new power technologies. Cotton was king in the expansion of the American economy between 1818 and 1839 as the cotton trade provided the impetus for the opening up of new land to cotton planting and new markets. In New England, the manufacture of textiles, leather, and shoes grew in response to new markets. Greater specialization and the search for greater efficiency in manufacturing accompanied market expansion, so by the late 1840s manufacturing rather than the cotton trade had become the main impetus for economic expansion.[1]

The ascendancy of manufacturing in the Northeast and in other regions owed a great deal to skilled labor and entrepreneurship. As manufacturers and machinists adapted foreign inventions to American needs and inventors applied their ideas to labor-saving technology, they developed a pool of generic and specialized skills that made the creation and spread of new technology possible.[2]

The transition from skill in the hand to skill in the machine, from artisanship to mass production, which took place over several generations in the early nineteenth century, was the crucible in which technical literacy was forged during the early nineteenth century. Skills developed through hands-on experience were not far divorced from the machines that replicated these skills. One simply could not learn without experiencing the tool or machine, and one could not very well understand the operation of a machine without seeing it move. The skill that once belonged exclusively to the workman was built into the machine. Skill in the machine was accompanied by the need for more sophisticated technical skills and more managerial, interpersonal skills by apprentices and operatives who sought socioeconomic mobility.

The skills needed in power technologies, selected manufacturing processes, and machine tool shops were diverse and aligned with a hierarchy of labor found in shop and manufacture, ranging from elite machinists and toolmakers to operatives. In between were repairmen and foremen who needed to know how to manage manufacturing processes and how to repair a broken machine. Repairmen and machinists still had high-order manual skills, but they also needed an overall picture of how machines operated.

Building the skill into the machine prompted a change in priorities for employers and educators. "People" skills and attitudes became increasingly important with the growth of "self-acting" machinery. Technical skills, of course, were not discarded. The skills and knowledge of machinists, particularly those in the machine-tooling industry, encompassed a thorough understanding of process and design along with actual hands-on performance. These men formed a technical elite indispensable to the design and development of machine-making tools.

WATER AND STEAM POWER

Water Power Innovation in power technologies was necessary for the growth of the American economic engine. Though of ancient lineage, water power technology was studied and restudied by inventors and academics in the late eighteenth century and first forty years of the nineteenth. The steam engine captured the imagination of succeeding generations, but it was water, commonplace and less dramatic, that powered most large manufacturing establishments in the first half of the nineteenth century.[3]

The millwright was a key figure in waterwheel construction and gearing for power transmission. His skills brought together those of the carpenter, joiner, mason, blacksmith, wheelwright, and machinist. In laying out mills he needed to be familiar with hydraulics and surveying. As late as 1861, William Fairbairn described the millwright as a "fair mathematician" who knew "something of geometry, levelling and mensuration" and was able to "calculate the velocities, strength and power of machines." And, notes Hunter, he was the central figure in "the mechanical arts in his day."[4]

The selection of wheel type and dimension and the gearing needed to supply sufficient power for a specific mill site required some sophistication. Millwrights' handbooks were valuable if not indispensable aids in these matters. The translation of the millwright's knowledge into text was accomplished in the United States in large part by Oliver Evans' *The Young Mill-Wright and Miller's Guide* (1795), which combined the practical experience of Evans and Thomas Ellicott with current theory. For more than a half-century this work dominated the water-milling field.[5]

Tables, drawings, and plans for the construction of mills were probably the most accessible part of Evans' text, though he made every effort to put into simple prose the background for calculation and the principles of motion of levers, friction, and fluids.[6] The *Young Mill-Wright and Miller's Guide* began with a review of the "mechanical powers." Evans even thought it necessary to explain the arithmetic signs ($+$, $-$, $\times$, and $=$) going further than most to indulge those with poor educational backgrounds. At the same time, however, he included tables of experiments performed on mills.[7]

Evans described the disparate traditions of French and American waterwheel and turbine construction. He warned that quantitative theory had "severe limitations," noting that "in treating of the elementary principle of hydraulics, it is necessary to proceed upon theoretical principles." He added, however, that the processes of art, in which the motion of water is concerned, deviate so significantly from the deductions of theory that the latter must be considered an imperfect guide for the practical millwright and engineer.[8]

The empirical tradition of American millwrights served them well, but they were handicapped by their lack of scientific and mathematical understanding.[9] Because they lacked formal academic training, self-study was often the only way to acquire the knowledge necessary for mill construction. Knowledge of construction techniques was decentralized and accumulated regionally. For the millwright who designed and built mills on streams and tributaries, trial and error testing was sometimes the only source of information other than word-of-mouth advice obtained on visits to other mill sites. This, however, was precisely the situation that manuals and lectures on mechanics sought to remedy.

Gradually the millwright was displaced from center stage by the hydraulic engineer. This slow process, which accompanied the evolution of the waterwheel into the reaction wheel and then the turbine, was affected by factors other than technology, including available capital and location of markets. It was still recognized, however, that an old waterwheel, unless damaged or simply worn out, could meet a wide range of production demands.

As the crude wooden parts of waterwheels and the unmachined castings used in reaction wheels were replaced by the finely machined parts for turbines made in advanced machine shops, trial and error methods were combined with the theoretical studies of French engineers.[10] Still, even in the textile centers of New England, where studies of Fourneyron were known, empiricism remained the rule. Using elaborate experiments but little theory, Uriah Boyden, a legendary American inventor and self-trained civil engineer, carried out experiments and achieved success as a builder and designer of "hydraulic facilities." Yet his labors were inefficient, and work that took him months probably could have been accomplished in minutes with the help of calculus.[11] Even the famous work of James Francis, *Lowell Hydraulic Experiments* (1855), remained wedded to experimentalism rather than mathematics.[12] Though they borrowed from the theoretical literature on hydraulics, Boyden and Francis kept their faith in experiment and empirical data. Their work was a creative synthesis of tradition and theory, but it was left to others with a better grasp of theory to see the "potentials" they had missed in their designs.[13]

The importance of water power to the American economy in the early nineteenth century was not matched by steam until mid-century, but it was steam that made unprecedented demands on American technology as the century progressed. As the prospects for steam power increased with expanded markets, so did the necessity for precision techniques in machine construction.[14] Even though technological considerations were often minor factors in the choice of power, in some instances the absence of knowledge needed to repair and maintain steam engines was determinant. In these cases, careful planning was required to make certain that men with the required skills were available.

The growth in use of stationary steam engines was slow before 1840, but by 1860 several factors had come together to produce a sudden surge.

These included an increase in the size and number of cities, more production involving interchangeable parts, and the development of capabilities for greater precision in metalworking.[15]

The increase in the number of large-scale manufacturing establishments made initial costs of investment in equipment less important. In addition, there was increased concern with low unit operating costs. The need for greater efficiency spread across all dimensions of production, and, correspondingly, the engineer replaced the millwright in large manufacturing concerns. The technical merits of improved steam engines came to the fore along with the additional requirements in skill and technical knowledge as uniformity of motion became a key determinant of the quality and the volume of products.[16] Schools for mechanics, libraries for apprentices, and mechanics' journals all responded to the widening gap between theory and practice in power technologies. Individual workers, of course, found their own solutions.

The Promise of New Power Technology

In the early nineteenth century the difficulties of developing steam power and overcoming technical problems are illustrated by the experiences of Robert Fulton and John Fitch. For Fulton, the most difficult problem to be solved was the mechanical linkage between engine and paddle wheel. His qualified success on the river Seine in 1803 (the machinery was much too heavy for the vessel) led to a less ambiguous success in 1807 with the launching of the *Clermont* on the Hudson.[17]

Fitch's problems with steam propulsion stemmed from his ignorance of basic mechanical principles. His able mechanic, Henry Voight, later recalled that "the Steam boat company miscarried . . . entirely owing to [Fitch's] want of mechanism; he was the most deficient in that respect of any man I ever knew that professed it; . . . nor could he make any mechanic understand what he wanted." Fitch's workmen were also ignorant, said Voight: "I had no conception . . . that it would have employed so great a length of time merely to acquire the art of making a steam engine—an art familiar in England, but of which all the artisans I could ever converse with in America [were] entirely ignorant. Thus we had to explore an unbeated [*sic*] path, and did not ascertain the true course until we had wandered into a thousand wrong Rodes."[18]

Compared with marine engines, stationary steam engines required greater uniformity of motion.[19] This, and efficiency, eventually became the overriding concerns of mill engine builders in the late 1840s. Many mill engines (high pressure, noncondensing steam engines) were unsophisticated and imprecise, but manufacturing fine textiles, printing on paper and cloth, machining metal, and shaping wood demanded greater precision.[20] Planers and drilling machines to bore small holes became common in large establishments. Dimensional accuracy grew more crucial with higher engine speeds, and mechanized metalworking gradually replaced handworking. A pool of knowledge and skills gradually accumulated for future use.[21]

The mill engine served a capital- and labor-scarce America well in the first half of the nineteenth century.[22] George Corliss' automatic valve cutoff engine (AVC), patented in 1849, then set the stage for a new era of steam engines. Before Corliss, relatively little was known of the principles of thermodynamics that underlay the use of steam, so improvements in engine design focused on better mechanical arrangements of moving parts rather than on the dynamics of converting the heat content of fuel to energy. Mechanical efficiency rather than fuel efficiency was of primary concern.[23]

As engines became more sophisticated, the need increased for mechanics with knowledge of and experience in the construction and management of steam engines. Oliver Evans' *Abortion of the Young Steam Engineer's Guide* (1805) provided mechanics with the principles of steam and guides to its use, including diagrams and tables. But even with Evans' manual and those that followed, such as James Renwick's *Treatise on the Steam Engine* (1830), steam was not easily understood. Mechanics learned to deal with the difficulties attendant with greater precision and increased uniformity of motion, and, most important, with new valve mechanisms capable of regulating more precisely the expansive power of steam. The millwright's knowledge of waterwheel construction, however, did not transfer to the understanding of the moving parts of the steam engine. Gradually he was replaced by the engineer, who understood the importance of efficiency and economy and the necessity for designing AVC and valve gear systems to replace the old (and worthy) sliding valve.[24]

The rising demand for steam resulted in the growth of iron founding, but the building of steam engines was still frequently done on an ad hoc basis in blacksmiths' shops. Recalling his days as an apprentice, John Fritz, a leading iron manufacturer and mill designer, remembered that in 1838 a mechanic "would have to make his own drawings and patterns, make his own forgings, and fit the work all up, without tools, except makeshifts." As Purcell has noted, the significant fact is not that "a small-town blacksmith had to improvise in building an engine in 1838, but that he could even build a workable engine." This situation would change radically by mid-century with the standardization of steam engine parts.[25]

Fig. 1.1. "Casting the Cylinders," Novelty Works, New York City. From *Harper's Magazine*, May 1851. Photo courtesy Smithsonian Institution.

The knowledge needed to design, make, and repair steam engines demanded new theory and practice even though tradition still weighed heavily in small shops. As the blacksmith and small-town engine builder failed to keep up, they became objects of derision. With conceit bordering on arrogance Edwin Freedley remarked in 1858 that there was a "marked difference between the quality of the labor that can be obtained in the country and in the towns. In fact, in or near large cities only can labor of the first quality be obtained."[26]

The new trade of the machinist emerged as a combination of blacksmith-
ing and iron founding, but with the added dimension of applied physics
(mechanics). Applied physics was virtually indispensable for shops designing their own engines and those filling the orders of large manufacturers
(see figs. 1.1 and 1.2). As with water power, the most practical information related to cost and efficiency. The principles of thermodynamics were
strange compared with those of hydraulics. Thus practice continued to lag
behind theory.

Disaster rather than curiosity may have been the most powerful reason
to understand thermodynamics.[27] The response of the Franklin Institute
to the increasing frequency of boiler explosions and the unpredictability
of steam as a source of power was one of many educational responses to
new power technologies between 1830 and 1860. To review this response
in detail would take us too far afield, however. What is important is that
the increased power demands of manufacturing and the move from wood
to iron construction in power technology placed difficult new demands on
those who would educate and train mechanics.

Fig. 1.2. The machine shop. From *Scientific American* 14, no. 25 (26 February
1859). Photo courtesy Smithsonian Institution.

Greater efficiency was the byword of large-scale manufacturing. In textile centers and locomotive manufactures, machinists were pressed to integrate the qualitative, empirical tradition of the American millwright with the mathematical tradition of the French. In textile manufacturing particularly, the empiricism of the visual and tactile began to merge with and set the boundaries for the mathematization of machinemaking. The knowledge needed to improve the efficiency of manufacturing often was developed locally and was determined frequently by local geography, fuel availability, and marketing considerations. Yet wherever precision machinery was necessary it created an educational imperative that was not easily met. Technical literacy grew slowly, but the precedents set in the first half of the nineteenth century were cumulative. Gradually they formed the foundation for rapid institutional growth in the postbellum era.

THE CASE OF TEXTILE MANUFACTURING

Growing recognition that the proper interaction of capitalization, geography, fuel, markets, and technologies produced greater efficiency, and larger profits set the stage for the on-site development and implementation of new methods of manufacturing. The case of textile milling is probably the most important example of attempts to synthesize new knowledge, techniques, and market factors to achieve greater profits.

Jeremy has observed that American mechanization of textile manufacturing was a response to a "severe shortage of unskilled labor" that necessitated labor-saving devices.[28] Textile manufacturers had two basic ways to innovate: they could create more versatile machines or replace manual operations with machines.[29] Both vertical integration ("either the elimination of an operation or the mechanical continuity of two consecutive operations") and mechanization of manual tasks were fundamental to mass production in textile factories. Both were innovative by nature and required a pool of technical skills and knowledge beyond what operatives could offer.[30]

The major technical effects of the vertical integration and increased mechanization of manual operations were twofold. First was the movement toward high-speed power looming in textile manufacturing, and second was the change in the skills needed by operatives. Automatic fault detection (mechanical "stop motions") was a major labor-saving device, making the vigilance of the operative less important. As the skill was built into the machine, the management of quality was tightened, and skills needed by operatives, foreman, and managers were redefined.

Innovation gradually moved from empiricism to greater reliance on scientific knowledge. The empirical bias of innovation, however, was never far in the background in textile manufacturing because productivity varied so much at each processing stage. Innovation at one stage made for obsolescence in another, and overcoming such variability required both technical and managerial expertise. The technical literacy that emerged under these conditions transcended mechanism and took its meaning and significance from the system of mass production itself.

Textile manufacturing, like other mass-production operations, required numerous skilled workers to assemble, repair, and alter the large machines and power trains needed for continuous operation. In the first and second decades of the nineteenth century, farmer and village mechanics were crucial to the success of manufacturing. In these decades a "competent mechanic," Gibb observes, could hang a waterwheel, rig shafting, and "work a true plane surface with tools which he had made himself."[31] He was a generalist—a carpenter, millwright, and toolmaker. By 1850, however, the manufacture of machinery took place in large shops that had heavy and expensive tools and employed men with specialized skills. Textile machinery was no longer a blacksmith's sideline, as it had been in 1813. Rather, the shop that could supply machinery for an entire mill was in a strong competitive position.[32]

The introduction of power looms, such as those used by the Boston Manufacturing Company at Waltham, spurred the growth of large on-site shops headed by a master mechanic. Paul Moody's inventions at Waltham illustrate the empirical foundations of technical literacy in manufacturing. When Francis Lowell returned from England, bringing with him a drawing of Horrocks' dressing machine, it fell to master mechanic Paul Moody to make the machine.[33] The major problem Moody faced was the warping of the wooden rollers that conveyed the yarn into the sizing solution. Because they warped easily they could be used for only a short time. Moody first tried casting a shell of pewter around the rollers, but this, says Gibb, was "beyond the manual skill of his foundrymen." Moody's brother David suggested using soapstone to cast the molds. Moody instead made the rollers themselves of soapstone, thus solving the problem and setting a design precedent for the Waltham dresser.[34] Other examples include Moody's epicycloidal gearing system for his "double speeder" that effected sequential changes in the speed of the bobbin. The essential point, however, is the same. In the machine shops of large manufacturers a pool of technical knowledge had been created, making greater profits possible.[35]

MACHINE MAKING AND MACHINE TOOLING

Accounts of nineteenth-century manufactures suggest that there were three major elements in successful manufacturing. First was an understanding of shop organization and its relationship to the overall manufacturing process, including the necessity for skilled and specialized labor and labor-saving machinery. Second, it required an understanding of the need for innovation and the relation between innovation in one manufacturing process to innovation in another. Third, it was necessary to understand changing markets and to identify windows of opportunity. Understanding market opportunities and the possibilities of transferring technology from the manufacture of one type of item to another allowed Matthias Baldwin, for example, to move from manufacturing bookbinder's tools and cylinders for calico printing to manufacturing stationary steam engines to building locomotives.

Success in large-scale production required machine-tooling innovation beyond the capabilities of small shops. The lack of skilled labor was a major concern, particularly in machine tooling and in the making of gauges for standardizing parts. Thus, in the 1830s and 1840s, "educated mechanics" slowly replaced unskilled workers. This, of course, was more true in machine shops than in routine assembly operations. In machine shops, drawing and drafting were important skills, as was understanding the basics of mechanical motion. The aim, as one account said, was to produce "machines which shall, with the least skill on the part of the workman, be able to produce the best work in the largest quantities."[36]

The specialization of function in manufacturing both de-skilled and re-skilled work, which required a pool of knowledge and skills widely applicable to different manufacturers. Building the skill into the machine, moreover, required the key element of precision (as differentiated from accuracy relative to a standard of measurement) that was part of early efforts at interchangeability.[37]

Machine shops and machine tooling were crucial in the transfer of new skills to various manufacturers, as they increased the power and precision of mass production. Rosenberg provides us with the useful concept of "technological convergence" to understand the educational implications of early nineteenth-century industrial organization.[38] Technological convergence in the machine tool industry, he says, relied on a "pool or reservoir of skills and technical knowledge" that could be applied to common problems across manufacturing specialities. In 1820 ad hoc production of machines built to the specific requirements of the user characterized machine making. Between 1840 and 1880, however, manufacturers began to share solutions to machine-making problems as they diversified their products. Diversification, not specialization, was the key to diffusing new knowledge in the form of innovations and solutions to common problems. Technical skills in the machine-tool industry thus grew within the context of "decentralized sources of power" and the sharing of metal-using technology.[39] Shops and manufacturers that shaped and formed metals became "learning centers," notes Rosenberg.[40]

Once a particular problem was solved in one area of manufacturing, the solution became part of a reservoir of knowledge that could be used elsewhere. The Blanchard lathe, the turret lathe, and milling machines developed in association with armsmakers, for example, helped to solve the problem of interchangeable parts for other manufacturers. Specialization still took place *within* particular manufactures, however, as in the making of accurate patterns and standard inspection gauges for armories. This "vertical disintegration" within manufactures (the tendency toward specialization by separate firms) accompanied technological convergence *across* industries, and together they made possible the intensive specialization that characterized the second half of the nineteenth century.[41]

Machine shops, whether independent or part of manufacturing establishments, were indispensable to mass production. In them apprentices (see fig. 1.3) brushed shoulders with inventors, machinists, and entrepreneurs.[42] Many machine shops of the 1830s were simple affairs, usually containing a lathe, vise, grindstone, and chest full of assorted hammers, chisels, files, and wrenches. In the Rockdale community, built along Chester Creek in Delaware County in southeastern Pennsylvania, most spinning mill factories employed two or three people who specialized in repair. Mechanics were called on to assemble parts ordered from other machine shops. Carpenters repaired wooden parts, replaced pins and bolts, and installed card clothing; tinsmiths made large cans for slivers; blacksmiths forged; and machinists turned rollers.[43] Larger shops like those of the Sellers in Upper Darby, Pennsylvania, Oliver Evans' Mars Works in Philadelphia, Horatio Allen's Novelty Works in New York City, and the West Point Foundry had several departments with lathes, a blacksmith shop, a foundry for castings, a pattern room and a drafting room, and an assembly area for parts of larger machines, such as locomotives or stationary steam engines.[44]

Machine shops were noisy, the work was hard, and accidents were common as shafts and pulleys broke or hot metal spilled. The excitement was immense, however, as evidenced in the reminiscences of George Escol Sellers, a famous Philadelphia machinist. The organization of work con-

Fig. 1.3. Young man at the lathe. From "Schools and the Means of Education Shall Forever Be Encouraged: A History of Education in the Old Northwest, 1787–1880," an exhibition of Ohio University Libraries. Photo courtesy Ohio University Libraries.

trasted sharply with the efficient floor plans of larger manufacturing concerns, yet George Sellers' description of the construction of early papermaking machinery is an important reminder of their importance to the development of American industry.

It was here that Sellers learned to draw, model, and profit from others' errors. Here he learned the value of mastering mechanical principles before attempting new inventions. He tested ideas against the experience of others more knowledgeable, and he cooperated with others to bring the various parts of an engine together.[45] In a memorable account Sellers testifies to the power and influence of Henri Mogeme, an itinerant German craftsman and a born teacher. "I never went into his shop that I did not learn something," said Sellers. "He was always ready to answer my questions and mostly with some illustration. . . . Mogeme was a capital teacher:

when explaining anything to me it would be as if I was entirely ignorant. He would say, 'No understand without beginning right.' "[46]

Much of the success of early-nineteenth-century machine shops depended on machinists' use of state-of-the-art lathes.[47] The pool of skills and knowledge that accompanied technological convergence derived from empirical testing and from the application of mathematical and scientific principles. Gear-cutting machinery was immensely important in overcoming the limitations of low-speed belt and pulley drives. Many of the features of the industrial lathe were eventually incorporated into specialized milling machines, planers, shapers, and gear-cutting machines—testimony to the integration of shop experience, visual acuity, and the theoretical solution of difficult geometrical problems in practical machine shop operations.[48]

The methods of gear cutting for clocks and mill wheels were important precedents for machinists but were of limited value in solving problems in gear cutting for high-speed machinery and for iron and steel gearing.[49] The mathematics of gear design based on epicycloidal and involute curves had been worked out during the late seventeenth and eighteenth centuries, but machine designers were not familiar with this work because it was not in a usable form—that is, in tables and rules that could be applied by using a compass and scale. Consequently, until the 1830s workshop methods relied on the experience of machinists and on "rule of thumb" methods.[50] This situation was indeed the nemesis of educators, who sought to persuade machinists to abandon tradition for innovation. Most machinists did not have the mathematical knowledge necessary for the production of precision gearing, either because it was not in sufficiently usable form or because machinists themselves were not sufficiently literate. Work went on, of course, but educators and advocates of technological progress through education struggled to locate the nexus of theoretical and useful knowledge necessary for the education of machinists and inventors.

THE "AMERICAN SYSTEM":
INTERCHANGEABILITY AND UNIFORMITY

Precision tooling and gauging placed the dream of interchangeable parts within the grasp of manufacturers. The concept of interchangeability that underlay the American system had fascinated early-nineteenth-century machinists, entrepreneurs, and political leaders, including Thomas Jefferson, who was aware of the potential usefulness to the United States of French musket production methods.[51] The concept grew in importance as maintenance and repair problems promised to be greatly simplified for mass-produced manufactured items.[52]

The "American system" built the concepts of interchangeability and uniformity into mass production using sophisticated gauging techniques, automatic stop-motion mechanisms, variable speed control, and advanced cutting tools.[53] Federal armories and the private sector both played major roles in developing the manufacture of interchangeable parts. Work done at the Springfield, Massachusetts, armory, the work of Eli Whitney at Mill Rock in Whitneyville, Connecticut, and John H. Hall's system at Harpers Ferry, West Virginia, contributed substantially to the movement toward interchangeability of parts.[54]

Donald Hoke suggests that the private sector of the American economy was far ahead of the government armories in many respects.[55] The private sector, Hoke argues, held the technological lead from 1807 to the mid-1820s, then shared the lead with the armories until the late 1840s. By the 1860s the private sector had again taken the lead. Early in the movement toward interchangeable parts, says Hoke, wooden clock manufacturing was the key industry even though it never was more than a minuscule part of the American economy.[56]

Hounshell, unlike Hoke, gives high marks to the U.S. armories for developing a system of interchangeability. He demonstrates, however, that in the manufacture of the sewing machine and the McCormick reaper, interchangeability developed very late. In the United States the interchangeability system began with the work of two private armsmakers, Simeon North and Eli Whitney, under contract to the War Department.[57] But the American system of interchangeability flourished under the watchful eyes of Roswell Lee and George Bomford at the Springfield armory and John H. Hall at Harpers Ferry. It was in the armories, too, that the Blanchard lathe for turning gun stocks was implemented.

At Harpers Ferry armory, Hall was instrumental in the development of precision manufacturing through "fixture design." Fixtures were used to hold an object in a machine tool securely during the machining operation. Fixtures, however, were not perfect, and "each time an object is fixed in a machine tool, a certain amount of inaccuracy creeps into the operation." Over time, the errors are multiplied. To solve this problem, Hall devised the "bearing point"—the point on the machine serving as the standard of reference for all operations performed on the piece being machined. This practical and conceptual breakthrough effectively diminished the multiplier effect of errors.[58]

The overall importance of the armory system was threefold. First, it set precedents for government subsidizing of arms production, even though it did not actually reduce the cost through interchangeability. Second, it provided a laboratory for solving problems of interchangeability, including gauging, fixture design, single-purpose machines, and the organization of machines for production in large quantities. Third, it trained generations of machinists who spread the word about interchangeability and taught others the virtues and operations of the armory system.[59]

The American system was far more than a process for mechanical innovation. As high-speed production increased, it was imperative that entrepreneurs seek out machinists and technical experts with good managerial skills to oversee production.[60] Just as economy was the mother of invention in mechanism, as David Pye suggests, it was also the mother of new management techniques.[61] Said the master machinist James Burton of the Hall Rifle works: it was "not an occasional machine, but a plant of milling machinery by which the system and economy of the manufacture was materially altered."[62] Interchangeability and uniformity—the salient features of the American system—were established within the complex culture of production itself, altering both the organization and the psychology of work. The old system of a small group of artisans working individually gave way to specialization that demanded a synchronous response of worker to machine but not the manual skills of artisanship. Moreover, the psychological distance of worker from product increased as thousands of parts were produced with a likeness and speed beyond the capability of the artisan.

The skills needed in precision machine making (particularly precision screw cutting and the making of plane surfaces) were crucial to large-scale, efficient manufacturing. Building the skill into the machine, moreover, had the effect of changing the skills needed by operatives. The general mechanical skills possessed by the farmer-mechanic were replaced by the specialized skills of the expert machinist. The diffusion of basic mechanical knowledge proceeded apace as machinists and engineers responded to diversification in manufacturing by helping to create a pool of general knowledge applicable across different manufactures.

The management of quality was tightened in due course. Trial and error testing was probably still the norm, but mathematics and science were gradually employed by those controlling the quality of interchangeable parts. Integrating the stages of production required greater planning and a mind-set that recognized the relations among machine shop, manufacturing, interchangeability, and large-scale capitalization. The demands of production shaped a new technological imagination just as they required new skills from those responsible for innovation, efficiency, and quality.

THE CHANGING WORKFORCE

Apprentices and Journeymen The evolution of mass production and interchangeability, together with technological convergence, altered the rules
of work. At the same time, it redefined the opportunities for young apprentices and the role of women in the workforce. The salient features of the
craft tradition—mastery of the entire production process, exclusive knowledge of production techniques, predominance of hand tools, and ownership
of tools by the artisan—were undermined as skill was built into the machine. Competing with the craft tradition was the factory, characterized by
specialized, mechanized production and large employer-owned machines.
Opportunities for innovation and initiative were many in early-nineteenth-
century factories, but the skilled worker was no longer his own boss, as
the artisan had been.[63]

In the early stages of the decline of apprenticeship that followed the
American Revolution, the master-to-learner relationship prevailed in technical matters, but much education was given over, by indenture, to evening
schools.[64] The moral content of the traditional master-apprentice obligations died hard. When Frederic W. Lincoln spoke before the Massachusetts
Charitable Mechanic Association in 1845 he observed the absence of in-
dentured apprentices among the membership. He urged his audience not
to "shake off the responsibility" of acting as "guardians, and friends" for
youth who needed the character training that was part of traditional apprenticeship.[65]

Printed moral advice to apprentices did not disappear. In fact, fear for
their moral decline may have caused a temporary resurgence in the numbers of advice and self-improvement books. The publishers of these works
were part of the large confederacy of institutions—apprentice libraries,
lyceums, and evening schools—that emerged as alternatives and comple-
ments to public schooling in the three decades preceding the Civil War.
These self-improvement books contained advice that was a secularized, updated version of that in earlier manuals, but they still addressed the time-
honored virtues of punctuality, accuracy, temperance, and self-discipline.
What many of the authors actually advocated was the formation of proper
reading and study habits that, it was presumed, would translate into economic opportunity.[66]

Independence and control over one's work declined as manufacturing
processes were standardized and products mass produced. Mechanics' periodicals, for their part, distinguished between workers who retained control
over their own success and operatives, who occupied the lower rungs of the

occupational ladder and were the "permanent wage earners of an industrial work force."[67] This distinction between mechanics and operatives is not a neat one, but it was used by contemporaries, and there is little question that periodical literature for mechanics stressed the ideal of upward mobility and the dangers (both moral and economic) of becoming mired in tedious, routine, unimaginative labor. In fact, this distinction of the mid-nineteenth century was a modification of one used in the late eighteenth and early nineteenth centuries, when, as Kornblith notes, it was "mental engagement that set the mechanic apart from the common laborer, who supposedly relied wholly on his physical attributes and gave no thought to the purpose of his toil beyond provision for his own subsistence."[68]

The uncertainty created by economic dislocation devalued apprenticeship and undermined the master's authority, as well as the secrets of trades themselves.[69] The most telling blow to the apprenticeship system was the cash wage. Ironically, as it undermined the apprenticeship system, it also created an opportunity for acquiring technical knowledge. Unless one grew up as the son of a machine shop owner, the way to learn about machines was to travel from shop to shop.[70]

The deskilling of some American workers and the reskilling of others were selective, but most occupations eventually were affected. Machinists were perhaps among the last to experience the loss of status that accompanied building the skill into the machine. Those with the broad perspective that resulted from managing large enterprises marveled at the interrelationships between one production stage and another. Machinists whose skills were crucial to innovation shared in the status associated with applying science to technical improvements. Their skills, in fact, were part of the romance of the machine celebrated by such technology enthusiasts as Jacob Abbott, a children's author, who wrote of the "calm and steady dignity with which the ponderous engines continue their ceaseless toil," the "real dignity and real grace in the movements which they perform," and the "multitude of wheels and pulleys, and bands that mingle and combine their motions with the revolutions of the machinery."[71]

This was the romance of the machine age—for some at least. The rise of capital-intensive manufacturing, with its attendant mechanization, however, also deskilled many production operations that had belonged to journeymen. Henry Brokmeyer, a talented journeyman and not very enthusiastic union supporter, put it well when he observed Mike and Jake, two Irish journeymen whose "craft was their entire life." Said Brokmeyer with the deepest irony: "Of the relation of their craft to the productive industry of the world as a whole, they know nothing; of the reciprocal interdependence of that industry, each craft or function upon all, and all upon each, they know nothing."[72]

Women in the Workforce Deskilling and reskilling among male workers were paralleled by changes in women's work. In shoe binding and textile mills women faced low pay, long hours, and the dislocation brought about by mechanization. Women were increasingly locked in to low-skilled jobs. In shoe binding, for instance, the introduction of the wooden peg and the sewing machine to sew leather drastically altered women's work, requiring them to move into the factory in greater numbers to work full time or purchase their own machines and work at home.[73] In the artisan tradition, shoe binding was known as women's work aptly named because the women and children who performed it were isolated from the shop culture of male shoemakers. Women did not work *with* men but, rather, kept them supplied with sewn uppers. As shoemaking moved to factories women remained in the low-status, low-wage work of sewing uppers.[74]

The percentage of women employed in the manufacturing labor force in the early nineteenth century belied their major role in the transformation to an industrial society. Perhaps only 10 percent of women actually worked in manufacturing establishments prior to the 1840s, but their importance in the production and processing of cotton far outweighed their numbers. In the South female slaves were crucial to the harvesting of cotton, and in the North the spinning and weaving skills of entire families, young native-born New England women recruits, and later those of Irish birth were critical to the development of large-scale textile manufacturing.

In the more sophisticated and mechanized mills of Lowell and Waltham, Massachusetts, women operatives were forced onto the lower rungs of the labor hierarchy.[75] In her *Loom and Spindle, or Life Among the Early Mill Girls*, Harriet Robinson recalled that there were four "classes" in the mills. These were, at the top, the agents, the "aristocrats" and "autocrats" of the mill, followed by the overseers, "a sort of gentry" made up of "ambitious mill hands" who had worked their way up. Next was a third class of operatives, the "girls" or "men"; and, at the lowest level, the "lords of the spade and shovel," who lived in shanties.[76] Women were not part of the labor force that directed textile production but were subject to the commands, rules, and often harsh treatment of overseers. Perhaps because of this, women in both milling and shoe binding emerged as leaders in the infant but vigorous labor movement of the 1840s.

The development of the high-speed power loom removed children from the textile operative workforce and increased the percentage of young men and women. Technological changes in spinning and weaving decreased the economic value of young women who spun at home. Bringing cash wages home to the family seemed a better alternative.

The millowner defined women as cheap labor, in accordance with their traditional subordinate status in the household economy. This cultural fact, combined with the diminished value of their skills that were taken over by mechanization, resulted in a gender-based hierarchy of wages in mills. Skilled jobs went to men, and women and children tended the new high-speed spinning machinery. Men could expect to earn 50 to 65 percent more than women.[77]

By the early 1840s demands for greater profits and increased production in textile mills intensified the pressures on the workforce of young women, as overseers received premiums for increased production. Paralleling and reinforcing this custom were the introduction of heavier and faster machinery and the practices of speeding up machinery, assigning extra looms to women, and reducing piece rates. Although the work load increased, take-home pay for women was the same as it was in 1823, and the seventy-five-hour week remained in place.

The cash wage was a powerful incentive for young women to migrate to Lowell, the "city of spindles," but the romance of the machines that powered the mill and processed the cotton also beckoned them to the new age of manufacturing. Like Daniel Webster, who anthropomorphized the power of textile machinery, they were fascinated by these "active agents" that were "guided by laws of science."[78] "In the mill," said S. G. B. [Sarah Bagley], a contributor to the *Lowell Offering*, "we see displays of the wonderful power of the mind. Who can closely examine all the movements of the complicated, curious machinery, and not be led to the reflection, that the mind is boundless, and is destined to rise higher and still higher: and that it can accomplish almost any thing on which it fixes its attention."[79]

The discipline of the mill taught young women "daily habits of punctuality and industry; it was, in fact, a sort of manual training or industrial school," reflected Harriet Robinson. The attention young women paid to the cultivation of the intellect was a conspicuous feature of the early mill experience in Lowell.[80] The rose-colored picture painted by Harriet Robinson was not shared by all. *Factory Tracts, Factory Life as It Is*, published by the Female Labor Reform Association of Lowell in 1845, documents the condition of wage slavery and presents a bleak picture of the intellectual culture of the operative. The difference in these views may be a result of Robinson's stress on the early years at Lowell, but it is also possible that the observers studied different groups within the mills themselves. John Clarke, an agent of the Merrimack Mills, noted in 1841 that "290 of our girls attended school during the evenings of the last winter" and that "124 of the females now at work in the Merrimack Mills have heretofore taught school." In 1842 he observed that in the mills there were "40 females including sweepers and other hands, who cannot write their names; of this number 30 are Irish."[81]

Judging from the case of the Lowell mills, mechanization had a far from simple effect on the intellectual culture of factory women. Labor surely was stratified by gender, but within each gender the effects were uneven and probably depended on educational background. A realistic appraisal was probably given by one "Julianna," who acknowledged in 1845 that some girls rose above the "obstacles of factory life" but that "few have the moral courage and perseverance to travel on in the rugged paths of science and improvement, amid all these and many other discouragements." Julianna concluded that those operatives who devoted little time to self-improvement had little to offer their husbands and were jeopardizing the "mental and intellectual character of future generations of New England."[82]

CONCLUSION

The demands of production shaped the technological imagination and formed the bedrock for educational expectations and technical literacy. Translating the demands of production into educational requirements was not only a matter of identifying required occupational skills but was something much broader—a new way of looking at production that demanded a synthesis of shop experience, a strong perceptual element in the form of spatial and tactile acuity, and formal academics. In short, production demanded and helped to create a technological culture.

The educational implications of new technologies and the reorganization of production in an emerging industrial economy were, as we shall see, addressed by the leaders and educators of mechanics' institutes and by mechanics' advocates in the periodic press. From workshop to factory there were requisite skills and knowledge that ranged from an understanding of materials to proportional drawing to calculations for gears. Given the fact of technological convergence and the pool of generic skills needed for manufactures to diversify their operations, mechanics, entrepreneurs, and educators in mechanics' institutes all concentrated on transmitting the generic knowledge and transferable skills necessary for innovation. Bridging the gap between formal instruction and the empiricism of the workshop was exceedingly difficult. That difficulty, however, was aggravated by structural inequalities related to age, gender, and ethnicity in the workforce.

Building the skill into the machine and organizing manufacturing to produce uniform and interchangeable parts required the integration of technical skills with the predominant values in the new forms of production. Efficiency, punctuality, and accuracy became part of the larger moral and civic context for technical literacy. Beyond this, however, was the recognition that the workplace was the pragmatic test of creative energy in the form of innovation and invention. It was not only a trial by fire but also a test of individual and collective ingenuity. Here the generic skills related to spatial cognition, visual acuity, and the logic of science and mathematics were tested by putting the skill into the machine under the constraints of cost reduction and increased production. Here success was measured by meeting the challenge of the production process itself.

2

THE CONTENT AND PEDAGOGY
FOR SPATIAL THINKING:
DRAWING AND MODELS

THINKING SPATIALLY

Many of the skills required in shops and manufactures required nonverbal spatial skills. At their highest levels these skills had been mastered by machinists and ironworkers who built, repaired, assembled, and often helped design or modify machines for mass production. To be a master machinist required a sense of design, a mastery of the characteristics of materials, and a holistic view of the manufacturing process. Even operatives needed a modest degree of eye-hand coordination and, if they were to move to the level of overseer, an understanding of the sequence of production and the floor layout required for maximum efficiency. The apprentice who lacked visual-spatial skills had little future as a machinist.

Spatial cognition or spatial thinking, a nonverbal way of representing material culture, was a basic element in technical learning and literacy. To bridge the gap of "coming up against the world physically, on the one hand, and looking and talking about it, on the other," educators worked to link the "grammar" of traditional literacy to spatial thinking and its referents in mechanized manufacturing.[1] This meant, first, integrating the literacy of traditional language with the principles of natural science mediated by numeracy and the symbols and logic of mathematics. Second, it meant linking science and the machine through drawing and modeling.

Spatial descriptions, like traditional verbal expression, reflect not only the object being represented but also the prior knowledge of the observer. The distinction between meaning and structural representation is important and may provide a clue to how meanings embodied in the verbal representations of traditional literacy were linked to nonverbal, spatial representation.[2] To link the structure of nonverbal, material culture with the culture of traditional literacy became a central task for educators.

In the case of machines and even relatively simple implements there were several possible levels of representation: the sketches accompanying patents; the models that accompanied patents; analytic diagrams, idyllic sketches, and woodcuts in journals; and descriptive narratives. Diagramming, in contrast with other language systems, notes Doblin, "is generally not linear-sequential in its method of communication." That is, it is "presentational," a configuration of symbols rather than a string of symbols. Illustrations giving a three-dimensional view of a farm implement with measurements, for example, or giving an isometric perspective of gears presumed certain nonverbal skills.[3]

Historians of technology, especially Eugene Ferguson and Brooke Hindle, have made it clear that technological innovation was strongly perceptual and relied heavily on spatial thinking. In his well-known essay "The Mind's Eye: Nonverbal Thought in Technology," Ferguson observes that "many features and qualities of the objects that a technologist thinks about cannot be reduced to unambiguous verbal descriptions." "All of our technology," he continues, "has a significant intellectual component that is both nonscientific and nonliterary." The designer, he reminds us, "thinks in pictures."[4]

In *Emulation and Invention* Hindle also points to the spatial mode of thinking supported by analytical, logical thought (a fundamental condition for technological development) that "flourish[ed] especially in the United States in its early decades."[5] The spatial thinking of design is decidedly different from the determinism of science, but the two are combined in the creative process of machine design. The knowledge of physical properties of materials and the linkage of one machine component to another complement the design process itself.[6]

While drawing obviously is necessary to design, it is only one component of the process. Design, as David Pye has pointed out, is always based on "trial assumptions" and verified in practice. The geometry of the system—a machine, for example—must be compatible with the desired result, but no amount of geometry will design a machine. Rather, geometry enables the designer to verify assumptions early in the design process without building a prototype. More than other elements of design and invention, it is economy, not necessity, that is the mother of most inventions. "A requirement for convenience is simply a diluted requirement for ease and economy," Pye says.[7]

Bringing together the spatial skills associated with mechanical thinking and a knowledge of kinematics proceeded slowly in American machine shops.[8] Watts' celebrated four-bar linkage, which traced the approximate straight line necessary to allow a piston rod to move "up and down perpendicularly" in an efficient manner, made possible both his own success and developments in large machine tooling, particularly boring mills, capable of boring steam engine cylinders.[9] Watt's four-bar linkage for "parallel motion" did not, however, trace a perfectly straight line, and the mathematical solution to the problem of finding linkages that did occupied keen minds for years to come.[10] The discovery of mathematical solutions to mechanical linkages brought kinematics into the academic fold, where, with statics, it formed one of two branches of elementary mechanics.[11] This division of the study of mechanics was used in the curriculum of the Ecole Polytechnique and was introduced at least as early as 1824 in the reorganized curriculum at the U.S. Military Academy at West Point.[12]

Up to this point the science of mechanics was classificatory in nature. There were calculations, of course, but they were not the heart of the study. Despite the work of Robert Willis, which shifted the study of motion from description to analysis, and the work of William Rankine, who applied Willis' work to the analysis of velocity, a great divide remained between the formal study of kinematics and practical mechanics.[13] Theories had not produced new mechanisms, yet machinery, including machine tools, advanced rapidly in sophistication, a fact, notes Ferguson, that "could only be accounted for by an increase of information with which the individual designer could start."[14]

In the early nineteenth century, craftsmen usually worked from freehand drawings. An apprentice would have been lucky to be in the workshop of William Mason and Rufus Tyler, Philadelphia machinists; Mason taught youngsters to use mechanical drawing instruments.[15] Increasingly, though, there was a place for drawing based on descriptive geometry, both as a method to attain precision (in stone cutting and carpentry, for example) and as a means to represent objects. As a means of representation, descriptive geometry became increasingly important for educational purposes and for design in machine shops. It was a long way, however, from the Mongean methods and mathematics dealt with in Claude Crozet's *Treatise on Descriptive Geometry* (1821), written to be used at West Point, to early shop practice in Philadelphia, New York, and Cincinnati.[16]

Spatial cognition, vernacular artistic expression, and invention were closely related in the perceptual worlds of mechanics, artisans, and architects. Those who studied inventions and inventors in the early nineteenth century were also acutely aware of the close relation between the process of invention and other artistic endeavors.[17] Their remarks were sometimes intended to glorify the process, but their insights came from close observation. For mechanics in general, it was a matter of sensitivity and aesthetic sense. Said a self-promoting piece in *Scientific American* in 1851: "How grateful to the eye of a mechanic is perfection in machinery, or works of art of any kind."[18] In the same issue, Thomas Ewbank spoke of poetry as "the art of invention." In his essay "Artists of the Ideal and Real" he called both poets and inventors "children of inspiration," differing "only in the media of its manifestation." Tropes, springs, and pulleys all yielded to the artist's imagination. Ewbank's estimate of the status of inventors was wishful thinking, but his concern was real enough. These "artists of realities," as Ewbank called them, were no longer "mean and servile" nor "ignoble and scandalous." They were poets of modern technology, and Ewbank waxed eloquent when he pictured them carrying a "magic elixir" and rising to a rarefied atmosphere not occupied by "common mortals."[19]

Voiced in the rhetoric of evangelism, these hyerbolic panegyrics to the gods of art and technology were nonetheless grounded in the perceptual and intellectual tasks of machinists and inventors. Language was "auxiliary" to mechanical innovation in many cases. The "grammar of the machine," as Anthony Wallace called it, was sequential rather than classificatory, as was the grammar of language. The language of the machine could be discovered in its motion and in the spatial relations of its parts. In spite of attempts to teach general scientific principles, day-to-day mechanical improvements often derived more from experience and old technologies than from new knowledge.[20]

Machinists and mechanics thought within a paradigm that was difficult to express in written language and difficult to learn outside shops and manufactures. It was guided by experience and visual representation and was inseparable from production itself. Many parts and positions of a machine had only generic names. If put into words, they might have to be described "by such circumlocutions as 'the 137th spindle from the left,' 'the lowest step of the cam,' or 'the upper right hand bolt on the governor housing.'"[21]

Recent studies of spatial cognition and visual, nonverbal thought help us to understand more clearly the historical challenge faced by late-eighteenth- and early-nineteenth-century educators interested in technical learning. These educators were forced to grapple with the limitations of language itself, with the fact that the categories and classifications of verbal expression do little justice to the particulars of spatial experience.[22] Kouwenhoven reminds us that there is much in our attitudes toward language that asks us to "disregard the evidence of [our] senses."[23] In short, language disassociates us from material culture in its several dimensions, including technology.

The potential dissonance between language learning and nonverbal thought is troublesome for the learning of technical knowledge. Olson and Bruner probably are correct in contending that the artificial separation of knowledge from its medium in traditional schooling led to a gradual denigration of experience as an independently legitimate source of abilities.[24] A parallel development in the history of technology itself is suggested by Edwin Layton; technology, he says, has been devalued in its own right and made subordinate to theory.[25]

It is likely that many mechanics were asked to play the dangerous game of divorcing concept from experience and perception, of burning the bridge of experience only to be left without the skills necessary to reconstruct it.[26] In matters of the practical arts and technology the difference is between the logos *in* the technē and the logos *of* the technē.[27] "Coming up against the world physically, on the one hand, and looking and talking about it, on the other," observes Caws, "represent two complementary and to some degree separable kinds of involvement with it."[28] If the history of technical learning is any guide, Caws probably understates the case.

DIFFERENT LEVELS OF REPRESENTATION: DRAWINGS AND MODELS

As skills for representing the material culture of machines and production, drawing and modeling more accurately reflected the language of the machine than the grammar of the text. Descriptive geometry became increasingly important for the design of machine tooling and production machinery. For the mechanic, the utility of drawing was undoubtedly more important than the mathematics and Newtonian physics that rationalized it. This was so even though the concept of mechanism itself was at the heart of the Newtonian physics that underlay instruction in mechanical principles. The "truth value" of mathematics for the mechanic lay in design, workmanship, and production.

Drawing: An Illustration from the Workshop Mechanical drawing was a basic skill for the mechanic and important to the invention and building of machinery. As a boy, the machinist George Escol Sellers learned to sketch as a matter of course and later attended a private class taught by William Mason, a maker of philosophical instruments and small tools. "A good style of mechanical drawing was taught in Philadelphia long before the want of a mechanical publication was filled," remembered Sellers. William Strickland, an architect, also "was always ready to lend a helping hand to young beginners."[29] Drawing to scale, however, was difficult even for master craftsmen, so full-size drawing boards were common. "In the smith shops," said Sellers, there were "two great boards jointed together. On one of them was half of the set of levers drawn to full size for the large engines and on the other were the levers for the village engines which the blacksmiths worked to for the curves." To make these drawings, Sellers recalled, "part of the time I was obliged to lie on my belly and use my arm as radii for the curves with father standing by directing the changes of the trial marks I made."[30] This indeed was empiricism at a most basic level.

A poignant example of the difficulty of visual representation and the generation gap that was emerging in technical learning was recounted by Sellers in a portrait of John Brandt, a master mechanic. Brandt was a self-made inventor and smith who eventually rose to foreman of the Pennsylvania Railroad shops at Parkesburg and later became master mechanic of the New York and Erie. According to Sellers, Brandt invented a machine for fastening teeth into the leather of a textile carding machine. The machine, as Brandt designed it, had nine distinct movements generated by cam studs on a brass barrel, "not unlike the barrel of a hand organ or musical box." Sellers recalled that his father had explained a similar machine to Brandt, showing him the separate cams on a single shaft that made the different motions, but with "steadier and less jerky motions than the short stud cams on his brass barrel." Brandt asked "to be left alone with the old machine that he might study the cams," and he then proceeded to dismantle the machine. Sellers found him with his pocket knife "carving out of shingles the forms of the various cams." The young Sellers then offered to draw the parts for Brandt, whereupon he discovered that Brandt "did not understand the simplest plain drawings." Said Sellers: "His pocket knife was his pencil, and his habit [not unusual among older workmen] was to carve models out of wood and to adjust parts by trial, a kind of rule of thumb."[31]

Brandt had been engaged by Sellers to make more carding machines, and Sellers recalled that he came to him the next winter, in 1828, with a proposal to teach the younger man to make his own forgings if Sellers would "give him some instruction in machine drawing." Brandt believed that "no man could be a good working mechanic without being able to make his own forgings" and that the young Sellers, "with proper attention and desire," could learn "in a few weeks" what usually took "four or five years' apprenticeship" to learn. It was an interesting proposal because Brandt and Sellers would serve as helpers to each other. It was a humble move for Brandt but the mark of an excellent, instinctive teacher.[32]

When it came his turn to teach Brandt drawing, Sellers recalled that he "thought it would be an easy task to make a good mechanical draughtsman of a man who, with such facility, carved with his pocket-knife the forms he wanted to produce with his hammer." There was no problem with manual dexterity, and Brandt easily learned to "copy line drawings with neatness and accuracy." But, noted Sellers, it was "purely mechanical," a telling remark on the pure empiricism of Brandt's skill. Sellers remembered that Brandt was "mortified by not being able to understand sketches." "A verbal explanation of any portion of a machine was clear to him, but the moment a sketch in illustration was made all was confusion." [33]

Sellers realized that all Brandt's thinking was "full size." He could not reduce to scale. Full size and scale could not be "carried both in his mind at the same time," said Sellers. Sellers continued to work with Brandt on full-size drawings, but "some ludicrous things occurred," he recalled. When showing Sellers a full-size drawing of a crank, Brandt asked Sellers to reduce it to half size, to which Sellers responded, "why don't you do it. . . . You have two centers on a line." Brandt replied that "yes . . . I have done it, but it don't look right." Sellers complied, and Brandt remarked that "it looked too small." "Measure from center to center, and you will find it right," said Sellers. Brandt walked away and soon came back with both drawings cut out, saying: "I have weighed both. There is something wrong. The half size does not weigh one-fourth as much as the full size." (When all dimensions of a plane figure are reduced by one-half, the area becomes one-fourth of the original area.)[34]

The episodes of being taught apparently were anxious for Brandt, and books only confused him. "At one time," continued Sellers, Brandt "became very despondent" and said "he felt his own ignorance, that he was too old to begin, too old to go to school," but would try with a private teacher who would promise "to keep his secret." "If he could only be taught how to learn, he thought he could do the rest; but he was sensitive on the subject, and did not want it known that at his time of life [over 40] he was beginning." [35]

A tutor was engaged for Brandt, and it was agreed that the "first step in instruction must be entirely oral." Brandt's studies continued during 1828 to spring 1829. Later he took the job of foreman at the Pennsylvania Railroad shops at Parkesburg. When Sellers visited him he found that Brandt's office walls were "covered with working models of eccentrics, rock shafts, and steam valves, *all full size*." When asked about them, Brandt replied, in what must have been a plaintive tone, "It is best, I think, that way."[36]

DRAWING INSTRUCTION: THE RATIONALE, PEDAGOGY, AND CRITICISM OF THE COMMON SCHOOLS

In mechanics' institutes, where apprentices and journeymen attended classes and lectures on science, mechanic arts, and mathematics, mechanical drawing was viewed as basic to the process of inventing and making machinery. As early as 1814 Thomas Cooper defined the three requirements to be a civil engineer. They were a "habitual facility in drawing and designing with neatness and accuracy," a "profound knowledge of mathematics," and a "full knowledge of the modern science of chemistry."[37] Drawing, noted the *Journal of the Franklin Institute,* was more difficult than was usually recognized. One or two quarters of instruction were not sufficient, said a columnist, and students must be industrious enough to follow through with the program of drawing.[38]

In many ways the story of John Brandt represented the end of one era and the beginning of another. Advocates and founders of mechanics' institutes moved early in the nineteenth century to offer courses in drawing and geometry. The Franklin Institute, for example, gave instruction in drawing in the winter of 1824–25; there were forty pupils enrolled. An observer of the program in 1826 noted that the course in "geometrical drawing" served a wide range of occupations and taught pupils "knowledge of designing."[39] By 1828 mechanical drawing was listed as part of the high school curriculum.

Learning *about* drawing was no substitute for developing drawing skills, however. Drawing was the quintessential hands-on subject and, along with mathematics, was considered by Walter Johnson of the Franklin Institute a subject requiring a close teacher-student relationship.[40] Johnson, always alert to the limitations of the lecture method and verbal learning, addressed the problem of visual representation in his essay "On the Utility of Visible Illustrations" in the *American Annals of Education and Instruction* in 1833. The eye, he said, "claims pre-eminence among the available means of gaining and establishing all our real knowledge." Johnson acknowledged that "questions of abstract and metaphysical science are seldom capable of being reduced to the form of visible representation," but in the physical sciences and natural history he listed six methods and their purposes for "visible illustrations." Most important were "artificial models," "graphic representations" giving "perspective," outlines and diagrams giving general impressions, and symbols representing the "magnitude, number, proportion, and efficacy" of objects.[41]

Drawing was, as one author in *The American Polytechnic Journal* put it, one of three "languages," the other two being algebraic formulae, and "ordinary" language. Drawing was the most readily comprehended of the three, he argued, and even when poorly executed it gave "*some* idea of the subject represented, without the circumlocution of a wordy description, or the necessity of a long, and, in some cases, expensive preparation, to appreciate the '*a* plus *x*' of the formula." In the same journal, however, the editor complained that drawing as a "branch of education . . . has been too much neglected heretofore by the artisan." "The art of drawing, with mathematical accuracy," the editor continued, "is often absolutely necessary, and always useful to every operative, as well as to the engineer and architect."[42]

Those who had first-hand experience with successful machine design appreciated the importance of visual representation in general. In the common schools, however, drawing was a low-status affair when compared with reading, arithmetic, and geography. With few exceptions, practice in drawing at the elementary level accompanied instruction in geography and penmanship. Some high schools offered drawing, and many taught geometry, though the emphasis was not on spatial constructions but rather on mathematical proofs. Drawing was also a part of the curriculum in normal schools, but it did not rival rhetoric, ancient languages, grammar, English, and mathematics.[43] As late as 1857 the author of "Instruction in Drawing," published in the *Connecticut Common School Journal* and reprinted in *The American Journal of Education*, complained that "every talent, but that for art, is duly cultivated at school, or, at least, a foundation laid for it; and why should this be made an exception?"[44]

Educators in mechanics' institutes and schools operated by trade associations were generally staunch supporters of common schools, but they were also some of their harshest critics. They shouted, cajoled, and used virtually every rhetorical flourish to reshape the common school curriculum to provide a useful education for mechanics and farmers. Editors of journals never argued for transforming a common school education into a vocational one. They did, however, lobby common school educators to teach drawing—and teach it well—along with science and mathematics.

For their part, common school advocates of more drawing began by observing that the subject generally was missing from a common school education or that, if present, was poorly taught. Speaking of the proposed institution for instruction in the "practical arts and sciences" in Massachusetts in 1825, one author noted that "to be able, in half an hour, to make, with a lead pencil, a sufficiently correct picture of any common house, apartment, bridge, tool, or instrument that we see, to serve as a model to copy from, is certainly no trifling attainment."[45]

The persistent criticisms and recommendations in such journals as the *American Annals of Education, The American Journal of Education, The Western School Journal, The Common School Journal,* and *Common School Assistant* attested to the common schools' reluctance to change. The issue was the familiar one of the "crowded curriculum," and the debate was over what type of knowledge was most valuable. Frequent complaints about the "verbalism" of common school instruction were heard: "Words, words, words," as one essayist put it. At its best, said critics, mere verbalism was simply confusing; at its worst it was preparation for eristic discourse.[46] Complaints about verbalism were often accompanied by pleas for greater emphasis on arithmetic, science, and drawing and for more attention to the mastery of the "basics" in these subjects.

By 1838 pressure to include drawing in common school education was mounting, along with complaints about the focus on ornamental drawing and the fine arts. It was not drawing as a "polite accomplishment" that was needed but, rather, drawing as a different language, a way of *"defining, experiencing, and retaining* some ideas," said J. S. Buckingham in *Common School Assistant.*[47] The point also was made in *The Common School Journal:* "Drawing, of itself, is an expressive and beautiful language. A few strokes of the pen or pencil will often represent to the eye what no amount of words, however well chosen, can communicate."[48]

In a series of essays in *Common School Assistant,* Buckingham defended drawing on grounds of both mental discipline and utility. The faculties and attributes of the mind to be developed through drawing were memory, conception, imagination, abstraction, comparison, reason, and taste, he said.[49] The utility of drawing was seen in everyday occurrences that spread new ideas: "If we learn to draw a likeness of a kitchen utensil, or a farming implement, and in our travels see an article, whether it be a plough or chopping-knife, which we perceive at once, is better than the one we use at home, we are able to make a drawing of it, and thus carry home the improvements of others," said Buckingham.[50] The way to self-improvement, it seems, lay not only in books but in observing and recording the improvements of others.

A similar argument appeared in *The Common School Journal:* "Everyman should be able to plot a field, to sketch a road or a river, to draw the outlines of a simple machine, a piece of household furniture or a farming utensil, and to delineate the internal arrangement or construction of a home."[51] To illustrate the utility of drawing in a changing economy, the author of "Writing and Drawing" noted that the "master-architect, the engraver, the engineer, the pattern designer, the draughtsman, moulder, machine builder, or head mechanic of any kind . . . acknowledge that this art [of drawing] is essential and indispensable." "We now perform by far the greater part of our labor by machinery," the author continued, and "whatever will advance the mechanic and manufacturing arts . . . is especially important here; and whatever is important for men to know, as men, should be learned by children in the schools."[52]

Drawing Texts Early-nineteenth-century drawing texts were divided into two general categories: those emphasizing drawing as a tool of the fine arts and those using drawing as an applied art. For example, R. Dagley's *Compendium of the Theory and Practice of Drawing and Painting* (London, 1819, 1822) stressed the role of drawing in the education of a gentleman, presenting it in the larger moral and aesthetic context of "refined" judgment. Good models were necessary in youth, said the author, to avoid "whatever is vulgar, unmeaning, and offensive to refinement."[53] Charles Blunt's *Essay on Mechanical Drawing* (London, 1811), on the other hand, offered a course in practical geometry. Blunt's explanations of general principles were direct, often to the point of being incomplete, but there were sixty-three illustrations, ranging from basic figures to perspective drawings of a sawing machine, mechanical screws, a rectilinear machine, and other machines used in manufacturing and raw materials processing.

George Birkbeck, an advocate of the working man and the president of the London Mechanic's Institution, offered instruction in the common geometric features of both fine and applied arts in his adaptation of Baron Charles Dupin's *Mathematics Practically Applied to the Useful and Fine Arts* (1827). Inspired by his observations of the education of the laboring classes of Glasgow, Dupin had lectured at the Conservatoire des Arts et Metiers on the application of geometry to arts and manufactures. He recognized the threat to France of highly skilled labor from England and Scotland and believed it was his patriotic duty to devise a method for teaching the application of geometry and mechanics to all the arts.[54] Birkbeck's preface to Dupin's work likewise spoke of the ascendancy of the British worker, criticizing such works as Olinthus Gregory and Lee's *Mathematics for Practical Men* and *Elements of Arithmetic, Algebra, and Geometry* for their failure to demonstrate the practical applications of geometry.[55]

Because there were few elementary drawing texts produced before the mid-nineteenth century, learning to draw was difficult for both teacher and neophyte, regardless of whether instruction took place inside or outside the common school. Such texts as *The Oxford Drawing Book* (1825, 1845), *Linear Drawing Book* (1843), *First Book of Drawing* (1846), and *Initiatory Drawing Cards* (1844) included instruction in drawing basic shapes but emphasized ornamental and landscape drawing.

In most elementary and intermediate texts, the sequence of instruction varied little. The essential lines—vertical, horizontal, and oblique—were introduced first, usually with a warning, or at least a reminder, that the child should master these with a steady hand before moving on. Next came the standard shapes: circle, triangle, and rectangle. At this point, depending on whether the emphasis was on utility or ornamental drawing, the child either learned the concepts of horizon and vanishing point or continued to work on geometric forms. To the extent that drawing and geometry were integrated, students were expected to master the concepts of point, line, surface, and solid.

By the 1840s the reasons for teaching drawing in public schools were well rehearsed, and they ranged from the utilitarian to the aesthetic. Yet authors of texts in the 1840s and 1850s still felt compelled to remind teachers and students that "drawing is essential to all good education, and eminently useful in every branch of manufacture and art," wrote the author of *A Progressive Course of Inventive Drawing on the Principles of Pestalozzi* (1851). "It aids the artisan in carrying out the productions and designs of the man of science and cannot fail to make him better understand the end for which he labors."[56]

In texts on drawing, the student met a new vocabulary that included words like oblique, concave, convex, parallel, perspective, acute, obtuse, curvilinear, geometrical, linear, aerial, vanishing point, horizon, foreshortening, isomorphic, and orthographic. Such words were sometimes introduced with little or no explanation. But Charles Blunt's *Essay on Mechanical Drawing*, however, brought together an understanding of optical illusion and mathematics in his lessons on linear perspective. His work was well illustrated with lessons on practical geometry, including those of an elementary nature, such as erecting perpendiculars and subdividing lines into equal parts, along with the more difficult tasks of inscribing octagons and squares in circles, drawing elevations of wheels, and delineating the spirals of a screw. Blunt's essay was not for the beginner, and mechanics who had not already studied elementary drawing must have struggled.

A. Cornu's *Course of Linear Drawing* (1842), adapted from the French polytechnic schools, also brought together the mechanics of drawing and geometric principles. Lessons ranged from elementary ones to those demanding the construction of scales, projections, and proportional representations. Students who had not received extensive instruction in elementary and intermediate drawing would not have understood the following explanation or been able to carry out the drawing: "In a screw with square threads, we must determine the two spirals generated by the vertices of the angles on the exterior of the cylinder, and those generated by the vertices of the angles at the interior of the cylinder; and although the form of the generating square is concealed by the thickness of the thread generated, we will easily determine by the process pointed out, the spirals given by the vertices A and B, by means of the height of the space A A', and of the horizontal projection of the exterior half-cylinder; as also those described by the interior vertices C D, by means of the horizontal projection of the interior half-cylinder."[57]

Though texts were few and authors despaired over the poor drawing instruction offered in the public schools, there is some evidence that drawing instruction evolved along the lines of child-centered Pestalozzian methods, which were introduced to American educators in the 1820s. The *American Journal of Education* in 1829, for example, explained Pestalozzi's rationale and methods of instruction, noting that the entire system conformed to the laws of nature.[58] Reprinted material from English publications also informed American educators about applying Pestalozzi's hands-on, perception-based methods to drawing instruction. The *Mechanics' Magazine and Register of Inventions and Improvements* of New York City, for example, enthusiastically endorsed the recommendations of the Society for Diffusing Useful Knowledge on the teaching of drawing to the "poorer classes." According to the essay, drawing should conform to Pestalozzian principles. And those who enter trades after leaving school would secure the greatest advantages if they "develop and cultivate a taste for beauty and symmetry of form." The result would be beneficial for "all branches of our national industry."[59]

In England, Richard Lovell Edgeworth and Maria Edgeworth's *Essays on Practical Education* (1811, 1815) was far ahead of its time in analyzing the perceptual linkages among modeling, invention, and mechanics.[60] The Edgeworths noted that "an early use of rule and pencil, and easy access to prints of machines, of architecture, and of implements of trades, [were] of obvious use" in teaching about mechanics. Models of such common items as furniture, bellows, and grates would help children comprehend basic principles of mechanics. Drawing itself would promote the "habit of abstraction" and the knowledge of perspective, improve taste, and be "useful in facilitating the knowledge of mechanics." Having had instruction in drawing and observing models, children presumably would be able to easily comprehend the structure and use of real machines.[61]

An Introduction to Linear Drawing (1828), translated from the French of M. Francoeur by William Fowle, attempted to fill a gap in public school education. Like the Edgeworths' book, Fowle's was characterized by an emerging awareness of the importance of sequencing instruction according to child development. Fowle's observations led him to believe that teaching the drawing of geometrical figures should be presented in order of "difficulty of execution, rather than in order of theorems."[62] His work began with basic geometric figures: drawing right lines, dividing them into segments, and extending their length. It included practice in proportionality—for example, adding squares or cutting a square. Numerous examples of applied geometry were included as students learned ornamental drawing by sketching Tuscan, Doric, Ionic, and Corinthian columns. Having gained experience in actual drawing, the student then moved to formal operations involving definitions and calculations. Thus, for example, the student was asked to calculate the unknown third side of a triangle and the area of a parallelogram and to find the volume of a prism and cylinder.

When Rembrandt Peale published his *Graphics; A Popular System of Drawing and Writing for the Use of Schools and Families* (1841), he defended both the utility and the academic importance of drawing, that "simplest of languages." The language of drawing was "spoken by the draughtsman" and became "the law and guide of the workman," said Peale. "Geometry, Mensuration and Surveying are founded on its elements," he continued, and geography is "greatly facilitated to the eye which is accustomed to drawing."[63]

Peale devoted considerable space to Pestalozzi's advice on education, particularly that on the advantages of teaching drawing and penmanship together. (Pestalozzi had demonstrated that drawing, as a general branch of education, was a "means of leading the child from vague perceptions to clear ideas" and that the skills of drawing were preliminary to the teaching of writing.) Writing, said Peale, "is nothing else than drawing the forms of letters . . . , little more than writing the forms of objects."[64]

Based on lessons learned while implementing his method at Central High School in Philadelphia, Peale devised an improved manual and "Directions to Teachers." His directions specified a sequence of twenty-seven guidelines for instruction that incorporated several fundamental principles. These principles led the student from the drawing of Roman, English, and German letters to a knowledge of "form" and "relative proportion" and an "application of the rules of parallel comparison—perpendicular, horizontal and oblique; as well as the proportions and directions of curves, chords, and triangular situations." Even the student who already wrote a good hand, said Peale, would "derive advantage from understanding the application of drawing to define the peculiar characters of writing."[65]

Peale defended drawing as the "law and guide of the workman." He was sensitive to the range of talent encountered by teachers, and he offered specific advice on "freedom in sketching." He also emphasized accuracy through drill but warned that students' work need not "have the appearance of ruled lines, as if intended for drawing machinery or architecture." Instead, it was satisfactory for students to demonstrate a "general correctness, like the resolute furrows of a well ploughed field."[66]

Like Peale's work, *The Common School Drawing Master*, which was published as a series in *The Common School Journal* between 1844 and December 1845 and was based on Peter Schmid's [Schmidt's] "Guide to Drawing," aimed to take advantage of students' natural curiosity and allow them to develop confidence in their abilities. It avoided the intimidating language of most academic disciplines. Moreover, Schmid claimed that his method obviated the need to train teachers to be specialists in drawing, which appealed to budget-minded school boards. Financial exigency, he observed, was the primary reason that drawing was not offered in common schools.

Schmid's method had broad appeal. It was ideal for "self-teaching students," no small matter for a subject necessary "to the education of every mechanic" and to "family use." The work was also a foundation to the further study of perspective geometry. By learning "scientific perspective," Schmid argued, students would be prepared "to draw objects in perspective of their own invention." Lest the student be deceived, however, the author reminded his readers that the science of perspective "never, by itself, taught the art of drawing *nature* in perspective." That "requires an eye practiced; and these lessons give practice to the eye and hand."[67]

Schmid's method was characteristically Pestalozzian in its use of material aids. He used nineteen blocks proportioned to inch cubes (one-half inch, one and one-half inch, and two inches). The cubes were arranged in a variety of configurations for students to draw. But Schmid warned teachers that the mere use of blocks did not constitute his method. Rather, he said, teachers should sequence their lessons so that each scholar's "powers of observation" would "gradually unfold."[68] In all cases the eye needed to be educated first, and mathematical rules of perspective would follow.[69]

The proper method of teaching drawing was far from settled at mid-century. Whether drawing a straight line was the mark of success was much in dispute, with some teachers insisting instead that the drawing of curves was both natural and more pedagogically sound in linking drawing, geometry, and sketching. The use of models was also controversial, as was the degree to which drill should predominate over drawing from nature.[70] Whether Pestalozzian methods made the same headway in practice as they did in textbooks is unknown, but it is probably safe to say that the forces of reform did not completely subdue the defenders of tradition.

The rightful place of drawing in the common school curriculum also remained in question in spite of its obvious utility in the workplace and its acceptance in mechanics' institutes, engineering colleges, and in the periodical press devoted to science and mechanics. Occupational utility was an insufficient ground for the defense of drawing in the common school. Explanations of its necessary relations to other subjects gained it greater favor. Thus, for example, its utility with respect to geometry was a strong argument in its favor, as was its contribution to the student's perceptive faculty, allowing him or her to represent what was "really" seen.[71]

Drawing surely had made some headway in the common schools, but not enough to satisfy proponents of technical learning. What little drawing was taught left the mechanic ill prepared for mechanical drawing. *Scientific American* was still, in 1851, urging mechanics to learn to draw. Said an inspirational essay on upward mobility for young mechanics: "Every machinist should learn to draw, so should every carpenter, and do not be content until you fully understand, and construct every machine, apparatus, or whatever it may be, and can take charge of and superintend every branch of business connected with your trades."[72]

Models Models played an important part in invention and innovative manufacturing processes. They were a standard part of the patent application procedure and were justified as such on grounds of public utility (display), feasibility (so that a skilled workman might understand and construct a full-sized operating machine), and clarity (so that the operation of the invention was clearly understandable to patent examiners).[73] With or without the rules of the patent office, however, modeling was common for inventors, mechanics, and experimenters. Their value was well put by John Fitch in 1786 when he and his machinist Harry (Henry) Voight built a model of a crank-paddled boat. "Perhaps this model gave us a greater . . . opinion of our abilities than we really merited," said Fitch, yet "it elucidated the principles so fully that it could hardly admit of a doubt but the next which we made, would be nearly perfect."[74]

The use of models allowed reviewers of patents and associations, such as the Franklin Institute and Munn and Company, to evaluate inventions. Thus the reviewers were concerned with the characteristics of acceptable models. Among the observations of Walter R. Johnson at a monthly meeting of the Franklin Institute in 1847 (a meeting at which Mr. Herron's model of a railroad bridge was exhibited) was a list of criteria or "conditions to be fulfilled in constructing *models*." Johnson listed three conditions, for a successful model: correspondence of the model, proportionally, to the "structure"; identification of materials in the model and structure; and "proportional accuracy" for joints and tensions by which the parts are "compacted together."[75] These criteria, in effect, were those to be met by any well-built machine.

Johnson's conditions were applicable to a wide range of purposes in the use of models. In general, models were used in three distinct ways: for display, demonstration, and experimentation. For mechanics' institutes, demonstration was probably the most crucial. In advocating the formation of mechanics' institutes "in every town and village in our country," the editor of *Scientific American* noted the importance of models in teaching and invention and recommended that instructors build models that "could be taken down and put up with screws and pins, so that they could be explained in all their parts and uses."[76]

The case for using models in teaching paralleled that of drawing. As with drawing, the Edgeworths' essays on practical education elucidated the relation between pedagogy and utility. Toys, for the Edgeworths, were the perceptual and conceptual links between the world of material culture and the development of verbal and nonverbal communication in early life. Maria Edgeworth recommended that children make "models of common furniture" that they would use as toys. The various parts should be labeled so that they could be assembled and disassembled, and "all their parts . . . might be seen distinctly." The labeling would allow children to associate the names "with realities" so "they will neither learn by rote technical terms, nor will they be retarded in their progress in mechanical invention by the want of language." Models, said Edgeworth, amuse children before they "can use tools." From models of furniture, children could go on to build "architectural models" and "models of simple machines." "Gradually," she said, children would construct "models of more complicated machinery," including spinning wheels, looms, paper mills, windmills, and waterwheels.[77]

Edgeworth pictured model building as a prelude to direct observations made on trips to manufactures. When children had acquired a "general idea of the whole," she said, they were prepared for the "explanations of the workmen" and "would understand some of the technical terms which so much alarm the intellects of those who hear them for the first time."[78] This knowledge, along with the experiences of invention and working in wood, brass, and iron, helped prepare the student to learn the principles of mechanics.

A review of J. R. Young's *The Elements of Mechanics* in the *Journal of the Franklin Institute* in 1834 acknowledged the importance of "geometrical constructions" and "experiments with models" in teaching mechanical science. The reviewer went on to say, however, that "neither of these methods is without limit," primarily because they do not have the generalizability of the analytic method.[79] Here was a hint at the emerging educational controversy over empirically based methods versus analytic-scientific methods of teaching the principles of mechanics. Still, models remained important in the educational program of mechanics' institutes.

The use of models was detailed in Robert Brunton's American edition of *A Compendium of Mechanics* (1830). In his essay on isometric perspective in this book, Farish explained isometric drawing and remarked on the use of models and the need for drawing to represent them.

Farish, a lecturer at Cambridge University, explained that in his course he exhibited "models of almost all the more important machines which are in use in the manufactures in Britain." Economy of space, he observed, dictated that he not retain "permanent and separate models, on a scale requisite to make them work," because it would have been difficult to find a warehouse large enough. To solve the problem, Farish procured an apparatus that would demonstrate the principles of machinery and how the parts fit together. The parts, made of metal, were strong enough "to perform even heavy work," Farish said. Included in the "kit" were geared brass wheels, axes of various lengths, bars, clamps, frames, and "whatever else might be necessary to build up the particular machines which are wanted for one lecture."[80]

Farish quickly recognized that his assistants had difficulty interpreting his drawings, so he combined his work on models with a method for drawing machinery from an isometric perspective. He found this method "much better adapted to the exhibition of machinery." Farish went on to learn about isometric drawing and then wrote his essay on the application of the isometric perspective to various objects, including wheels, axes, cylinders, and arches. He concluded that the isometric perspective was applicable to "almost every thing which occurs in the representation of models, of machines, of philosophical instruments, and, indeed, of almost any regular production of art." In addition, he believed that the method could be carried out by a "person who is but little acquainted with the art of drawing" and that the "information given by such drawings is much more definite and precise than that obtained by the usual methods, and better fitted to direct a workman in execution." It was, in short, ideal for workmen, students, and teachers alike.[81] In fact, as will be seen, instructors in mechanics' institutes and colleges made frequent use of models, as did those who popularized scientific principles on the lecture circuit. Models, like drawings, were the gateways to design and to understanding the principles of mechanics.

CONCLUSION

The case for teaching drawing and modeling was based on the highly visual and tactile environment of production and shop experience. For the machinist, particularly, the language of drawing and modeling was necessary to translate the motion of machinery into three dimensions. Transmitting that information more efficiently into print then became the task of those who both understood motion and could represent it graphically and pictorially. Design and even repair of machinery were creative processes that could be described in words, but they were were difficult to carry through without the special skills of drawing and modeling.

Like production itself, on-site repair, maintenance, and innovation were done within the context of efficiency and cost considerations. Individuals with even a passing acquaintance with mechanics and kinematics understood their usefulness in setting the boundaries of what was mechanically possible. But such individuals also understood that science was not design; in order to make or fix a machine one had to conceive of its operations spatially. They understood both the limitations of ordinary language in describing motion and location and the limitations of abstract formulae in making mechanical calculations to take account of the special circumstances in each manufacture.

Drawing and modeling increasingly became part of the repertoire of skills of the successful mechanic, especially the machinist. For operatives these skills were not crucial, although to become one with the machine they had to visualize its operations and react synchronously. For the machinist and repairman, however, expectations were high. Both were absolutely necessary to the success of the manufacturer. Unreliability was a manufacturer's nightmare, and downtime meant lost profits. On-the-spot innovation was often expected if a flaw in design could not be dealt with at its source. Those who found it difficult to think spatially and were unable to draw and model were not of much value to a manufacturer who needed to avoid mechanical breakdowns to keep his mill running.

Educators responded to the need for greater facility with spatial thinking, although their efforts were far from systematic and their success limited. At the elementary level of instruction it was the *skill* of drawing and the manual dexterity needed for building models that received most attention. Drawing, as a skill, was seen simply as a different way of writing. Moreover, it fit nicely with the emergence of Pestalozzian hands-on methods of teaching.

At more advanced levels of schooling, educators sought to link the skill of drawing to rules of perspective geometry. One way to do this was to incorporate the study of perspective geometry into the curricula of mechanics' institutes and high schools. Yet, more basic skills had to be taught first. Most teachers in common schools had little facility with drawing and modeling, so they, along with their students, became the targets of reformers' recommendations.

Education reformers stressed drawing as a useful skill as opposed to a refined accomplishment. They understood that drawing was a "language" and that, like other languages, it had a grammar. They appreciated, moreover, that drawing and the making of models were creative acts and that the product was to be understood as a whole, not merely as an assembly of parts. Thus they were prepared to argue from the high ground of art as well as from utility, and aesthetics and utility thus became the twin pillars on which the case for spatial thinking and its related skills were educationally justified.

3

THE HERITAGE OF NATURAL
PHILOSOPHY, MATHEMATICS,
AND PERSPECTIVE GEOMETRY

As educators came to grips with the demands for knowledge arising from new technologies and new ways of organizing production, they also sought to link the empiricism of the workplace to theoretical foundations in science and mathematics. Spatial thinking and its related skills were crucial bridges between theory and practice. These skills, however, did not bring the mechanic fully into the world of science. In fact, it is likely that mechanics as a broad class of workers did not have the educational background to access scientific knowledge through traditional methods.

The pedagogical problems educators faced in helping public school students, farmers, and mechanics to achieve technical literacy were rooted in part in the epistemological difficulties of natural philosophy itself. The teaching of natural philosophy had been the mainstay of scientific education and was considered by mid-eighteenth-century educators important to a thorough understanding of technological progress. Yet the heritage of Bacon notwithstanding, the marriage of the technical and the scientific was a formidable challenge. To better understand the dilemma facing educators attempting to synthesize mathematics, science, and technology, it is helpful to consider the development of natural philosophy, or, as it was variously called, physics and natural science.

From the thirteenth to the mid-seventeenth century, Aristotelean classificatory schemes were dominant in natural philosophy, giving order to a
broad array of subjects.[1] Despite the eventual union of mathematics and
natural philosophy in the science of physics, natural philosophy and mathematics were sharply distinguished in theory and pedagogy. Natural philosophy, said the entry in the *Library of Useful Knowledge* (1829), "teaches
the nature and properties of actually existing substances, their motions,
their connection with each other, and their influence on one another." While
the truths of natural philosophy "depended on matter of fact . . . learnt by
observation and experiment [and] never . . . discovered by reasoning at
all," the truths of mathematics are "wholly independent of facts and experiments" and depend "only upon reasoning."[2] But disputes over the proper
role of mathematics, with its ideal geometric constructions in determining
causation, remained an obstacle to the integration of mathematical and scientific knowledge.

Newton's great synthesis in the seventeenth century allowed natural
philosophers and mathematicians to tap a rich vein that promised to unite
science and mathematics in the common problem of understanding motion.
Newton succeeded like none before him in capturing and representing the
heart of science in mathematical expression justified empirically and experimentally. But to natural philosophy he also left the thematic (both
moral and metaphysical) content of science. Textbooks of the early nineteenth century dealt with all three dimensions of scientific thought: empirical, analytic, and thematic. Thematic content was much more evident in
books for younger audiences, who lacked the mathematical skills for analysis.[3]

During the eighteenth century much scientific work took place in the
context of natural philosophy. The beliefs that God's mysterious ways were
mathematical and that his design for nature was an efficient one were
widely accepted. The mechanics of the universe had been divorced from the
metaphysics of Aristotle. Nature had been geometricized, then mathematized, but the dynamics of the universe still belonged to God.[4] Just as nature
was the perfect machine, so was God the great engineer. That works of
nature could be understood inductively had been demonstrated by Locke
in his theory of sensation and his rejection of "innate" ideas. That *all* could
share in the discovery of nature was the bequest of Francis Bacon and an
inspiration for many attempts to popularize science through formal and demonstrative lectures.[5]

The Legacy of Francis Bacon

The role of Francis Bacon's "point of view"—a philosophy of induction tied to a scheme for classifying all knowledge—in early-nineteenth-century American science has been scrutinized and vigorously debated by historians of science and technology. Few question that science in that era was utilitarian in spirit or that the method of induction was highly prized. Most disputes focus on the value of Baconian science to further scientific development and the degree to which Baconian science may have obstructed the integration of scientific and mathematical studies. Although Bacon's contribution (or lack thereof) to scientific progress was not a major issue in the teaching of American science and natural philosophy in the early nineteenth century, his scheme for a new taxonomy of human knowledge raised important issues for those attempting to integrate natural philosophy, mathematics, and technology.

Bacon's scheme for redefining the relations of the "types" of knowledge assumed the traditional divisions of philosophy—natural, moral, and metaphysical—each distinguished by its objects of knowledge: nature, man, and God, respectively. Theoretical natural philosophy was divided into physics and metaphysics, corresponding to the two "operative" sciences of mechanics and magic. Bacon's pyramid of knowledge allowed the student and scholar to move by induction from empirical observations to abstract levels of physics and metaphysics. At both levels, consideration of the material and efficient causes of physical phenomena led to reflection on the formal and final causes of metaphysics. From the empirical foundations of mechanics and the mechanic arts to the study of metaphysics, the method of induction was tied to mankind's "mastery over nature."[6]

Bacon's pyramid of knowledge had the effect of more efficiently relating the mechanic arts to the higher branches of science.[7] But Bacon warned that knowledge should not be reduced too quickly to "arts and exact methods." The danger of such a reduction, for Bacon, was that the work of the imagination could be stifled, even though knowledge might be refined when accommodated to action. With this warning Bacon argued that a deeper understanding of science must rely on an inductive procedure leading from the particular to the universal.[8]

Bacon battled against speculative philosophy, but he knew that practical knowledge, isolated as pure technique, could no longer be nurtured by philosophy.[9] Although he grew to respect the craftsman, notes Farrington, Bacon understood that "inventions were few, casual, and limited in scope compared with what they might be."[10] Uniting theory and practice was the objective of his "inginary" (an engine house or shop), a part of Solomon's house in his utopia on the island New Atlantis.[11] Bacon contrasted the history of the mechanical arts, those "happy omens" of progress, with philosophy, a statue drawing "crowds of admirers" but unable to move. His aim was to revolutionize production and invention, which in itself provided a test of man's knowledge of nature. The pyramid of knowledge was his strategy for victory over scholasticism and the foundation of his plan to establish an enduring peace between truth and utility. Both, he argued, should lead to action, not argument.[12]

Bacon's taxonomic solution to the integration of the practical and the theoretical gave more prominence to the mechanical arts by allying them with natural philosophy itself. The epistemological implication of man's interaction with nature was summed up in *Novum Organum:* "What is most useful in practice is most correct in theory."[13] The practical effect of this dictum was to reintegrate experience and contemplation. What Bacon advocated was what the Enlightenment of the eighteenth century eventually did so well: to compile an "encyclopedia of the arts and crafts as a basis for a true philosophy of nature." In Bacon's analogy between language and the process of discovery and understanding we see the dilemma of linking verbal expression and experience. Just as the alphabet, syllabification, and constituent parts of sentences are the building blocks of language, the forms of nature (not Platonic, but very Aristotelian) allow us to spell nature's words and "make new words for ourselves." Through the study of nature's language, Bacon suggests, we are led to look behind appearances and description to principles of formal operations.[14]

Bacon was suspicious of the abstractions of mathematics but acknowledged their importance to the study of natural philosophy.[15] In his revised *Advancement of Learning* Bacon noted that mathematical demonstrations "only show how all things may be ingeniously made out and disentangled, not how they truly subsist in nature; and indicate the apparent motions only, and a system of machinery arbitrarily devised and arranged to produce them, . . . not the very causes and truth of things."[16] In short, he protested that mathematics was not of experience but physics was. The key point is that the Baconian heritage emphasized the importance of the inductive method and a philosophy of experience that relied on the tangible and visible rather than the idealizations of mathematics.

Bacon and Nineteenth-Century American Science

By the time the Baconian view of science came to reign in nineteenth-century America the marriage of physics and mathematics had been consummated in Newtonian mechanical philosophy. Analytic geometry and calculus had increased the predictive power of mathematics, and perspective geometry had reemerged in the early nineteenth century as a new tool for design and drawing. In spite of these changes, physics was still taught as part of natural philosophy, and the tension persisted between the empirical foundations of science and the deductive (idealized) method of mathematics. The fact that physics was taught as part of natural philosophy allowed questions about the physical universe to be confounded by metaphysics and moral philosophy. Yet the teaching of natural philosophy could not, in many cases, be separated from a religiously conservative climate of opinion. Thus the analytic division between physics and metaphysics that was part of the Baconian tradition broke down under the stress of religious orthodoxy.

The Enlightenment tradition carried with it into the nineteenth century a mechanical philosophy that had expurgated the Aristotelian concepts of form, substance, and accident. Yet the problem of causation and the concept of force made the collision of physics, metaphysics, and theology inevitable: what was the origin of force, where was its location, how was it to be measured, and did it apply equally to living and nonliving things? Even leaving metaphysical questions aside, there remained knotty problems of measurement: was force proportional to velocity, to the change in velocity, to the square of velocity? [17]

The fact that these questions were asked within the context of natural philosophy made them difficult to answer without provoking religious and moral controversy. Yet attempts to avoid such controversy were the stuff of both natural theology and a theology of nature. Theology and science achieved a tenuous peace in the nineteenth century, not because the conflict between materialism and theology was resolved philosophically but because the politics of religion restrained the claims of science.

There was little conflict between science and religion in the early nineteenth century, says Daniels, because theologians were the gatekeepers of "an important part of the cultural values to which the new profession [of science] had to appeal if it were to become firmly established." Thus scientists had to "supplant" theology, not "displace" it. The compromise was delicate but simple. Science explained *how* God worked his way according to lawful principles. Science could not explain God's plan. The findings of science, when properly interpreted, however, "could be used to reinforce belief in the benevolence of God, and consequently, to impress upon men the necessity of obedience to His laws." Scientists subscribing to natural theology, for their part, used nature to demonstrate God's existence. Conventional theology was wary of science but allowed scientific principles to demonstrate the workings of God.[18]

The uneasy peace between theology and science, and the alliance of science with eighteenth-century views on progress purged of its association with deism, cleared the way for a Baconian philosophy of science in the United States by the mid-1820s. Isaac Newton and Francis Bacon were frequently lumped under the heading "Baconian" by writers during the 1820s and 1830s. Yet, as Daniels has observed, they were not referring to Bacon's elaborate scheme of speculative philosophy or Newton's mathematical proofs of the laws of motion. They focused on Bacon's empiricism, his appeal to the study of facts, his advocacy of the inductive method for discovery, and his use of the deductive method to classify observations.[19]

The Baconian method was a process of collection, description, and classification. Through this process the laws of nature were then deduced. At this point, however, scientists in nineteenth-century America found themselves on the horns of the Baconian dilemma: Bacon's arguments could be used to justify the utility of science, but his own scheme was largely classificatory. The preoccupation with classification in turn undermined the search for explanation. "Science is but a collection of well-arranged facts," said an essayist in *Scientific American* in 1852. Even physicists were inclined to accumulation of data rather than theory, to application rather than explanation. Joseph Henry stood alone as an American physicist with a "European reputation" for analytic reasoning.[20]

In his *Discourse on the Baconian Philosophy* (1844), Samuel Tyler taught that Bacon's philosophy was one of experience that relied on a psychology of perception and used both the method of observation to collect facts and deduction to classify them. Classification itself often relied on identity by analogy, a permissible method for Tyler, who was willing to invoke the basic law of identity in his deductive method. Tyler's epistemology and metaphysics (theology) also accepted a parallelism between mind and nature instantiated by God.[21] Natural theology and Baconian philosophy were united in the voice of God. Perhaps the clarity of God's voice increased, for one in six leading scientists was a clergyman's son, and many who taught science in college had studied theology.[22]

The most obvious shortcoming of Bacon's empiricism was its inability to connect observations, no matter how multitudinous, with the processes of change. The "science of analogy" seemed to provide the answer. It was Francis Wayland—a leading representative of Scottish philosophy, author of "The Philosophy of Analogy," and president of Brown University—who brought the usefulness of the science of analogy to the attention of American scientists. Analogy provided a solution to the problem of unobservables. Based on the assumption that nature was uniform, it could be inferred that the "unknown would correspond with the known." From this theory of correspondence it followed that the unknown could be predicted from the known. Behind this reasoning lay the assumption that nature was created by an intelligent, rational being and that the explanations of natural phenomena would, in turn, correspond to the "character" of their creator.[23]

The virtual identification of the method of analogy with the method of science—the "final step," so to speak—was made by James Whelpley in 1848. Whelpley argued that the method of analogy could be applied to all phenomena, from atoms to man's spirituality. The result, says Daniels, was to make the method so general and so undiscerning that it could be used to prove anything. By extending the method to all domains of observable phenomena and by making logic a part of that method, Whelpley went beyond Wayland and even reintroduced the doctrine of final causes that Bacon himself had banished. Indeed, the inner reasoning of American science had retreated some three hundred years. The irony, of course, was that the closer American scientists came to Bacon the easier it was to see that pure induction was inadequate to address the problem of unobservables.[24]

Mathematics and Physics For early-nineteenth-century American scientists the work of Isaac Newton epitomized the great synthesis of natural philosophy, the foundations for which were the laws of gravitation and motion. It was during the eighteenth and nineteenth centuries, also, that the mathematical expression of the famous laws of motion and the law of gravity moved from simple equations for single particles in motion to partial differential equations expressing the motions of many interacting particles.[25]

Newton provided a mathematical description rather than a physical explanation of nature's grand mechanical design.[26] His model was made clear in his *Mathematical Principles of Natural Philosophy*, a work organized, like Euclid's *Elements*, in a deductive manner using definitions, axioms, theorems, and corollaries. Newton had indeed linked mathematics and mechanics at a conceptual level unknown to his predecessors, so much so that mathematics provided the concepts needed to describe the mechanisms of motion.[27] For all his mathematization and his use of fluxions (calculus), however, Newton's own thinking and the process he used to work out solutions to mathematical problems were geometrical in nature. This is crucial to our understanding of how early-nineteenth-century educators conceived of the relations among mechanics, geometry, and drawing.[28]

The Newtonian world view that permeated natural philosophy was premised, in part, on the union of geometry and mechanics. Abstract geometry was an impossibility in Newtonian physics, and Newton himself displayed an aversion to handling geometrical problems algebraically. His physicalist and realist conception of mathematics led him to view the spatial relations among physical bodies as "sensible measures." That is, space, for Newton, was accessible to sense perception; it was not a "useful fiction," as are the coordinate systems of modern physics.[29]

The importance of Newton's physicalism and the Newtonian world view was immense, for it dictated the relations among geometry, mechanics, and drawing as branches of study. Geometry, said Newton, was founded on mechanical practice. "The description of right lines and circles, upon which geometry is founded, belongs to mechanics. Geometry does not teach us to draw these lines, but requires them to be drawn, for it requires that the learner should first be taught to describe these accurately before he enters upon geometry, then it shows how by these operations problems may be solved. To describe right lines and circles are problems, but not geometrical problems. The solution of these problems is required from mechanics, and by geometry the use of them, when so solved, is shown."[30] In a direct but elegant way Newton thus spelled out the nexus among those branches of study needed to understand *his* mechanical system.[31]

Newton had indeed built a mathematically configured and efficient model of a "regular dynamic system." The search for efficiency and general principles proceeded both on physical and mathematical fronts. In both cases, though, differential and integral calculus were the methods of choice.[32] This followed from their mathematical power and their ability to demonstrate the economy of nature.[33]

Lagrange's calculus of variations and his publication of *Analytic Mechanics* (1788) marked, as did Newton's *Principia* in the previous century, a giant synthesis of mathematics and a theory of motion. Lagrange made energy and the principle of least action the cornerstones of his edifice.[34] The edifice was, as Kline has noted, mechanics "treated entirely mathematically," and Lagrange himself boasted that he needed no physical referents or geometrical diagrams.[35] "There are no figures in this book," he announced. "The methods I demonstrate here require neither constructions, nor geometrical or mechanical reasoning, but only algebraic operations subject to a regular and uniform development."[36]

The confidence of eighteenth-century mathematicians bordered on hubris. In this "heroic age" of mathematics, equations seemed to seduce men of reason. Yet as the nineteenth century opened, mathematicians found that they had divorced their system further and further from experience. Equations were seductive, and differentiation and integration seemed to need no justification other than their being possible.[37]

The uncertain relation of calculus to experience had a great deal to do with the inability of mathematicians to separate calculus from space intuition and geometry. The conceptual development of calculus took place irregularly. Newton had developed a generalized procedure for calculating instantaneous rate of change, and Leibniz, the famous philosopher and mathematician, had clarified the doctrine of continuity. Yet calculus was still conceptualized within the contexts of geometry and motion, that is, as "geometrical magnitudes." Calculus was almost two centuries away from discarding geometry, from separating a numerical concept of limit from a "geometrical representation." Even by the mid-eighteenth century intuition rather than logic still played a large role in the "reasonableness of calculus."[38] The separation of mathematics from the sensory world had been slow but irresistible. On the one hand, mathematical concepts had become more useful, but at the same time they grew more epistemologically divorced from nature. This dilemma, in fact, is inevitable in geometric thinking. Pure analytic geometry—geometry resting on theorems that are analytic—is true only insofar as it is devoid of factual content. Physical geometry, on the other hand, is usable only to the extent that it can be connected to empirical science. The irony is inescapable, as Einstein once noted: "As far as the laws of mathematics refer to reality, they are not certain; and as far as they are certain, they do not refer to reality."[39]

The Special Cases of Descriptive and Projective Geometry The historical division between algebraists and geometers is well known. Since the seventeenth century the perceptual and conceptual skills that divided them became more obvious, ironically, because the mathematical tools to join them became more developed. Leibniz observed that there are geometers who "by greatly stretching their imagination" are, in the words of Alexandre Koyre, able to see into space and "to trace therein a multitude of lives, and perceive their relevance and relationship without confusion." Historically, Desargues and Pascal represent geometric problem solving, and Descartes and Leibniz represent problem solving through equations. These modes of analysis are not mutually exclusive in a psychological sense, but the logical distinction is clear enough. For the geometrician "a conic section is an event in space, [and] an equation is no more than an abstract, remote representation." For the algebraist, the "essence of a curve is precisely its equation, [and] its spatial form is only a projection—something which is secondary and at times even useless."[40]

In the early nineteenth century, the logic of Euclidean geometry was still the mainstay for spatial representation both because of its long and useful history and because it could be expressed in deductive form.[41] Projective geometry, as an extension of the Euclidean system, received attention from Gaspard Monge and Jean Victor Poncelet in the late eighteenth and early nineteenth centuries. The major goal of projective geometry was to identify the properties of geometric figures which applied to any projection of those figures.[42] Although the logic of projective geometry, like that of mathematics in general, was under severe stress in the early nineteenth century, its intuitive sense and obvious utility for problems of design and graphic representation made it easy for scholars like Poncelet to overlook its shaky logical foundations. In fact, geometers often scorned algebraic methods.[43]

The immense importance of descriptive and projective geometry as a method of nonalgebraic problem-solving and the heuristic and technical value of geometric thinking (not only drawing) has been made clear by William Ivins' work on the "rationalization of sight." As a pictorial representation, says Ivins, perspective gives us a reciprocal, metrical picture of objects in space. At the perceptual level, size and shape constancy allow for perspective. The artist, for example, provides depth cues that allow the viewer to see a painting in perspective, though the perspective is never really complete.[44]

Perspective, however, is far more than perceptual. At the conceptual, problem-solving level, perspective allows us to map the exterior relations of objects as their location changes while assuming the invariance of their internal structures. What was a law of nature in science could thus be represented spatially. Technology made the same assumptions about external variance with a change in location accompanied by internal invariance.[45] In effect, the grammar of perspective allowed the technical and the scientific to be linked for all practical purposes without challenging the logic of science or the utility of the technical.

In his *Art and Geometry, A Study in Space Intuitions*, Ivins observes the very different perceptual (leading also to conceptual) bases of tactile and visual operations. The hand "knows objects separately" and cannot trace simultaneous movements of objects nor perceive multiple objects with a single awareness. But the eye has a point of view. Visually, objects are seen in relation to one another, and in many cases the meaning or understanding of an object depends on its relation to another object.[46]

The "perspective" of vision, as opposed to the tactually "here" of the hand, makes three-dimensional perspective possible; that is, it creates in two dimensions the representation of objects as they appear relative to one another in three-dimensional space. Moreover, as Ivins notes, perspective moves beyond the metrical (quantity and measurement) geometry of Euclid, which is grounded in the "tactile-muscular assumptions of congruences [coincident superimposition of two figures] and parallelism."[47] The difference between a visual and tactile awareness of parallelism is clearly described by Ivins: "If we get our awareness of parallelism through touch, as by running our fingers along a simple molding, there is no question at the sensuous return that parallel lines do not meet. If, however, we get our awareness of parallelism through sight, as when we look down a long colonnade, there is no doubt about the sensuous return that parallel lines do converge and will meet if they are far enough extended."[48]

Most mathematicians between the mid-seventeenth and early-nineteenth centuries were preoccupied with the analytic geometry of Descartes and Fermat and the calculus of Newton and Leibniz. In these areas, science and mathematics thrived on the progress of each other. But neither the work of Desargues nor of Pascal attracted wide attention from mathematicians until Monge published his *Geometrie descriptive* (1798–99) and Poncelet his *Traite des proprietes projectives des figures* (1822).[49]

In the early nineteenth century the utility of descriptive geometry overcame its logical defects, though it did not resolve them. Logical weaknesses were ignored in favor of profits. In fact, Ivins has argued that without perspective geometry, modern machinery "could not exist." The mechanization of life in the nineteenth century certainly had sources other than mathematics, but without the latter, technological advance would have been at a standstill. The nineteenth century surely was a great age of mechanization, and the technique of invention itself was rationalized by perspective geometry.[50]

CONCLUSION

Virtually every debate about the study and application of natural philosophy reflected the struggle to replace a qualitative, classificatory method for studying natural phenomena with quantitative methods expressed in the abstractions of equations expressing space and number. The fundamental challenge was to express the world of experience while transcending it, and to seek, in the idealized, permanent forms of mathematics, a counterpoint to the flux of experience. This was the challenge in most debates over the application of natural philosophy. Both verbal classifications and numbers were, at one level, rooted in experience, just as the idea of space was rooted in place and the "attributes" of materiality were rooted in the auditory, visual, and tactile senses. At another level, however, space was an equation, not a place; gravity was an equation, not a feeling; and the lever exerted force, not movement. The problem to be solved, then, was how the grammar of nature should be represented and expressed. Thus the old philosophic issues of correspondence and the parallelism of mind and nature weighed heavily on those seeking to express nature's will and, by indirection, God's.

As we see in the next chapter, these problems were dealt with pedagogically in the organization, sequence, and format of textbooks and periodical literature. The same problems, however, were part of the Baconian heritage popularizing scientific study. In fact, the pedagogical issues could not be separated from the Baconian viewpoint of American science during the first half of the nineteenth century. Thus, for the teacher, as the following chapter will illustrate, the problem became one of representing the principles of natural philosophy in a scientifically legitimate but teachable way.

Bacon, as it turned out, was both part of the problem and part of the solution. It was the doctrine of scientific utility—a faith in the inevitability of human progress through scientific study—that allowed American educators to justify their purpose and method for teaching science. Bacon's alliance of the mechanic arts with natural philosophy and his insistence that the former not progress in isolation from the latter was a welcome message to devotees of scientific study. So was, for that matter, Bacon's distrust of verbalism. Yet, for all that, Bacon distrusted mathematization, fearing its separation from the world of experience. Moreover, he never provided an alternative, nonclassificatory method for uniting the discrete observations of inductive science. His descendants in the world of scientific popularization and pedagogy inherited the dilemma. Educators struggled repeatedly with this issue both within the context of Pestalozzian methods and the demands of mental discipline in the traditional curriculum.

The problems of applying mathematics to the study of nature were mirrored in the teaching of mathematics itself. Equations were descriptive, not explanatory. They opened the door to nature but did not explain it. On these grounds the study of mathematics could be justified as a tool for scientific study.

But there were other justifications. Mathematics was justified as a practical tool in commerce and mensuration and also as a way to develop mental discipline. Here again method mirrored epistemology and its unresolved difficulties. This was evident in the different demands that geometry and algebra placed on students. Both, of course, required deductive reasoning. For most people, geometry was probably justified by experience even after they had muddled through Euclid. Perspective geometry, because of its obvious utility, bridged experience and technology with nature. Algebra, however, was a different matter, because many perceived it as "outside" of experience. It dealt with the relation of knowns to unknowns, and its mission could not be fulfilled through induction. For the practical man and student both, it often obscured expression, just as for the mathematician it clarified and crystalized expression into a beautiful symmetry.

The following chapters illustrate how perspective geometry and drawing, and the empirical, analytic, and thematic content of natural philosophy and mathematics, along with their epistemological problems, became evident in pedagogy itself. Here, too, the broad themes that made the union of science and mathematics possible were also played out in the organization and content of instruction. As in the shop and factory, so in the text and classroom the worth and clarity of theory was tested by utility.

4

Teaching Natural Philosophy

Conceptual, methodological, and classificatory problems plagued natural philosophy at the outset of the nineteenth century. The roots of the problems were both epistemological and ontological. Despite these difficulties, the term *natural philosophy* remained in wide use, reflecting the view that all natural forces could be uniformly explained and that there was an essential unity to the otherwise increasingly specialized sciences.[1] Natural philosophy had largely rejected what Jahnke and Otte call "substance concepts" in favor of relational and functional concepts. The language of science changed also as it embraced the language of mathematics and moved away from a perceptual foundation. Perspective geometry alone seemed able to bridge the perceptual and the conceptual.

Scientific instrumentation made the diversity of empirical reality increasingly evident and enhanced the necessity of expressing that diversity in relational and functional vocabulary. The language of natural philosophy had ontological *and* heuristic value. It was a language of exploration and control. It created possibilities but tamed them by analysis, experiment, and the absolutes of scientific materialism. In mathematics the conceptualization of number as relation, not substance, aided scientific expression itself and helped to build the bridge between algebra and geometry.[2]

Experimental philosophy, especially that reflecting the claims of the Scottish Common Sense School of philosophy, had long been a vehicle for popularizing the physical sciences, chiefly physics, in the form of mechanical philosophy.[3] Literally, experimental philosophy was teaching natural philosophy "by experiments in a mathematical manner."[4] Early-nineteenth-century textbooks in physics, though few, often described experiments that could be used to illustrate the principles being explained. Few, however, demanded mathematics beyond the elementary level, and most emphasized the practical benefits of studying natural philosophy.

It was axiomatic for authors of texts, encylopedias, and dictionaries of the arts that the study of natural philosophy led to progress in the mechanical and chemical arts. The historical link between the craftsman and scientist was strong. Kuritz observed that "the republican ideology of Franklin and Jefferson was imbued with the need to link science to craft skills and to show the applicability of science to utilitarian goals."[5] Guralnick has noted that only a small minority—an aristocracy of the classical intellect—opposed the linkage of science to material utility in college education. Professional scientists interested only in research did not dare ignore arguments for utility when it came to requests for funds.[6]

It is difficult to know how broad the readership for scientific literature was, but the range of reading difficulty in scientific textbooks was great. Using the Flesch formula for reading difficulty, a sample of seventeen books on natural philosophy published from 1785 to 1859 shows the books to be far more difficult than the level represented by McGuffey's *Third Reader*—a level that was probably average for mechanics and farmers who had attended common schools.[7] Instruction in natural philosophy at the elementary-school level was virtually absent in the first two decades of the nineteenth century.

Collegiate education in science, though experiencing some growth, was woefully out of date. For example, William Enfield's compilation *Institutes of Natural Philosophy, Theoretical and Practical* (first published in the United States in 1802) was widely used at the collegiate level, but much of the material from which it was drawn was a century old. *The American Journal of Science* in 1820 noted of this "ill-digested compilation" that "the Institutes of Natural Philosophy will be found in examination to be little more than an abridgement [and] . . . the compiler of this work, while setting with his pen in one hand and his author in the other, appears never to have indulged for a moment the illiberal suspicion that his author might be in the wrong." The errors of the original, said the reviewer, were "faithfully transcribed into his abridgement."[8]

The Baconian view of science provided a rationale for scientific study among adults. *The American Journal of Education*, borrowing from the *Library of Useful Knowledge*, advised its readers in 1828 that the study of science "makes men more skillful, expert, and useful in the particular lines of work by which they are to earn their bread, and by which they are to make it go far and taste well when earned." The study of science was one step on the ladder of upward social mobility. Said the essayist: "It gives every man a chance, according to his natural talents, of becoming an improver of the art he works at, and even a discoverer in the sciences connected with it."[9]

The Baconian model easily merged with Whiggish tendencies in American thought. This view of science, as Slotten observed, helped to blend scientific inquiry with the desire for moral order, the foundations for which could be found in natural theology buttressed by natural science, and progress in the form of technological and industrial growth. For those attempting to give science a place beside classical studies in the early-nineteenth-century collegiate curriculum, however, the technical and instrumental meanings of science were subordinated to its potential for contributing to mental discipline. It was only when scientists sought to justify higher levels of investment in apparatus and faculty that utility became a claim equal to that of developing higher cognitive powers.[10]

Introductory Textbooks in Natural Philosophy

Most of the books published in natural philosophy in the early nineteenth century were written by only a few individuals. A sample of books published between 1820 and 1852 shows that nearly half of the books on physics published in the United States were by a single writer. Most of the remaining books were by eleven other authors. The science of mechanics was dominated by a few individuals as well, with about half of the books written by three writers. Mathematics books, particularly elementary- and intermediate-level ones, served a more rapidly expanding market than did the physical sciences. Even here, however, almost 70 percent of the works were written by fifteen authors.[11]

Two problems plagued introductory textbooks in the physical sciences in the first half of the nineteenth century. The first, observed *The North American Review* in 1851, was "that the physical sciences involve the application of mathematics, and sometimes of its most subtle and intricate departments. . . . The physical [science] student needs the helping hand of mathematics to expound to him the theory of the instruments which he uses." Visual acuity was another source of difficulty. In fact, said one reviewer, "we believe that a geometrical eye is quite as indispensable to the success of the mathematician as a geometrical mind." Because visual representation and geometric reasoning were crucial to scientific learning for many students, learning the principles of perspective geometry was imperative. These principles, it was inferred, could overcome deficiencies in the "instability of vision." The failure to master solid geometry, it was added, "originates as often in this organic peculiarity of vision, existing to excess, as in any deficiency purely intellectual."[12]

Because acceptable texts were difficult to find, the same reviewer offered criteria by which to judge their quality. Comprehensiveness, accuracy, and clarity were foremost considerations. Although the analytic method of instruction had the advantage of leading the student through a process of discovery, it was not the preferred method. According to the reviewer, instruction should be offered in the synthetic mode, which took the student through the history of discovery and instructed him or her in the "great laws" of the subjects. Finally, concluded the reviewer, "no pains should be spared by the author and teacher" to impress upon the student the "unity of nature, and the intimate connection of the physical sciences as they stand out before the mind of the Creator."[13]

This advice on the use of the synthetic method differed markedly from that offered by another reviewer in the *Journal of the Franklin Institute* some two decades earlier. Here it was argued that the "analytic method . . . has been too much neglected in the universities and academies in this country." The reviewer said that "the progress of invention in higher mathematics" unbound the principles of mechanics from "geometrical constructions" and "experiments with models" and made it possible to generalize scientific findings through mathematics. The analytic method was "our main support when experiment and geometrical construction fail."[14] Here, in a pedagogical nutshell, was the epistemological controversy about the proper place of mathematics in scientific study.

Before the surge in common school reform in the late 1830s, there was little pressure to offer instruction in the physical sciences in public schools. In academies, colleges, and mechanics' institutes, the last of which offered evening instruction to apprentices, science was increasingly popularized, however. George Gregory's two-volume *Lectures on Experimental Philosophy, Astronomy, and Chemistry* (1808) was a highly readable, illustrated introduction to the standard branches of natural philosophy: mechanics, astronomy, and chemistry.

Descriptions of instrumentation and apparatus played an important part in *Lectures on Experimental Philosophy*, and the book was virtually free of numbers. The laws of nature are discovered through experiment and observation, Gregory explained, and this "positive test of experience" separated the modern scientist from the ancient one.[15] Historical narrative appeared alongside definitions of terms and scientific vocabulary. Simple experiments using common apparatus found in the home, shop, and manufacture were described. For example, atmospheric pressure was explained through illustrations of vent holes and vent pegs in liquor casks and the "valencia," an instrument used to sample liquor from bung holes in the cask. The forces of the pendulum and of oscillation were illustrated by simple drawings, and the parallelogram of forces was illustrated by a drawing of a boat being towed on a canal. The principles of optics were illustrated with sketches of the eye, hand, and mirrors.

Like Gregory, Thomas P. Jones, professor of mathematics at the Franklin Institute, helped to introduce an audience with diverse interests to the basic principles of the natural sciences. Jones used Marcet's *Conversations on Natural Philosophy* (1826), which was written in the format of a family dialogue, presumably to illustrate that the erudite could be made palatable when placed in a familiar setting. The choice of dialogue with female protagonists was significant given that women regularly attended evening lectures at the Franklin Institute. Jones added questions at the bottoms of the pages and a glossary to Marcet's book.

Almost forty years after Gregory's work on natural philosophy, Almira Phelps's *Natural Philosophy for Schools, Families, and Private Students* (1846) appeared. Phelps was a teacher at the Troy Female Seminary, the principal of the Patapsco Female Institute, Maryland, and a sister of Emma Willard. She had years of experience in teaching the natural sciences and was sensitive to the difficulties in mastering the vocabulary, notation, and different levels of visual representation needed to understand natural philosophy. Phelps covered the standard topics of motion, mechanical powers, hydrostatics, pneumatics, acoustics, optics, electricity, magnetism, and astronomy. The treatment was verbal and practical, and the concepts were illustrated by sketches and examples from common experience. In the short section on mechanical powers the author made certain that students were introduced to various types of motion and their general applications to machinery. The labor-saving benefits of machinery were illustrated. "Females are greatly indebted to science for labor-saving machines of various kinds," wrote Phelps. "The carding machine has superseded the tedious and laborious use of hand-cards, giving the wives and daughters of farmers not only an exemption from severe toil, but more leisure for mental improvement."[16]

Concern with the practical benefits of studying science was carried into Phelps's "lectures" on drawing and perspective, a subsection of the study of optics. As with so much of Phelps's previous work and that of Emma Willard, visual representation was important. Natural philosophy did not traditionally deal with foreshortening, vanishing point, light, and shade.

Pedagogically, however, it made sense to ground the abstractions of optics in the experience of vision.[17]

By the 1840s the number of texts in the physical sciences had increased significantly. Denison Olmsted's work was a staple of the market addressing audiences at both the secondary school and collegiate levels. Olmsted's *Compendium of Natural Philosophy* (1833, 1842) for schools and academies assumed no mathematical education beyond the rule of three (proportions). Calculations were kept to a minimum, and illustrations were numerous. Questions on the text were printed at the bottom of the page. The following lesson on the screw and inclined plane illustrates the simplicity and clarity of expression: "When a road, instead of ascending a hill directly, winds round it to the summit so as to lengthen the inclined plane, and thus aid the moving force, the Inclined Plane becomes a screw. In the same manner a flight of stairs, winding around the sides of a cylindrical tower, either within or without, affords an instance of an inclined plane so modified as to become a screw. These examples show the strong analogy which subsists between these two mechanical powers; or rather, they show that the screw is a mere modification of the Inclined Plane."[18]

Olmsted also wrote a text for college audiences titled *An Introduction to Natural Philosophy: Designed as a Text Book for the Use of the Students in Yale College* (1831–32). The book included numerous mathematical formulae using standard scientific notation, but the level of mathematics stopped short of analytical geometry and calculus. It did not contain any "mathematical expressions for the laws of electricity and magnetism" or, as Guralnick notes, any of the "then well established connections between electricity and magnetism."[19]

By the mid-1850s Richard Parker's works on natural philosophy were competing with Olmsted's for a place in the academies' curricula. Parker's *School Compendium of Natural and Experimental Philosophy* (1856), designed for grammar schools and academies, was noticeably free from equations; it instead stressed definition and classification. It contained numerous illustrations and diagrams, and a section at the end featured 202 figures, including illustrations of balloons, pyramids, waterwheels, pulleys, presses, Archimedean screws, fire engines, steam engines, and locomotives and steamboats.

Parker was meticulous with language, emphasizing proper distinctions between physics and metaphysics, observation and experiment, and science and art. In addressing the poorly conceived notions about science in the public mind, he explained that science and art were not properly distinguished by some. Art, said Parker, is a matter of "practice and perfor-

(11.) Which would have the stronger attraction on the earth, a body at the distance of 95 millions of miles from the earth, with a weight represented by 1000, or a body at the distance represented by 95, and a weight represented by one? *Ans.* As $\frac{1}{90300000000000}$ to $\frac{1}{9025}$.

(12.) Supposing the weight of a body to be represented by 4 and its distance at 6, and the weight of another body to be 6 and its distance at 4, which would exert the stronger power of attraction? *Ans.* The second, as $\frac{6}{16}$ to $\frac{4}{36}$.

108. THE CENTRE OF GRAVITY.—As every part of a body possesses the general property of attraction, it is evident that the attractive force of the mass of a body must be concentrated in some point ; and this point is called the centre of gravity of the body.

What is the Centre of Gravity of a body? 109. The Centre of Gravity of a body is the point about which, all the parts balance each other.

110. This point in all spherical bodies of uniform density will be the centre of sphericity.

111. As the earth is a spherical body, its centre of gravity is at the centre of its sphericity.

112. When bodies approach each other under the effect of mutual attraction, they tend mutually to approach the centre of gravity of each other.

113. For this reason, when any body falls towards the earth its motion will be in a straight line towards the centre of the earth. No two bodies from different points can approach the centre of a sphere in a parallel direction, and no two bodies suspended from different points can hang parallel to one another.

Fig. 3.

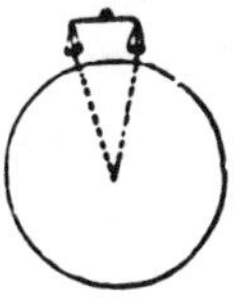

114. Even a pair of scales hanging perpendicularly to the earth, as represented in Fig. 3, cannot be exactly parallel, because they both point to the same spot, namely, the centre of the earth. But their convergency is too small to be perceptible.

What is a Vertical Line? 115. The direction in which a falling body approaches the surface of the earth is called a Vertical Line.

No two vertical lines can be parallel.

116. A weight suspended from any point will always assume a vertical position.*

* Carpenters, masons and other artisans, make use of a weight of lead suspended at rest by a string, for the purpose of ascertaining whether their work stands in a vertical position. To this implement they give the name of *plumb line*, from the Latin word *plumbum*, lead.

Water-wheels are there? the Overshot, the Undershot and the Breast Wheel.

291. The Overshot Wheel receives its motion from the weight of the water flowing in at the top.

Describe the Overshot Wheel. Fig. 37 represents the Overshot Wheel. It consists of a wheel turning on an axis (not represented in the figure), with

Fig. 37.

compartments called buckets, *a b c d*, &c., at the circumference, which are successively filled with water from the stream S. The weight of the water in the buckets causes the wheel to turn, and the buckets, being gradually inverted, are emptied as they descend. It will be seen, from an inspection of the figure, that the buckets in the descending side of the wheel are always filled, or partly filled, while those in the opposite or ascending part are always empty until they are again presented to the stream. This kind of wheel is the most powerful of all the water-wheels.

292. The Undershot Wheel is a wheel which is moved by the motion of the water. It receives its impulse at the bottom.

Describe the Undershot Wheel. Fig. 38 represents the Undershot Wheel.

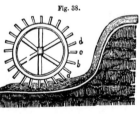

Fig. 38.

Instead of buckets at the circumference, it is furnished with plane surfaces, called float-boards, *a b c d*, &c., which receive the impulse of the water, and cause the wheel to revolve.

Describe the Breast Wheel. 293. The Breast Wheel is a wheel which receives the water at about half its own height, or at the

Fig. 4.2. An explanation of overshot and undershot waterwheels. From Richard Green Parker, *A School Compendium of Natural and Experimental Philosophy* (New York: A. S. Barnes and Burr, 1859), 82.

mance" while science is "the examination of general laws, or of abstract and speculative principles." The mechanic arts dealt with vocations in which tools, instruments, and machinery are employed. "A principle in science is a rule of art," he concluded.[20]

Parker's decidedly nonmathematical treatment of natural philosophy allowed him to join more easily the mechanic arts to mechanics as a science. There was no attempt to mediate the two by equations, but it was obvious that Parker expected the teacher to fill the gap. Thus, for example, he begins an explanation of the center of gravity with a definition in the traditional fashion (see fig. 4.1) but also notes the practical application to the mechanic arts.

Parker's format—with its emphasis on classification and definition, the absence of equations, and the conspicuous presence of word problems—was highly flexible. Even more important than this flexibility, however, were his numerous attempts to link practice and theory through illustration. For Parker, the presentation of natural philosophy and science was best done by linking the two to technology (see fig. 4.2). Parker was true to science and computation, but he avoided the obstruction (and elegance) of equations. Science and technology were the contexts for each other, though it is clear that the former informed the latter.

Science at the Common School Level

As the study of natural science expanded at the secondary school level, pressure mounted for more natural science education in common schools. The study of geography had long been one of the few potential sources of technical and scientific information for the very young. Its emphasis, however, was descriptive rather than analytic at the elementary level. At advanced levels there was mathematical analysis in physical geography and astronomy, but this approach required at least an introduction to geometry and trigonometry.

The justifications for teaching science emphasized utility and mental discipline. In common school journals, advocates for scientific study frequently appealed to the natural curiosity of students. Just as the essayist in "Self Improvement for Adults" spoke of gratifying the curiosity and the "feelings of wonder" evoked by the "extraordinary discoveries of Mechanical Philosophy," so the *Western School Journal* promoted the study of science at the elementary level by arguing that the "natural curiosity of children concerning the phenomena of nature, should be gratified." Such curiosity was God given, it was said, and every teacher and school was obliged to satisfy it.[21]

The *Common School Assistant*, with the help of J. S. Buckingham, crusaded with rhetoric and lessons on how to teach science. Recognizing the difficulty of obtaining suitable texts, the journal campaigned for practical and simple books that carried detailed sets of questions and answers but were not "dry and technical."[22] Natural philosophy and mechanics received a good deal of attention from the *Common School Assistant*, but chemistry received less. Examples of lessons were given through simulated dialogues, questions for students, and definitions of terms. All questions about natural philosophy were taken from the world of children rather than that of adults. The appeal was consistently made to curiosity, not to utility. Questions on mechanics were more advanced and appealed more to utility. Teachers were instructed to draw representations of "mechanical powers" on the blackboard, followed by description, explanation, and "interrogation."[23]

Finally, teachers were given explanations of familiar natural phenomena and were told of the significance of natural philosophy for other disciplines. Most lessons contained a moral, and sometimes a lesson was linked to geography or history. For example, the apparent exception to the rule that related heat to expansion and cold to contraction was explained by invoking God's "wise" decision to make it impossible for a river or lake to freeze completely. Likewise, the geographic, historical, and moral were all related to a lesson on sound and vibration in which the correlation of types of music to national character was described.[24]

By the mid-1850s some advances had been made in elementary instruction in natural science, including Richard Parker's *Juvenile Philosophy; or, Philosophy in Familiar Conversations, Designed to Teach Young Children to Think* and *First Lessons in Natural Philosophy*, an abridgement of the *Compendium*. There were nine sections to Parker's *Juvenile Philosophy*, each written in question-and-answer (catechetical) format. The child and, significantly, the mother, began each dialogue by focusing on familiar objects and natural events, including rain, steam, clouds, rainbows, vision, fire, and wind. These topics were the stepping-off points for further conversations about such concepts as color, condensation, light, reflection, heat, absorption, reflection, air, expansion, and pressure. Often concepts were simply described rather than given technical names.

The thematic content of science was strong in elementary textbooks. Moral philosophy, philosophic theology, and natural philosophy were thoroughly intermingled. Questions probing the causes of natural events were treated as part of philosophic theology. It was God who was responsible for the conservation of matter, and light was "so skillfully and beautifully mixed up together by the great God of heaven, that [it was not seen] separately, except in different objects." To study science was to learn that God designed all things for our "good" and should be praised "for all his goodness to you, and to your fellow creatures."[25]

THE USE OF APPARATUS

If apparatus were not available to teach science, then the "intelligent, ingenious and scientific teacher can always make some. Ingenious pupils could occasionally make it, if the teacher should not."[26] This was the advice given by *The Western School Journal* in 1842 to teachers who lacked the resources to teach science. The manufacture of scientific apparatus had become a small industry by this time, but the slow progress of public schools in making science a standard part of the curriculum gave many teachers little leverage for making demands on meager budgets. Even such well-known lecturers as Amos Eaton, who later helped to found Rensselaer Polytechnic Institute, made much of their apparatus sui generis.[27]

Instrument making for the purposes of manufacturing and scientific study made rapid progress in the eighteenth century. England was the leader, particularly in large-scale productions that had commercial value. French instrument making was confined to small-scale products. In the shops of England, particularly in those whose employees were expert in the use of lathes, workmen laid the technical foundations for scientific apparatus, and in France a renaissance of instrument making took place in the last twenty years of the eighteenth century.[28]

By the beginning of the nineteenth century, mechanical apparatus for popularizing science was abundant but expensive and therefore beyond the reach of many schools and colleges. Professors who lectured for a living were a ready clientele for scientific ("philosophical") apparatus and cheaper demonstration apparatus.[29] In their advertisements lecturers on natural philosophy usually made a point of mentioning apparatus. In the classroom, apparatus and drawings brought visual order to the abstract natural forces underlying the laws of mechanics. That both the visual and verbal were needed for classroom instruction was a widely accepted premise.

The first step for schools planning to expand their curricula to include science was to construct or provide a "cabinet." The cabinet, a tradition in mechanics' institutes and inventors' associations, served to display models and materials thought necessary to the educational mission of the organization.[30] Everything from stones to skeletons, levers, and electrical apparatus found a place. The articles were used as demonstration apparatus in the classroom and in exhibitions.

As pressure grew to include science in the curriculum of the common school, controversy over its use increased. Drawing on Pestalozzian principles of teaching, pedagogical liberals championed the use of apparatus. "The eye is a most powerful and efficient inlet of knowledge," said one essayist, and "on many subjects, a mere glance of that organ will do more than a course of reading and study for weeks or even months." A proto-progressive view that was rooted in the naturalism of Rousseau declared that "every child, in his earliest infancy, is a natural philosopher" as "he experiences the most intense delight, in his endless and endlessly varied experiments to ascertain the nature or properties of objects around him, and of the laws which govern them."[31]

In the same essay it was argued that apparatus and drawings aided children in learning science and mathematics. Verbal descriptions were not effective, the essayist continued, whereas shapes, models, and drawings were. "Geometrical diagrams and solids must be a valuable part of the furniture of every nursery and school room," along with globes, rocks, wood specimens and "a few cheap and simple articles to illustrate some of the most interesting and important principles of chemistry and natural philosophy."[32] In 1841 *The Common School Journal* concluded that the "necessity of apparatus is becoming more and more general." Objects and experience came first and "afterwards the statements, deductions, and generalizations, which are founded upon them."[33]

During the 1830s and 1840s Pestalozzian thought, the rejection of verbalism rooted in Bacon's own rejection of a philosophy of words, and the experience of lecturers in educating adults merged in a convincing argument for the use of "visible illustrations." Walter Johnson of the Franklin Institute was an ardent spokesman for the use of visuals, creating a taxonomy for their use by drawing on the insights of his experience and on a new understanding of the learning process. There were six methods for illustrating the principles of science, said Johnson. Objects could be used in their natural (whole) state or in an "imperfect" (dismantled) state, he said. Artificial models could be substituted for the original objects. "Graphic representations, combining the advantages of lights, shades, and perspective," and "outline figures, or mere diagrams," were acceptable though no substitute for the real thing. Finally, "mere symbols" could convey the "relations of objects in regard to magnitude, number, proportion, and efficacy."[34]

Johnson did not argue that every method was suitable in every circumstance. He did say, however, that the practical application of scientific principles ought to be understood early in a student's development. Therefore, the wise teacher *illustrated* scientific principles first, leaving until later the mathematical foundation and abstract reasoning that accompanied their explanation.[35]

The easy acceptance of Newtonianism in America provided a philosophic foundation for the growth of a small but important apparatus industry. Attempts to popularize science grew, as did the potential market for demonstration apparatus or "mechanisms." George Chilton claimed in 1800 that he was the only educator in New York "teaching by artificial representation." Benjamin Silliman, the American chemist who had learned "the art of lecture demonstrations at the Royal Institution in London," wrote that "speaking to the mind through the eye was a very successful mode of imparting knowledge."[36]

Josiah Holbrook, the leader of and publicist for the lyceum (public lecture) movement, began manufacturing demonstration apparatus for the public schools in 1828. Timothy Claxton, a leader of the mechanics' institute movement in England and maker of philosophical apparatus, had come to Boston in 1826. In 1829 he "interviewed" with Holbrook and discussed several items that might be manufactured for lecture purposes. Said Claxton: "From this interview I may date the commencement of my making philosophical instruments as a regular business."[37]

Making apparatus to be used in public schools did not require the skills of an artisan, but it was an artisan who was called on to create more sophisticated equipment for colleges. Cost was a major consideration in making apparatus, notes Warner, and marketing, not manufacturing, became the biggest challenge.[38] Those responsible for making school budgets eventually began to set aside money for apparatus. The essential equipment needed for demonstration was listed by one lecturer in 1830 as a timepiece, maps and globes, a blackboard, and an abacus or a numeral frame. Desirable apparatus included optical instruments, an air pump, pneumatic apparatus, and a steam engine.[39] Eleven years later the scientific and mathematical apparatus listed for the New York City schools included a machine to illustrate angles, chords, sines, tangents, and so on; geometrical solids; tellurium; a tide globe; a frame of pulleys and levers; an electrical air pump; and chemical apparatus.[40]

The school apparatus business and science instruction secured footholds by mid-century. The Holbrook School Apparatus Company used the motto "Good enough for the best, and cheap enough for the poorest" in the 1850s. For lyceums and schools, Holbrook suggested, among other things, an arithometer, geometrical figures, illustrations of levers, pulleys, wheel and axle, wedge, screw, an inclined plane, an orrery, a pneumatic cistern, blow pipes, glass tubes, cylinders, an air pump, and labeled specimens for geology.[41] A *Teacher's Guide to Illustration* explained the use of apparatus. Any doubt about the market for educational apparatus should have been allayed by the Ohio State Commissioner for Common Schools' statement that sixteen thousand dollars had been spent on "orreries, telluriums, terrestrial globes (both solid and hemispheric), outline maps, numerical frames, geometrical solids, and chemical and philosophic apparatus."[42] Visible illustrations had certainly come of age.

INTRODUCING ADULTS TO SCIENCE

Public lectures were a common means of popularizing science in the early nineteenth century, though few written versions survive. The introductory address to Walter Johnson's series of lectures on natural philosophy provides some indication of what would have been learned by those attending. Like the introductory chapter of many texts, Johnson's introductory lecture spelled out the benefits of scientific study, including its usefulness, its importance in mental discipline, and its moral value in nurturing the habits of mind and body that produced industrious citizens. Johnson outlined the course of study, which was organized into two parts: mechanics, which was divided into the theoretical and the applied, and natural philosophy. The subtopics were the standard ones of the laws of motion (solids and liquids), specific gravity, air, light, heat, electricity, and magnetism. Chemistry was taught only as it applied to the mechanical properties of matter. Astronomy received only minor attention because the twenty lectures were not intended for "nautical gentlemen."[43]

Apropos of his intended audience at the Franklin Institute, Johnson emphasized the practical and minimized the mathematical: "It is not . . . to be forgotten that the class must consist in part of persons to whom the *elements* of natural philosophy are not yet familiar." He was sensitive to potential critics who might view the lecture method as too superficial and assured his audience that he would not indulge in showmanship. Unlike many philosophers, said Johnson, he would "descend from [the] boundless 'domain of abstractions,' to the affairs of common life." In each lecture, he continued, he would "depart . . . from the usual routine" to give an "exhibition of the structure, and the explanation of the use, of various machinery."[44]

Johnson described two methods of using models. In the first he would exhibit "complete sets of machinery," and in the second he would analyze machines by explaining how each part demonstrated a leading principle of mechanics. Drawing would also be used, said Johnson. The objection to verbalism was clear in his remark that the "science of physics has far more to do with things than with words; contests about names, terms, definitions, and the spirit of dogmatism which led to these contests, belonged to the age which is gone by. . . . Sensible representations which the pencil can furnish" would replace the "dance of words."[45]

Johnson's remarks on mathematics suggest some misgivings and possible apprehension on his part. He explained that in order to understand physical science "some preliminary instruction in the science of numbers, in descriptive geometry, and in linear drawing is . . . indispensably necessary." He put his faith in elementary education and in the visual skills of the "practical man," noting that the latter would understand the elements of geometry. Indulgence had its limits, however, so he also announced that "mathematical demonstrations, . . . when *necessary*, will be concise and perspicuous as the nature of the subject will admit." Mathematics aside, Johnson knew the mechanical wisdom of his audience, and, with deference to their practical experience, gave "respectful consideration" to those who knew the "details" of machinery.[46]

In the early nineteenth century collegiate texts in natural philosophy were hardly suitable for adults with little common school education. Those who had completed a common school education but who had no background in science could read for self-improvement. The vocabulary and basic concepts of the natural sciences were challenging but still accessible to the novice through technical and engineering works that included elementary principles of physics and chemistry. Such early works as John Banks' *Treatise on Mills, in Four Parts* (1795), Thomas Fenwick's *Four Essays on Practical Mechanics* (1801), and Oliver Evans' *Young Mill-Wright and Miller's Guide* (1795, 1807) were not designed to give a comprehensive view of natural philosophy, but they did include basic descriptive information and calculations. The book by Evans was the easiest to read, though it presented material on gravity, elasticity, levers, hydraulics, and gears, which was difficult for the beginner. A reader of Banks' work learned of prime movers, mechanical advantage through levers, the laws of circular motion, centrifugal force, velocity, and gravity but in a language more difficult than that used by Evans. Banks' work required some mathematical background on the part of the reader, whereas Evans' seemed to have assumed virtually none. Fenwick's work included essays on waterwheels, steam engines, and mills, and his overall theme was teaching the young mechanic how to simplify machinery. This goal, coupled with some basic calculations on the center of gravity, velocity, and momentum, for example, allowed the millwright to build more efficient waterwheels.

Such multivolume works as the *Library of Useful Knowledge* and Abraham Rees' *The Cyclopedia; or Universal Dictionary of Arts, Sciences, and Literature* differed markedly from each other in difficulty. The former introduced the novice to natural philosophy and related mathematical concepts like logarithms. There was, however, a minimum of technical information, with the emphasis on definition and classification.

Rees' work, on the other hand, was reference material for serious students. It was a book of contrasts—from simple explanations of the purposes of machines to series of formulae, historical and etymological essays, and practical advice for engineers. The general entry for "machine" (eight pages) and categories of machines (four pages) cited major works in Italian, French, German, Latin, and English. It treated simple and compound machines, their purposes, the concepts of mechanical advantage, uniform motion, force, work, equilibrium, and velocity, and included mathematical formulae for work using fluxions (calculus). The entry for "machinery" (twenty-nine pages) included various definitions—machine, engine, and mill, for example—reciprocating movements, clutches, screws, and pumps.[47]

Nontechnical reading materials in the sciences became more available as the nineteenth century progressed. Such popular books as Alonzo Potter's *Principles of Science Applied to the Domestic and Mechanic Arts* (1840) and Dionysius Lardner's *Popular Lectures on Science and Art* (1845) introduced adults and youth to the principles of science and their application. Potter's work was diverse, but his message was that the arts were dependent on science: "We shall find that improvements in these arts have generally been preceded by discoveries in science; and that, when the latter has slumbered, the former have remained nearly stationary."[48]

Potter covered the obligatory laws of motion, inertia, heat, and steam. He dealt with the "elements of machinery," agricultural chemistry and machinery, and architecture. He included an appendix of about one hundred pages in which he attempted to explain the historical and educational significance of science while updating readers on progress in selected areas of American manufacturing.

Dionysius Lardner, a distinguished professor of natural philosophy at London University, lectured widely and compiled the essence of his lectures in his *Popular Lectures*. His aim, he said, was "to instruct and inform, and at the same time rationally amuse, those who have neither time, inclination, nor opportunity to cultivate mathematics, by which alone a strict professional knowledge of astronomy, mechanics, and physics, can be acquired."[49] Lardner translated mathematical proofs into "ordinary language" and included in his book illustrations, such as cross sections of a steam engine. To further simplify matters he used only round numbers.

Thomas Kelt and James Renwick wrote more advanced works that were still within the reach of those with a good common school education (probably six grades) and some experience with machines. Kelt's *Mechanic's Text-Book and Engineer's Practical Guide* (1849, 1854) was a two-part text. The first part was a compendium of technical information, including rules and tables for mensuration and calculation. The second, written by John Frost, was a series of inspirational essays, biographical sketches, and practical advice for the young mechanic.

Part one included many practical word problems. For example, it walked the student through the rules used for instrument settings for surveying, steam engine power, and boiler capacity. Kelt provided tables for square and cube roots, weights of various metals, air, and water, properties of chemical compounds and woods, and screw cutting. Word problems were presented in the rule and example format, such as that for screw cutting:

Rule. Divide the number of threads in a given length of the screw which is to be cut, by the number of threads in the same length of the leading screw attached to the lathe; and the quotient is the ratio that the wheel on the end of the screw must bear to that on the end of the lathe spindle.

Ex. Let it be required to cut a screw with 5 threads in an inch, the leading screw being ½ inch pitch, or containing 2 threads in an inch; what must be the ratio of wheels applied?

$5 + 2 = 2:5$, the ratio they must bear to each other.[50]

In part two Kelt, like Potter, set out to define the domain of technical instruction and to demonstrate its relation to liberal and scientific learning. Included were essays on changing a profession, professional attitudes and behavior, self-instruction, the social status of the mechanic, and moral and religious training. In addition, he criticized the absence of mental discipline in education, the blind devotion to the learning of rules, and the inflated ("gothic") jargon of scientific and technical instruction.

To elevate his status, said Frost, the mechanic must receive instruction beyond the technical. His mind ought to be disciplined by the study of Latin, Frost observed; his study of mathematics must transcend the learning of rules. In fact, he said, "it is . . . a serious and almost general complaint that few children, while at school, make any tolerable progress in arithmetic; [they] are incapable of applying the few rules which they have learned to the useful purposes of life."[51]

Renwick, a young engineer who was selected in 1820 to teach the "neglected" sciences at Columbia College, soon faced three of the obstacles that teachers of science had to overcome in the early nineteenth century: the absence of funds to purchase apparatus, the difficulty of justifying science as one of the several courses that developed mental discipline, and the poor preparation of students in mathematics.[52]

Renwick was a versatile and prolific writer, producing in close succession an edited version of a textbook for mechanics titled *A Compendium of Mechanics; or, Textbook for Engineers, Mill-Wrights, Machine-Makers, Founders, Smiths, etc.* (1830), *The Elements of Mechanics* (1832), *Applications of the Science of Mechanics to Practical Purposes* (1840), and *Treatise on the Steam Engine* (1830). *A Compendium for Mechanics* was moderately easy to read and assumed little mathematics background, as did his *Applications of the Science of Mechanics to Practical Purposes*, which was amply illustrated with woodcuts. His *Treatise on the Steam Engine* was specialized but only moderately difficult. He kept calculations to a minimum, preferring to concentrate on the history, applications, and construction of steam engines. *The Elements of Mechanics* was clearly the most difficult, although it was not, as the title indicates, the most technical.

The range of difficulty and the scope of textbooks on natural philosophy was broad. The degree to which adults could profit from self-study was obviously limited by their previous education, but popular works in the form of lectures allowed even the uninitiated to begin study. The mastery of more advanced texts was probably limited to those with a complete common school education. For those who had a good common school education but neither the time nor the patience for longer texts, a burgeoning periodical literature was available.

Periodical Literature Like textbooks, periodical literature was important in disseminating scientific and technical knowledge to apprentices, farmers, and mechanics. Such journals as *The Apprentice's Companion* (New York), *New York State Mechanic, Journal of the Franklin Institute, American Railway Journal,* and *Scientific American* delivered an array of information, lessons, and motivational essays to those whose formal education had not prepared them for scientific study. Those who were more advanced in their education and who sought further scientific and technical study could feast on essays explaining new inventions or stretch their minds on the latest scientific discoveries. Thus the range of reading difficulty varied greatly in journals like *Scientific American* and *Journal of the Franklin Institute.*

Using the Flesch readability formula, figure 4.3 compares the range of reading difficulty of two major journals written for mechanics—*Journal of the Franklin Institute* and *Scientific American*—with that of readers used in the common schools of the day. Included in the sample are essays

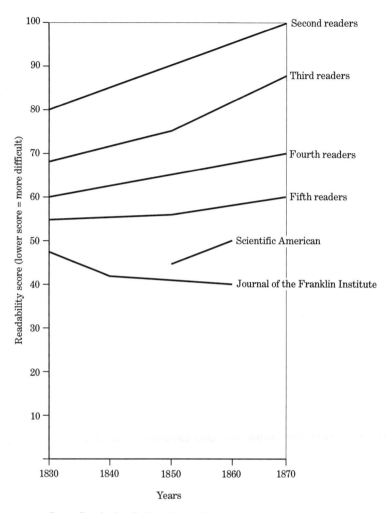

Source: Sample of textbooks and journals.

Fig. 4.3. Comparing the Average Readability of School Texts and Two Journals for Mechanics, 1830–1870

on mechanics and physics, chemistry, technology and manufacturing, and general essays of interest to mechanics as a broad class.

The Flesch formula for reading difficulty uses the textual features of average sentence length and number of syllables. The lower the number, the greater the reading difficulty. The formula does not take into account background knowledge of vocabulary or the logical structure of the sentences themselves. Nonetheless, it is informative when used to compare the difficulty of public school readers with other texts. Used in this way (not as a predictor variable to judge the grade level of current texts), it is clear that the textual features of periodical literature indicate a much greater reading difficulty on average than that for which most adults who attended public common schools were prepared. Whether technical, scientific, or general, essays in these journals were consistently more difficult to read than fifth readers.

Keeping in mind that most students during the period under study did not advance beyond a third reader, the difficulty of the literature surely restricted the audience for these periodicals. In fact, it was common for editors of popular science journals to lament the poor educational background of both their potential and actual readership. This was no doubt because their readership suffered, but they also believed that the study of science could result in socioeconomic improvement for the broad class of workers called mechanics.

As I noted in Chapter 3, the objection to verbalism was strong among those who taught apprentices and mechanics. The message could not have been put more clearly than it was in Gulian Verplanck's address before the Mechanics' Institute of the City of New York in 1833. Utility, pedantry, and verbal excess were on Verplanck's mind when he spoke of "the uniform tendency of all purely speculative and scholastic science to wander into visionary abstractions, to shroud itself in abstruse technicalities, and, above all, to substitute words of learned length, and rules or maxims of arbitrary authority, [for] simple and intelligible reason." Acknowledging that science had its "own peculiar terms," Verplanck nonetheless reminded his audience that science ought not be clothed in the "unnecessary garb of profundity and obscurity" and that "mental abstractions" should be replaced with seeing "how it works."[53]

Verplanck's message was part of the larger aim to demystify and democratize science. *Scientific American* complained in 1848 that science was known only within "Collegiate Halls"—"something that cannot be explained in common language but requires a peculiar jargon of its own." "Soldering names of wondrous length and thundering sound upon common plain facts to give them a *learned* appearance" did little to explain the facts of science. In fact, said *Scientific American*, the "more simple the language . . . the more confidence" could be placed in the author.[54]

The periodical press was remorseless in its attack on pseudointellectualism and incessant in its advocacy of science for everyman. Overcoming difficulties with language was but one aspect of popularizing science. Overcoming resistance to scientific study itself was another major task. Utility was probably the most compelling argument for the study of science, making its claim on both the individual and collective levels. At the individual level the strongest motivating argument was the claim that the study of science would contribute to upward socioeconomic mobility. At the collective level the most compelling argument was the contribution of scientific study to technological progress as evidenced in more efficient and more productive machine shops and manufactures.[55]

Encouraging the study of science was also part of a broader neo-Enlightenment message that political and economic progress depended on the union of science and art. To the broad appeal of individual and collective utility, advocates of the study of science added a moral defense. "Physical science," said an editorial in *Scientific American*, "has a direct moralizing influence upon society," meaning that the betterment and increased happiness of mankind could be attributed directly to scientific advance.[56]

Convincing the uninitiated that the study of science was worth the effort was the stuff of both lectures and editorials. The millwright must have been surprised indeed to hear himself labeled a natural philosopher because he was able to "make and calculate the power and effect of a water wheel, and explain the natural principles of its operations." "Mechanics, awake" was the clarion call of essayists who attempted to raise the level of scientific education among laborers and artisans.[57]

Because many adults and youthful apprentices lacked the background necessary to scientific study, journals stepped in to offer elementary lessons in science. Even the *American Railroad Journal and Advocate of Internal Improvements*, a leading journal in civil engineering, carried basic lessons in practical mechanics, discussing everything from cranks and spinning wheels to waterwheels and governors and the specifics of gearing.[58] Borrowing from such works as *Knowledge for the People, or the Plain Why and Because* and the *Book of Science, The Apprentice's Companion* ran a series of lessons on the screw, motion, weight, velocity, force, and the pendulum. Plain language with a minimum of calculations was the rule. From the half-column entry on the screw, for example, the student was to learn and apply the rule: "As the circumference of the screw is to the pitch, or distance between the threads, so is the weight to the power." The student was then expected to calculate the answer to the following question: "What is the power requisite to raise a weight of 8000 pounds by a screw of 12 inches circumference and a 1 inch pitch?" The answer: "As 12:1::8000:6662/ 3 power at the circumference of the screw."[59]

Other lessons were in the form of the familiar question and answer and examples were from familiar situations. Thus the question: "Why does a billiard ball stop when it strikes directly another ball of equal size, and the second ball proceed with the whole velocity which the first had?" The answer invoked Newton's third law of motion and also explained the effect of the elasticity of the balls on the rate of change in velocity.[60]

Scientific American was the preeminent journal for popularizing science in the mid-nineteenth-century United States and a virtual cornucopia of scientific information. For many it served to update patent laws and to disseminate information on inventions. As an inventor advocate and critic of U.S. Patent Office policy, it had no peer. For others, however, *Scientific American* was a gateway to the study of science, offering elementary and intermediate study on such topics as mechanical movements, optics, hydrostatics, and chemistry.

In its early years the journal took seriously its mission to upgrade its readers' knowledge of mechanical principles. For example, simple explanation and sketches helped to clarify the basic concepts of curvilinear and rectilinear motion.[61] "There is a great deal of ignorance among all classes respecting Mechanical Power," said a columnist for *Scientific American* in 1849. The writer then proceeded to explain the concept of mechanical advantage and to warn the ignorant mechanic that no combination of wheels, springs, and levers would ever produce perpetual motion. Two years later the publication began a five-part series on mechanical principles. The series began with general explanations of matter, weight, velocity, and gravity. The presentation, however, was disconnected though simply written. The next three essays dealt with gravity, action and reaction, momentum, and force. The treatment was largely nonmathematical, though simple problems with calculation were used to illustrate the principles.[62]

Other lessons followed. "Short Conversations on Mechanics," for instance, presented "weighty" questions in colloquial language. "Elementary Mechanics" dealt with human strength and horsepower. An essay by J. B. Conger explained the concept of force, illustrating the motion of a projectile with a drawing of a parallelogram of velocities. The elementary mechanics of waterpower were presented as a set of rules to be followed when calculating water flow from under and over a sluice.[63]

At a different level of sophistication altogether were essays in professional journals and in journals for mechanics. *Journal of the Franklin Institute* offered few elementary lessons, but the regular reader was kept current on scientific disputes, technical advances in machine construction, and expectations for those wishing to become engineers. Technical essays on the "General Rules for Proportioning the Length of Boilers for Stationary Engines," "Mechanical Engineering as Applied to Farm Implements," and "Field Practices of Laying Out Circular Curves for Railroads," appeared, along with articles like "What Constitutes an Engineer?" which explained "grades" of engineers, "each competent in his grade, but out of it often at a loss."[64]

Both the *American Railroad Journal* and *The American Polytechnic Journal* included material similar in difficulty to that in the *Journal of the Franklin Institute*. The mission of those journals, however, was more clearly professional, as they attempted to define the emerging role of the engineer in scientific and technical culture. They carried such articles as "The Engineering Profession" along with tables for civil engineers, and such essays as "Power of Traction of Locomotive Engines," "On the Theory of Gradients on Railways," and "Rules and Formulae for Constructing Machines and Parts of Machines." Essays without mathematics appeared on millwork, turning, cabinet making, and pen and pocket cutlery.[65]

Essays for engineers were, of course, far beyond the grasp of those with little formal education in science and mathematics. Yet learned essays illustrated the depth of reading available for self-improvement, and that depth offered a way for the relatively uneducated mechanic to measure his progress. In this way such essays served the spirit of emulation that pervaded the self-improvement literature of early-nineteenth-century America.

Conclusion

The study of natural philosophy in antebellum America cast a broad net, gathering under its panoply the study of physics, chemistry, natural history, and their relation to natural causes and divine will. Its thematic content linked the physical, moral, and theological. From a practical standpoint, however, it was mechanical philosophy (the study of the efficient causes of nature) that translated most easily into practical mechanics.

Those who taught and wrote about natural philosophy were sensitive to the problems of language that such study posed. Popularizers, especially, attempted to unite spatial-visual representation with written explanations; added to this were the skills of oral delivery. The use of scientific (philosophical) apparatus was common, though much of it was homemade until the market for its educational rather than research use was sufficient to sustain demand. Most essayists and textbook authors tried to avoid technical jargon and kept mathematical notation to a minimum. In fact, description rather than explanation was the predominant delivery. The level of reading difficulty in journals was severe enough without adding the subtleties of deductive thinking.

Utility and mental discipline vied for the allegiance of authors writing about natural philosophy. Many attempted a compromise between analysis and synthesis as methods for teaching natural philosophy. Utility had much to recommend it with its formulae for application found in tables and recipes for application. It appealed directly to the "arts" and promised profit through achievement in science. Utility was a powerful motivator, probably more so than mental discipline. Yet the latter was the gateway to the higher learning, which avoided a strictly vocational appeal in favor of learning belonging to gentlemen. For social mobility, mental discipline was required. Mental discipline, moreover, accompanied moral discipline, it was thought, and it was the latter that prepared a young mechanic for proprietorship or a management role in manufacturing. Here in natural philosophy the tension between the liberal and the vocational continued, as it did in the competing systems of instruction themselves. The fragile marriage of utility and mental discipline was held together only by the moral imperative of progressive enlightenment through scientific study and technological advance.

MATHEMATICS INSTRUCTION

TEACHING ARITHMETIC

As with the teaching of science, the teaching of mathematics was beset by pedagogical difficulties that grew out of epistemological problems and conflicting purposes of instruction. The purity with which some instructors and textbook writers approached their subject made it difficult to relate this abstract science to familiar experiences. Those who saw mathematics as relevant only to the clerk or bookkeeper likewise restricted its appeal.

To understand the problems of learning and teaching mathematics, including geometry, we must look at the texts and pedagogy of the early nineteenth century, when arithmetic instruction, including its application in coinage and mensuration, was in a sorry state. Few students owned a text; most used a ciphering book (blank pages) to record the lessons of the teacher. Looking back on his days in the Boston schools in 1810, one man observed that "no boy was allowed to cipher till he was 11 years old. . . . Any boy could copy the work from the manuscript of any further advanced than himself, and the writer never heard any explanation of any principle of arithmetic while he was at school."[1]

This state of affairs should not be surprising given the eighteenth-century view that mathematics was too difficult for those under age ten and often for those under age twelve. Because few children remained in school beyond age twelve, most of them received no instruction in mathematics.[2] Cohen studied sixty copybooks written between 1739 and 1820 and concluded that most were recorded in the hand of a child over age ten. The books, she observes, "trace a standard progression from addition, subtraction, multiplication, and division to the Rule of Three, single and double, inverse and direct." A few took up functions and decimals and the measurement of angles. Trigonometry and geometry were also taught in the applied context of surveying and navigation.[3]

Harvard College took a first big step for the few who could attend when in 1803 it began requiring arithmetic for college entrance. By 1816, Harvard required arithmetic through fractions and decimals, and by 1820 it required some algebra. Even so, the preparation of entrants was so poor that freshmen at Harvard, Yale, and Dartmouth in 1825 typically would take arithmetic and algebra. By the time they were seniors they would have taken geometry, trigonometry, and elementary conic sections. Twenty-five years later a senior at those institutions would have completed analytic geometry and calculus. A notable change had occurred by 1843, when Horace Mann reported that there were 2,333 students studying algebra and 463 studying geometry in Massachusetts.[4]

In the seventeenth and eighteenth centuries the primary purpose of arithmetic texts was to give readers useful information, particularly in trade and commerce. Arithmetic was the province of mercantile life, Cohen has noted, and "ready reckoners," as many books were called, testified to the "endemic lack of skill among tradesmen."[5] From ready reckoners to the formulae in so-called calculators, the emphasis was the same: give rules for quick calculating.

In the eighteenth century, mathematics was viewed as a subject too difficult for most, demanding a strong will and mental discipline. In spite of its utility, however, it was not a subject considered part of a good education. It was perhaps best left to geometers, craftsmen who made specialized mathematical instruments, clockmakers, a few teachers who tried to convince the public of its utility, and some compulsive measurers like Ezra Stiles, who described a spinning contest held in Newport as follows: "Spinning Match at my House, thirty-seven Wheels; the Women br't their flax— & spun ninety-four fifteen-knotted skeins: about five skeins & a half to the pound of 16 ounces. They made us a present of the whole. The Spinners were two Quakers, six Baptists, twenty-nine of my own Society. There were beside fourteen, &. In the evening & next day, Eighteen 14-knotted skeins more were sent to us by several that spun at home the same day. Upon sorting & reducing of it, the whole amounts to One hundred & eleven fifteen-knotted Skeins. We dined sixty persons."[6]

The tradition of practical arithmetics and calculators continued into the nineteenth century. Titus Bennett's *New System of Practical Arithmetic*

Particularly Calculated for the Use of Schools in the United States (1808, 1819) gave about two hundred pages of problems and rules, almost all of which were calculations with "federal money." Thomas Smiley's *New Federal Calculator: or Scholar's Assistant* (1825, 1830) was much the same. Thus, for example, the student was asked: "If 24 yards of cloth cost $47 87cts. 5m., what is the price of 1 yard?" or "When the given price is farthings, by what rule do you work?" or "If 834 dollars, at interest 2 years and 6 months, amount to 927 dollars 821/2 cents, what was the rate per cent. per annum?"[7]

Before 1820, Thomas Dilworth, Nathan Daboll, and Nicholas Pike dominated the market for arithmetic texts in the United States. Thomas Dilworth's *Schoolmaster's Assistant: Being a Compendium of Arithmetic Both Practical and Theoretical* was popular in the late eighteenth century and went through fifty-eight American editions though 1832. Dilworth, acknowledging in his introduction the importance of parental involvement in education, began his subject with whole numbers. He then proceeded to vulgar fractions, decimals applied to simple and compound interest, annuities and payments, and duodecimals (cross multiplication). Dilworth used the question-and-answer (catechetical) format that was to become familiar for the remainder of the antebellum period. Many of his simple problems involved addition and subtraction of measures of cloth, land, time, and motion. More difficult questions were in the form of word problems. The following question was typical: "Three Gardeners, A, B, and C, having bought a piece of ground, find the profits of it amount to 12L. *per annum*. Now the sum of money which they laid down was in such proportion, that as often as A paid 5L. B paid 7L. and as often as B paid 4L. C paid 6L. I demand how much each man must have *per annum* of the gain?"[8]

Daboll's text, like Dilworth's, also dealt with basic arithmetical calculations. It stressed commercial problems and included many extended computations. The problems of measures were similar to those in Dilworth. Other problems dealt with interest on annuities and pensions and with keeping merchant accounts. Daboll's text included methods of bookkeeping, short rules for "casting interest and rebate," and instruction on calculating the contents of surfaces and solids. There was no explanation of these calculations, but they were expressed clearly enough to be useful.[9] In fact, this method of instruction, featured in such texts as Joseph Stockton's *Western Calculator, or a New and Compendious System of Practical Arithmetic* (1818, 1839) and Uriah Parke's *Farmers' and Mechanics' Practical Arithmetic* (1822, 1854) continued to flourish in later editions during the "revolution" taking place in arithmetic teaching. The cult of utility probably reached its zenith in works like William B. Young's *Arithmetical Dictionary, or Book of Reference* (1847), a work of more than two hundred pages of tables.

Pike's *New and Complete System of Arithmetic Composed for the Use of the Citizens of the United States* (1788)—dedicated to James Bowdoin, governor of Massachusetts and president of the American Academy of Arts and Sciences—was the leading American-written arithmetic text, going through nineteen editions by 1822. Pike's work was more comprehensive than Dilworth's and Daboll's, and more difficult. Like Dilworth, Pike included many practical problems, and he supplied numerous tables on commissions, simple interest, expenses, and wages. Like an almanac, the book included calendar projections. It went far beyond Dilworth and Daboll, however, to geometry, trigonometry, logarithms, mensuration of volumes, algebra, and conics.

Pike's work also went beyond the usual arithmetic and calculator in its attention to concepts and calculations for acceleration, specific gravity, levers, wheels and axles, and screws. It was, indeed, a book for all people. The usefulness of the book at Harvard, Yale, and Dartmouth was clear, for it served those whose instruction in arithmetic was meager as well as those who came to college ready for geometry, trigonometry, and algebra. Though the treatment of these more advanced mathematical subjects was brief, a creative instructor could have done much to expand it.[10]

The study of arithmetic in the eighteenth and early nineteenth centuries stressed practical applications in commerce, mensuration, bookkeeping, navigation, and surveying. The format was "state a rule, give an example, and present exercises to be followed (or, in geometry, give proofs to be memorized)."[11] Given the assumption that mathematics was too difficult to explain yet useful enough to be learned, it made sense to state the rules in hopes that students would recognize the appropriate contexts for application. Even in practical books, notes Cohen, the effect of the catechetical format "must certainly have been to discourage and constrain the spread of numerical skills." This method of presentation, she explains, restricted the understanding of arithmetic to "commercial meanings."[12] The logic of mathematics could wait until another day.

The debate over whether the purpose of mathematics was to teach mental discipline or to provide practical applications beleaguered mathematics educators throughout the nineteenth century. These differences in purpose translated directly into disputes over pedagogy. Pressure had mounted during the late 1820s to apply Pestalozzian principles to learning, including the study of arithmetic. By 1830 the *American Journal of Education* was arguing that "ideas of number are among the earliest which children acquire. We soon learn to distinguish one, two, three, four, etc." Children, the essayist continued, experience numbers every day, and a perceptive teacher would see to it that the slate was used to record, through simple marks, the numbers of cherries, nuts, and other naturally occurring objects.[13] Similar sentiments were evident in the following year in the *American Annals of Education and Instruction*. One teacher observed that "when the child is old enough to learn to count objects around him, he is old enough to study Arithmetic." Again, however, the role of the teacher in sensitively preparing the way for the child was crucial. A slow, patient, sustained but not tiring approach was necessary, continued the author, who illustrated the dialogue between teacher and student in several scenarios.[14]

With the work of Warren Colburn the teaching of arithmetic was launched into a new era. Pestalozzi's ideas were prominent in Colburn's work, though Colburn said he had never read Pestalozzi. He was criticized for being too abstract and failing to implement lessons through objects as Pestalozzi did.[15] How many teachers heeded Colburn and Pestalozzi is unknown, but the tradition of teaching by rule did not disappear. Nonetheless, Colburn's work was still pronounced the "best that has yet appeared" by the author of "Prize Essay," published in *The Common School Journal* in 1840.[16]

Colburn eschewed "rules" in favor of "mental" or "intellectual" arithmetic—that is, the working out of problems, often orally, by analysis rather than through the application of rules. His approach to the teaching of algebra also epitomized his general method and was clearly stated in *An Introduction to Algebra upon the Inductive Method of Instruction* (1825): "to make the transition from arithmetic to algebra as gradual as possible [by] beginning with practical questions in simple equations, such as the learner might readily solve without the aid of algebra. . . . The most simple combinations are given first. . . . The learner is expected to derive most of his knowledge by solving the examples himself."[17]

Colburn's approach was inductive, perhaps in keeping with the Baconian climate of the age and certainly in keeping with Pestalozzian pedagogy. Other text writers followed Colburn's lead though they frequently departed from his principles. Daniel Adams published *Adams' New Arithmetic, in Which the Principles of Operating by Numbers are Analytically Explained and Synthetically Applied* (1840). Adams combined the best of the old rules with explanations and applications. In fact, the explanations were little more than descriptions of the arithmetical processes to be carried out. We do not know, of course, whether students were successful in using Adams' method.[18]

Colburn's attack on rules stemmed from more than his belief that they were unnatural for young children. Perhaps more important was his appreciation of numbers as language. The young child cannot successfully begin with the abstractions of numbers, said Colburn, because they bear no relation to "practical examples." Practical examples cannot be derived from abstractions, he continued, and the child must make the transition to the grammar of numbers. He cannot simultaneously conquer abstract numbers, figures, and correlative words. The result, said Colburn, is that the child learns only to perform the operations on the numbers without understanding the meaning of the operations themselves.[19]

Among textbook writers the analytic method was short-lived and its principles often violated. Joseph Ray's *Little Arithmetic. Elementary Lessons in Intellectual Arithmetic, on the Analytic and Inductive Method of Instruction* was ostensibly in the mode of Colburn. Yet, a comparison of the texts shows that Ray's method did not honor Colburn's dictum to begin with the practical.[20] Though he used illustrations and began his text with pictures of apples organized in rows corresponding to the proper numbers, the spirit of practicality was lacking. By the mid-nineteenth century the "science of numbers" had replaced Colburn's method in its pure sense. In fact, journals for educators carried detailed instructions on how to teach arithmetic, possibly because available texts simply did not take into account what practicing educators knew about the learning of young children.[21]

Teaching arithmetic by the "science of numbers" emphasized classification and deduction. Numbers were formally classified as concrete or abstract, simple or compound, and natural or artificial. Mathematical operations were carried out according to the principles that applied to each category. Little explanation was offered, and the emphasis was, as in the old works of Pike, Dilworth, and Daboll, on practical word problems. The same topics for application prevailed: interest, percentage, discount, payments, and coinage. A work like John Talbott's *Scholar's Guide to the Science of Numbers* went beyond arithmetic to geometry, though the treatment was elementary. Talbott even included ten pages on the mechanical powers.

In spite of the absence of explanation, there was a much clearer exposition of the processes of arithmetic in most post-Colburn texts. The mindless repetition in older texts was generally avoided, and the rules for various operations seemed to follow more naturally from practical problems. What Colburn had launched, others continued, despite the crosscurrents of conservative pedagogy. The revolt against rule-bound memorization was in full swing by the 1840s as Horace Mann criticized both the ineptitude of teachers and a pedagogy that stressed the right answer over the learning of principles. Utility ought not supersede the learning of principles, said Mann, for the result would be "too worthless an object to satisfy the desire or stimulate the ambition of any child whose faculties have not been misled or perverted."[22]

What Mann was advocating was mental arithmetic leading to mental discipline. Two years later he continued his attack on memorization, noting that he had seen older students who, having memorized numeration tables, still did not know the ratio of decimal increase. Mann contrasted the Prussian schools with American public schools, noting that the former began instruction earlier, practiced the basic elements much longer, and did not separate "the processes, or rules, so much as we do from one another." "In algebra, trigonometry, surveying, geometry, &c.," he continued, the teacher drew diagrams on the blackboard and accompanied them by explanations. Children were required to go to the blackboard and "solve problems themselves," a method quite different from that practiced in American schools, where the child held the text in the left hand and followed the demonstration with the forefinger of the right hand by pointing to the text.[23]

Teaching mathematics as the science of numbers was a standard approach in textbooks of the 1850s. In fact, the approach was a synthesis of the old and the new, a mixture of the practical of the early century and the new pedagogy of the 1830s, to which was added the mental discipline characteristic of collegiate studies. Charles Davies' formulaic texts were, perhaps, the best example.

Davies' texts proceeded from definition to explanation (description of the process) and application in practical word problems. The first part of his "improved" edition of *Arithmetic, Designed for Academies and Schools* (1852) began with the five rules of arithmetic, proceeded to practical application with "denominate" numbers, then followed with common (vulgar) fractions, decimals, proportions, practical applications in business, mensuration in geometry, and gauging. Later he defined and explained the standard arithmetic operations.[24]

Advanced students were later introduced to commission and brokerage. For example, a commission merchant was defined as a "person who buys or sells goods for another, receiving therefore a certain rate per cent," and a broker was a "dealer in money or stocks." A paragraph explaining the calculation of interest followed, and then a word problem: "What is the commission on $4396 at 6 percent?" More complicated problems concluded the chapter.[25]

Mental discipline—the cultivation of the mind's faculties—was always a major objective of mental arithmetic. Edward Brooks noted that arithmetic was a science of numbers, that it was much like synthetic geometry: "In arithmetic we have the same basis, and proceed by the same laws of logical evolution." [26] Pedagogically, the mental discipline of mathematics set it side by side with language studies. Its purpose was to "*quicken, strengthen*, and *develop* the reasoning powers" and to "cause the pupil to acquire the habit of *systematically classifying* his knowledge." These habits of mind, said John Stoddard, author of *The American Intellectual Arithmetic*, were of "infinite importance to a person in every condition of life." [27] It was a view that echoed the defense of mathematical studies as part of a liberal education. Mathematics, like the study of language, exercised the deductive powers and developed clarity and accuracy of thought. It was a subject where ratiocination achieved its greatest purity. [28]

TEACHING ALGEBRA

Horace Mann's estimate of 2,333 students studying algebra in Massachusetts in 1842 should be put in the perspective of the 10,177 Massachusetts students studying the history of the United States. Algebra was not even taught to most public school students in the United States. Nonetheless, in Massachusetts the number of students studying algebra nearly matched the number studying general history (2,571) and surpassed by a large margin the number studying bookkeeping (1,472). [29] As we have seen, the study of algebra was considered necessary to a proper understanding of natural philosophy.

The young student opening Charles Davies' *Elementary Algebra, Embracing the First Principles of the Science* (1842, 1851) was greeted by two protagonists, John and Charles, who introduced the basic concepts of algebra using apples, peaches, and pears.

1. John and Charles have twelve apples between them, and each has as many as the other: How many has each?"

In Algebra, we often represent numbers by the letters of the alphabet; that is, we take a letter to stand for a number. Thus, let x stand for the apples which John has. Then, as Charles has an equal number, x will also stand for the apples which he has. But together, they have twelve apples, hence, twice x must be equal to 12. This we write thus:

$x + x = 2x = 12;$

and if twice x is equal to 12, it follows that once x, or x, will be equal to 6. This we write thus:

$x = 12/2 = 6.$ [30]

After the introduction, John and Charles disappear as the young problem solvers and are replaced by nine pages of definition, including arithmetic signs, the signs for exponents and radicals, and parentheses for polynomials. From that point on, pages of practice equations and problems are arranged alternately. No doubt the practice equations were tedious, but some of the word problems restored algebra to the here and now. For example, the following might have convinced some skeptics of its utility:"8. A person engaged a workman for 48 days. For each day that he labored, he received 24 cents, and for each day that he was idle, he paid 12 cents for his board. At the end of the 48 days, the account was settled, when the laborer received 504 cents. *Required the number of working days, and the number of days he was idle.*"[31]

As the text progressed to equations of the second degree, to arithmetic and geometric progressions, and to logarithms, fewer and fewer practical applications appeared. In fact, one is struck by the divorce of algebra from the world of experience, even in some attempts to render it practical. For example, one could hardly conceive of the following unless the conversationalists had previously agreed to a test of wits:"17. A says to B, my son's age is one quarter of yours, and the difference between the squares of the numbers representing their ages is 240: what were their ages?"[32]

Davies' *Elements of Algebra: on the Basis of M. Bourdon* (1853, 1856) was a more sophisticated work than his *Elementary Algebra*. It began with the rules of elementary algebra, but it did not accompany them with practical examples, suggesting that this section was for review purposes only. Though the subtitle of the work promises "practical examples," the work is dense with equations and rules. The notable exceptions were the problem on the piling of cannon balls, one on calculating simple interest, and one on calculating compound interest. *Elements of Algebra* is a book for mental discipline; it was designed to develop "judgment" and "reasoning" and to provide the student with a stepping stone to calculus.[33]

At the highest end of the spectrum of difficulty was Lacroix's book—also titled *Elements of Algebra*—a work only for the hardy. Though authoritative, the language of the explanations was dense and unlikely to aid the student in the transition from arithmetic to algebra. In all fairness, Lacroix's work was a treatise, but the student who opened to page 1 found the following formidable explanation: "There are many questions, the solution of which is composed of two parts; the one having for its object to find which of the four fundamental rules the determination of the unknown number by means of the numbers given belongs, and the other the application of these rules. The first part, independent of the manner of writing numbers, or of the system of the notation, consists entirely in the development of the consequences which result directly or indirectly from the enunciation, or from the manner in which that which is enunciated connects the numbers given with the numbers required, that is to say, from the relations which it establishes between these numbers."[34] The language itself was fair warning of the abstruse study to follow.

TEACHING GEOMETRY

Before 1820 there were fourteen books on geometry published in the United States. *Hawney's Complete Measurer* (1801) was written abroad, as were the only three demonstrative (as opposed to applied) geometries by Simson, Playfair, and Legendre. Legendre's work, published in forty-two editions between 1819 and 1890, was unique in its "departure from Euclid's axioms and sequence of theorems" and in the use of algebraic symbols and proofs. Its staying power as a text is testimony to the enormous French influence on early American geometries.[35]

In the latter eighteenth century and antebellum period of the nineteenth century some students received their first exposure to geometry in arithmetic texts. Pike's *New and Complete System of Arithmetic* (1788) included a large section on mensuration of surfaces and solids, including arcs and sectors. Following the introduction to algebra, Pike included calculations for conic sections. The book did not deal with what was considered geometry proper, that is, the mastery of geometric logic in the form of proofs. It did, however, introduce the student to the practical aspects of geometry.

Texts like Davies' *Arithmetic, Designed for Academies and Schools* and his *Practical Mathematics with Drawing and Mensuration, Applied to the Mechanic Arts* did the same, though the latter was designed for the mechanic arts. Lines, angles, plane figures, and measures for carpenters, bricklayers, joiners, and slaters were dealt with in separate chapters. The final sections were an introduction to mechanical philosophy, including the laws of motion, mechanical powers, specific gravity, the use of logarithms, and the application of mathematics in calculating the strength of materials. The first part of Book Seven, which was the introduction to mechanics, introduced the student to basic concepts in mechanical philosophy, but it did not treat the subject algebraically. Rather, Davies gave only definitions of such concepts as matter, impenetrability, extension, inertia, atoms, attraction, force, power, velocity, acceleration, and momentum. The section on mechanical powers also contained definitions; these were accompanied by a few simple calculation problems that were part of the explanations of levers, pulleys, wheels and axles, inclined planes, and wedges.[36]

In most textbooks the rationale for teaching geometry was much the same as that for teaching mathematics in general. Geometry promoted the development of logical thinking, attentiveness, clarity of expression, accuracy of definition, and the distinction between "what is hypothesis and what is proof—between premises and conclusion."[37] Geometry was no subject for mindless repetition, though a good memory aided those trying to master proofs of theorems and their corollaries. The mental rigor required for the study of geometry was also one reason it was considered the "least feminine" branch of mathematics. In fact, as we see in Chapter 7, geometry became the test for proving the equality of men and women in mental discipline.[38]

Spatial representation and logic were united in geometry, but their union presented a dilemma for educators. Charles Davies' preface to Brewster's translation of Legendre's *Elements of Geometry and Trigonometry* for use in the United States clearly summarized the problem of integrating spatial representation, the logic of mathematics and philosophy, and verbal explanation of mathematical concepts.

Noting that the departure from Euclid's method was "generally regretted," Davies put the issue of joining the particular and the general this way: "The propositions of Geometry are general truths, and as such, should be stated in general terms, and without reference to particular figures." Even though the book contains numerous drawings that were adopted by others to ease the burden of beginners attempting to comprehend abstract propositions, this strategy, Davies thought, undermined the teaching of mathematics through rigorous logical demonstration. More generally, said Davies, the use of diagrams defeated one of the major purposes of learning mathematics, namely, to strengthen the "faculty of abstraction." It is not surprising, then, that problems of a practical nature were often thought beneath the dignity of formal proofs.[39]

Legendre's work followed, typically, the first six books of Euclid. Farrar's translation (1831) began with a review of "proportions" and presumed at least an acquaintance with the theory. Algebra was the tool, but there also was the hope of advancing the student in the study of algebra itself.[40] Substantial space in Legendre's book was given to circles and spherical trigonometry. Tables for logarithms and logarithmic sines were also included. Books one and two laid down the basic definitions and logical operations essential to geometric understanding. Definitions of such terms as axiom, theorem, problem, lemma, proposition, corollary, scholium, and hy-

BOOK II.

37

PROPOSITION IV. THEOREM.

*If there be four proportional quantities, and four other propor-
tional quantities, having the antecedents the same in both, the
consequents will be proportional.*

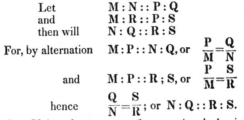

Let M : N :: P : Q
and M : R :: P : S
then will N : Q :: R : S
For, by alternation M : P :: N : Q, or $\frac{P}{M}=\frac{Q}{N}$

and M : P :: R ; S, or $\frac{P}{M}=\frac{S}{R}$

hence $\frac{Q}{N}=\frac{S}{R}$; or N : Q :: R : S.

Cor. If there be two sets of proportionals, having **an ante-**
cedent and consequent of the first, equal to an antecedent **and**
consequent of the second, the remaining terms will be **propor-**
tional.

PROPOSITION V. THEOREM.

*If four quantities be in proportion, they will be in proportion **when**
taken inversely.*

Let M : N :: P : Q ; then will
N : M :: Q : P.
For, from the first proportion we have M × Q = N × P, or
N × P = M × Q.
But the products N × P and M × Q are the products **of the**
extremes and means of the four quantities N, M, Q, P, and these
products being equal,
N : M :: Q : P (Prop. II.).

PROPOSITION VI. THEOREM.

*If four quantities are in proportion, they will be in proportion by
composition, or division.*

Fig. 5.1. An explanation of the theory of proportions. From A. M. Legendre, *Elements of Geometry and Trigonometry*, trans. David Brewster, ed. Charles Davies
(Philadelphia: A. S. Barnes, 1834), 37.

pothesis were then presented, as were the signs used in geometric equations, the axioms central to logical deduction, and the logic of proportions. In Brewster's translation (1834), the latter was illustrated in figure 5.1.

There was a range of difficulty in books devoted to the teaching of geometry. Most followed the time-honored format of stating a major proposition (theorem) and following with its proof, its corollaries, and their proofs, and derivative rules. Some, such as Matthew Dutton's *Elementary Treatise on Conic Sections, Spherical Geometry, and Spherical Trigonometry* (1824), included fold-out linear drawings and projections. *The Element of Geometry*, published by W. E. Dean in 1836, was organized into six books; a seventh book was on plane trigonometry. This last book was far less sophisticated, devoting a lengthy section at the outset to fifty-seven basic definitions.[41] As with the first book of *Element of Geometry*, other books also included definitions followed by theorems and problems arranged in relation to one another.

Geometry texts stood at a crossroads pedagogically. The logic of Euclid and the analytic geometry of Descartes demanded abstract thought but stopped short of dealing with the problem of movement and the laws of motion. Exercises in Euclid's proofs surely disciplined the mind, but they offered little to those interested in the applications of geometry. Sometimes texts tried to combine all aspects of geometry, including perspective geometry, but it was difficult to do all of it well. As in science, the periodic press attempted to rescue students from the abstractions of mathematics and to emphasize its applications.

TEACHING MATHEMATICS IN THE PERIODICAL PRESS

Writers frequently complained in mechanics, apprentice, and popular science journals about how mathematics was taught in public schools, but they promoted its usefulness for workers. The utility of algebra, however, was often doubted while that of geometry was applauded. Thus most attempts to fill the gap in worker's mathematical knowledge focused on the applied principles of geometry. These "lessons" were sometimes contributed by textbook authors, but they also took the form of "correspondence" and puzzles.

The *American Mechanics' Magazine* and the *Franklin Journal and American Mechanics' Magazine*, subsequently the *Journal of the Franklin Institute*, took the lead in educating mechanics about geometry. Editor Thomas P. Jones knew what many machinists knew through experience: that one could not design a machine with only a knowledge of geometric principles. He also knew that a machine without proper geometry would not work.

In its first year, 1825, a series on "practical" and "mechanical" geometry ran for most of the year. Some lessons were traditional proofs, others dealt with common problems encountered by mechanics, and still others were specific queries from readers. Thus, for example, the theorem which states that "if from the center of any circle a radius be drawn to the circumference, bisecting any chord, it will be perpendicular to the chord" was illustrated and followed by corollaries.[42]

Practical applications of the geometry of solids were contributed by T. S. Davies, whose preface to his series explained that little had been done to make geometry a popular study. Davies' series began with the following problem: "to transfer any given circle from the surface of a sphere, cone, or cylinder, to any flat surface." Other problems of drawing great circles and tracing perpendicular lines on a cylinder followed. Mechanical (rather than mathematical) solutions to finding circumferences, squaring the end of logs and planks, and finding the center of a circle with compasses and miter square only were included for the artisan with virtually no mathematical background.[43] As part of the emphasis on practical geometry in the 1825 series, problems from correspondents also were included. The following was a "Problem for Millwrights" much in the form of a word problem, but it was signed "A Man in the Moors": "There are to be four spur wheels; one of them is to have 99 cogs, and the other three to have 100 cogs each; they are all to work at the same time and into each other; and I want to know how they must be placed, so that two of them shall make 100 revolutions each, in the same time that a third wheel makes but one revolution: the solver may do what he chooses with the fourth wheel, only keep it amongst the rest. The thing can be done, and, when properly constructed, will form a very powerful and useful machine."[44]

As the *Journal of the Franklin Institute* shifted its focus from instructing mechanics to researching and writing for an emergent "professional" class, its essays on and demonstrations of practical mathematical problems grew more sophisticated. At a relatively low level of sophistication it carried essays dealing with "Rules for Solid Mensuration," in which Ellwood Morris, a civil engineer, explained simple rules for finding the volume of a cone and wedge. More difficult essays included calculations for bridge trusses and the trisection of an angle.[45] Drafting problems and their explanations were also included, and the essays often were accompanied by prefatory remarks on the usefulness of skills for making blueprints and representing the details of machinery.[46] As we have seen, specialized calculations for gradients and steam engines and trigonomic functions were also carried by the journal.

As journals for mechanics and engineers grew more specialized, it became more difficult to write and edit for diverse audiences. In 1846 *Scientific American* took up the cause of remediation in both mathematics and science. Here problems were included for the mathematically uninitiated. Problems and their solutions were sequenced from one issue to the next; they required, for example, the application of the rules of right triangles (the proportionality of their various sides and to the radius of an inscribed circle; see fig. 5.2). Non-numerical solutions (using rule and compass) were also given for cutting elbows and stove pipes and a leather covering for a cone. Wagon and carriage makers were given a rule for bevels by rule and draft.[47]

Given its mission to popularize science and to illustrate the utility of mathematics to the arts, *Scientific American* offered little mathematics instruction beyond the elementary level and none beyond the intermediate level. Its commitment to inventors (and to building the business of Munn and Company) did not require that it avidly promote mathematics, even though editorials expressed misgivings about mathematics instruction in public schools. It clearly was a limited utility that was sought, not a firm grasp of mathematical principles.

Other journals of more limited circulation also carried instruction in mathematics, particularly geometry. *The Apprentice's Companion* focused on geometry but assumed a common school education that included arithmetic, geometry, and trigonometry. A caveat to such preparation was given for those "but slightly acquainted with mathematics" by diagramming and defining a circle, angle, degree, chord, arc, tangent, secant, sine, and co-sine. In the same journal the basic facts of geometry were applied in other essays dealing with the parallelogram of forces.[48]

The *American Mechanics' Magazine* included essays explaining basic algebraic signs but devoted more space to practical and "mechanical" geometry. In 1825, T. S. Davies announced in the first of a series on "Practical Geometry" and "Mechanical Geometry" that "a knowledge of Geometry is so essential to the greater part of our practical mechanics, that it would seem surprising so little has been done towards rendering that science a *popular* study."[49] This substantial series began with the method for transferring circles from surfaces of spheres, cones, or cylinders to a flat surface. Other essays in the series included drawing bevel wheels in perspective, constructing right angles and triangles within circles, drawing arches, bisecting chords, and drawing tangents.[50] Even more sophisticated amoniac.

The solution of Problem 1, in your journal of last week, seems to depend on the proper-ty of right angled triangles, embodied in the following Proposition :—

In a right angled triangle, as the sum of the three sides is to either of the legs, so is the remaining leg to the rad;us of an inscribed circle.

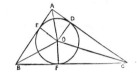

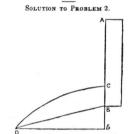

Let A B C be the triangle right angled at A, and E D F the circle inscribed in it, of which the radii O D, O E and O F, are drawn to the point of contact D E F. Now it is evi-dent, that

2. Area ABC=BA, AC. And also 2. Area ABC=2.AOB+2.BOC+2.COA=ABxOE+B CxOF+ACxOD=(as OE=OF) OD)AB+B C+AC. OD.

Hence AB+BC+.AC OD=BA. AC. And AB+ BC+AC : BA : : AC : OD. which was to be proved.

To apply this to the case in question. If AC be 16 and AB be 9, BC must be √16x16 x9x9=18 357. We have then this propor-tion, 16+9+18.357 : 16 : : 9 : 3.321=the ra-dius of the circle. Double this, or 6.642, is the diameter.   JOSIAH T. TUBBY.

New York, May 30, 1849.

SOLUTION TO PROBLEM 2.

Let A B denote the height or sides of the vessel. C the hole from which the water spouts in the parabolic curve D B. Draw the line D b and join B b so that the angles B b D shall be a right angle. Then B D is a maxi-mum, and since the angle b B D is constant B b is a maximum, also b D. But when D b is a maximum Db. tan. BDb=bB or 2 AC. tan. BDb=2 AC=AB or 2 AC (tan. BDb−1)=AB or 2 AC (1−tan. BDb)=AB :: AC= AB
                                                                                        ̄ ̄ ̄ ̄ ̄ ̄ ̄ ̄ ̄ ̄ ̄ ̄
                                                                                        2(1−tan. BDb)

Taking the positive value I find A C=9,433 feet, which was required.

RICHARD HINCHCLIFFE.

Ballard Vale, Mass.

[Mr. Hinchcliffe sent a solution of Problem 1 also. It was the same as Mr. Tubby's. We have received so many new problems, and solutions to those already proposed, that we have concluded to publish no more, as it re-

Fig. 5.2. A lesson in basic geometry. From "Use-ful Problems," *Scientific American* 4, no. 39 (16 June 1849). Photo courtesy Smithsonian Institu-tion.

lessons were found in *Mechanics' Magazine and Register of Inventions and Improvements*, including drawings for constructing curves for arches and equations for working drafts of ellipsoidal arches.[51]

As with science, the task of popularizing the study of mathematics fell to periodicals. Textbooks grew in number and responded to the growing demand for science and mathematics in common schools, but the preeminence of verbal and literary studies left only a modest space in the curriculum for additional subjects. Those interested in the education of mechanics and mechanics themselves were driven by the need to upgrade their skills as best they could. Editors appealed to a wide range of educational backgrounds, but they generally agreed that their mission was to further technological progress and individual upward social mobility through education. The study of mathematics was thus seen as part of a more comprehensive plan to bring together the practical demands of technology with the abstractions of mathematics.

CONCLUSION

Both the themes and the disputes in mathematics teaching in the first half of the nineteenth century were similar to those in the teaching of science. The pedagogy for each was debated, but with far greater rigor for mathematics. Moreover, the debate over whether geometric or algebraic thinking was most useful in mathematical solutions to problems stood quite apart from problems of scientific study. Issues over the internal logic of mathematics continued with little regard for the utility of mathematics as a discipline. This is not to say that its usefulness was ignored. Rather, it was a case of two parallel debates being conducted with only a limited understanding of their connections.

Behind the teaching of mathematics stood a mixed tradition that testified to its avowed utility in trade and commerce, yet was fraught with anxiety over its difficulty. "Ready reckoners" were testimony to the former. Beyond basic arithmetic was a land where only those of strong will and discipline dared to venture. Anything beyond arithmetic remained a speciality.

The spread of Pestalozzian methods, combined with Colburn's attack on rules divorced from experience, brought matters to a head in the 1820s. Colburn and his sympathizers insisted that the learning of mathematics proceed in "natural" ways. The rarefied, noncontextual world represented by algebra was not to be separated from sensory input and naturalistic scenarios expressed in "word" problems. Though they fell far short of their aims, Colburn and others sought to bring together the logical operations of mathematics and the world of experience. The pedagogy of "rules" did not disappear, but by mid-century mathematics textbooks had clearly shifted their ground as authors committed themselves to a science of numbers.

As with the teaching of science, disputes over whether utility or mental discipline was the primary aim of instruction were echoed in mathematics. The conflict, however, was selective. Geometry was clearly preferred over algebra for its immediate application to mechanical problems. The reason for that preference was obvious, for geometric principles and the rules of perspective geometry were easily applied through the visual-spatial skills of drawing. With algebra, utility was evident only in specialized applications, even though it was touted for its usefulness in developing mental discipline. As with science, the Baconian spirit collided with academic traditions rooted in liberal learning. For the latter, the purpose of mathematics was to develop the muscle of the mind, not unlike the purpose of the time-honored language instruction that dominated most curricula. For the former, mathematics was a skill to be applied. In joining the two, teachers faced their most difficult challenge.

6

New Educational Institutions for a New Society: Schools for Mechanics

"The mechanic is one of God's noblemen."—E. L. Magoon

The failure of the public schools to respond fully and swiftly to the educational demands of an emerging manufacturing society gave rise to educational alternatives in the private sector. To be sure, public schooling was successful in raising literacy rates to an all-time high in New England, in the old northwest, and in the eastern and central states, even though literacy remained stratified by region, age, socioeconomic class, and nativity.[1]

Yet the efforts of the public schools were directed toward civic literacy, and little effort was made to extend the concept beyond that imperative. School reformers believed in the importance of literacy to worker productivity and economic progress, but most viewed it in moral and political terms, not technological ones. Calls for the teaching of more mathematics and science were heeded slowly, even though pedagogical debates signaled increasing interest in these subjects. These calls, however, were often directed toward the goal of mental discipline unrelated to occupational utility and technological awareness. In fact, the liberal and the technical were frequently at odds despite efforts to unite them. The result was unsatisfactory for those who advocated education for occupational utility to the "mechanic class" and also for those who sought to justify the teaching of science as a means to achieve mental discipline.

Between 1818 and 1850 there were about one hundred mechanics' institutes and libraries formed in the United States. Slightly more than 40 percent of these were established in New England and the mid-Atlantic states between 1820 and 1840. About 13 percent were founded in the same period in the South and Midwest. In the 1840s, twenty of these organizations were formed in New England, the Midwest, and the South.[2]

The formation of mechanics' associations and institutes was both a response to economic insecurity and an expression of artisans' desire to achieve a social status worthy of their skills.[3] In New England, joining an association or institute was, as Kornblith puts it, an "act of self-definition" and a matter of setting old wrongs right. For many, the educational programs launched by these associations were attempts to secure for future generations the respectability missing from their own lives.

The collective action of these men did define their interests, cutting a broad swath across the socioeconomic topography of eastern and midwestern cities and towns. These interests were manifest in a broad range of activities, the most obvious of which were those encouraging economic independence. By defining the labor of the mechanic as the mainstay of progress, mechanics in turn defined their own place and their citizenship in an emerging industrial order.

Mechanics' associations differed in representation of mechanics as a group. For example, it was the breadth of the membership in Providence, Rhode Island, that was impressive, not its exclusiveness. Even so, the masters, not the journeymen, dominated the association.[4] The Massachusetts Charitable Mechanic Association in Boston (MCMA) was clearly more elitist in composition, though it represented the diversity of "artisan specialities" in Boston. Journeymen were excluded from the association, and within occupations the masters represented the upper half of the wealth distribution in real property. The members also clearly came from the upper half of the wealth distribution in Boston.[5]

A detailed breakdown of the occupational composition of two large mechanics' organizations—the MCMA and the Franklin Institute of Philadelphia—is given in table 6.1. The most significant occupational trends among the members over a forty-year period include the growth in numbers of metalworkers, workers in the applied arts, workers in manufactures, engineers, professionals, sales personnel, and clerks. The numbers of people in stoneworking, glassworking, leathermaking, shipbuilding, and apparel-making declined. In general, the changing distributions reflect the different demands of local economies, including the mechanization of some occupations. The one major exception appears to be woodworking, which remained high at MCMA and almost doubled at the Franklin Institute.

Table 6.1. Occupational Distribution as a Percentage of Membership in the Massachusetts Charitable Mechanic Association and the Franklin Institute, 1821–1860

Occupation and Manufactures	Date and Association			
	1821–1840		1841–1860	
	MCMA	FI	MCMA	FI
Metalworking	8.8	7.4	13.6	8.5
Woodworking	33.5	6.6	25.0	10.1
Stoneworking	12.2	3.8	10.6	2.8
Glassworking	.1	0	.1	0
Leatherworking	1.4	4.2	1.2	1.0
Shipbuilding	5.8	0	4.6	.2
Applied arts	6.5	10.0	10.1	9.1
Fine arts	9.0	2.7	10.0	4.1
Printing	4.6	2.9	3.0	2.4
Textiles	0	.9	0	.1
Apparel	9.6	3.6	6.0	3.2
Paper products	.9	2.0	1.6	.1
Food preparation	2.6	3.4	1.1	1.6
Manufacture	2.8	2.8	7.5	4.0
Professional	.9	19.7	2.2	18.6
Government	0	1.4	0	.9
Professional engineering	.6	1.2	2.4	4.4
Sales	0	26.7	0	19.5
Clerical	0	.4	0	8.8
Farm	0	.3	0	.5
Laborer	0	0	0	0
Service	.7	0	1.0	.1

Source: Membership records of the Massachusetts Charitable Mechanic Association and the Franklin Institute.

The broad range of occupations required mechanics' associations to serve members in a variety of ways, including offering mutual education. The associations strengthened the craft structure in their respective localities, helped to resolve disputes among members, and served as insurance societies by providing death benefits for widows and children. They sought to improve the image of craftsmen and craftsmen-entrepreneurs by linking their welfare with technological progress, inventive genius, the broad, democratic dissemination of useful knowledge, and an economic structure they presumed would reward competence, industry, and prudence.

Much in the American experience with mechanics' institutes resembled that of the British, particularly in Glasgow, London, and Manchester. George Birkbeck's efforts to organize mechanics' institutes were as legendary in England as they were in the United States. In fact, the renaissance nature of Birkbeck's accomplishments—he was a lecturer in philosophy and chemistry, a physician, an instrument maker, and an advocate of workingmen—was clearly inspirational, placing him on a pedestal among those who advocated more education for workingmen.[6]

In England and in the United States mechanics' associations and institutes were voluntary organizations promoting the greater diffusion of practical and scientific knowledge. "The object of our [mechanics' institute]," wrote George B. Emerson in 1827, is to provide practical knowledge to those in the "business of labor." Edward Everett, ardent promoter of technology, scientific knowledge, and self-improvement through education, likewise saw these institutes as illustrating and explaining the "principles of the various arts of life, and render[ing] these familiar to those who are to exercise these arts as their occupation."[7]

Everett's words were part of a larger message that basic literacy, the habit of reading, and moral discipline would lead an individual to prosperity. Everett's formula for the workingman was the intellectually productive use of leisure time and delayed gratification of material and animal wants. "Whoever has learned to read," he observed, "possesses the keys to knowledge; and can, whenever he pleases, not only unlock the portals of her temple, but penetrate to the inmost halls and most secret cabinets."[8]

In the early nineteenth century, mechanics' institutes and the educational activities of mechanics' associations served at least five distinct purposes. These included updating technical knowledge, preparing young men for mechanics' positions in manufacturing, increasing the skills of mechanics to a level that would distinguish them from operatives, promoting upward social mobility through liberal education, and building character to increase the chances of success in business.

In the name of both immediate utility and the elevation of the human mind, mechanics' institutes conducted numerous educational activities, including day and evening classes. Some of these were popular lyceum lectures and demonstrations; others were displays of scientific erudition. The Burlington Mechanics' Institute in Burlington, Iowa, cast a broad net, incorporating itself to "improve the members thereof in literature, the sciences, arts, and morals; for the establishment of a library, reading room, cabinets of geological, mineralogical, botanical, and other specimens; to endow and support a school for the education of the children of indigent mechanics and others, and to advance the social, intellectual, and moral conditions, of its members generally."[9]

The Franklin Institute also had a broad mission, but it focused increasingly on research as the century progressed. Nonetheless, like other mechanics' institutes, its aim was to abolish those "odious monopolies" in learning and to offer young men a practical education that borrowed heavily from natural science and philosophy.[10] Its special Franklinesque mission was to clear a path for the upward socioeconomic mobility of that broad class of workers called mechanics.

John Craig, in an address to the citizens of Cincinnati to promote a mechanics' institute, saw supporters serving the interests of citizens in general, but he warned of mindless mechanization and spoke strongly for "intelligent" labor.[11] Craig defined two onerous conditions that might result from ignorance among young men working for cash wages. The first was the "moral turpitude" resulting from workers being placed early in life in businesses that allowed "no opportunity of mental improvement." The second was the result of large numbers of employees being displaced by labor-saving machinery. In either case, however, it was their "gross ignorance" that led them toward moral degradation.[12]

Like other promoters of mechanics' institutes, Craig saw the education of mechanics in a broad light. Having achieved basic literacy, youth were to spend their evenings in school and at the library. Beyond that, Craig believed, should be a state-supported institution emphasizing advanced learning. A mechanics' institute, he said, ought to offer geometry, practical mathematics, drawing in perspective, principles of architecture, and mechanical and chemical philosophy, all of which should be explained in plain language and with apparatus. This, in addition to geology and mineralogy, he explained, constituted all the scientific knowledge necessary for the farmer, mechanic, and manufacturer.[13]

Nineteen years after Craig's address, the mission of the Ohio Mechanics' Institute had not changed. In a speech delivered at that time, E. L. Magoon summarized the essential features of educating mechanics. For the individual mechanic, said Magoon, education was a source of mental and moral discipline, a way of converting mental energy into action, and a "moral gymnasium of the soul."[14] Collectively, educated mechanics would be a powerful force for technical and scientific progress. Individually and collectively Magoon's image was that of the noble mechanic.[15]

In the early nineteenth century the terms *mechanic* and *manufacturer* were not clearly distinguished, especially before the development of large water- and steam-powered systems. Common usage, however, designated a mechanic as one who applied mind and hand in a creative and sometimes inventive process, "usually employing simple tools."[16] The mechanic class of workers covered a broad range of skills and production methods. Mechanic, artist, and manufacturer were easily united in small and medium-sized shops. This large middle ground, however, was usually distinguished from both the mercantilist and the laborer, respectively, at opposite poles of the occupational scale.

The mechanic arts creatively synthesized intellectual and manual skills, but the distinction between the fine arts and the mechanic arts was relative. Literature promoting the latter consistently portrayed the ideal of the mechanic-as-artist.[17] The liberal arts were quite another matter, however, and educators in mechanics' associations struggled to integrate the mechanical with the liberal.

The term *manufacturer*, which once signified a person who made articles by hand, came to refer to a person who used machinery but who was not necessarily a skilled workman. As the tendency toward artisan-turned-entrepreneur became more pronounced, however, a worker could easily be both mechanic and manufacturer. But as the terms became more distinct, the former identified small-scale enterprise and the latter large-scale.[18]

As the structure of labor changed, the portrait of the ideal mechanic changed as well.[19] The mechanic-as-craftsman became one with the mechanic-as-entrepreneur. Perhaps more important, however, was the new knowledge that underlay applied mechanics. By 1830 a praxis that fused science, craft, and art into one image had evolved.[20]

Periodical literature for mechanics forged a new image of the mechanic entrepreneur, whose virtues linked him to the craft tradition but whose business acumen drew him closer to an industrial economy in which vicious competition and capital accumulation were necessary to success. All this was still within God's law. Those who understood both its moral lessons and its physics were at a distinct advantage in the race for success.

In a period in which the cash wage was eroding the authority of the apprenticeship system, mechanics' associations and institutes experimented with ways to socialize prospective skilled workers in the virtues necessary for economic and social success. Within the context of an emerging industrial economy, self education and formal education allowed workers to avoid or move out of the ranks of wage earners. The operative and apprentice could embrace new technology, thus becoming "technological entrepreneurs," or submit to the will of others and remain operatives.[21] The jobs of machinist, toolmaker, and founderer required a knowledge of rudimentary physics and mathematics and the managerial skills (broadly construed as technique and moral demeanor) necessary for building a successful business. In addition, they needed to understand the overall production sequence vis à vis cost restrictions and markets in order to move to the entrepreneurial level.

Technical and Liberal Learning

The broad mission of mechanics' institutes was to wed the liberal and the technical so that upward social mobility and technical expertise could be achieved by both apprentices and adult workers. The aim of liberal knowledge was to develop an enlightened citizenry whose moral worth and verbal skills made them the cultural and intellectual pillars of the new republic. So-called "elevated" reading was one of the marks distinguishing those who advanced to foreman and employers from operatives. Technical knowledge was more specifically the avenue to innovation and profit. The union of these two layers of knowledge produced the "managing machinist," "the practical intelligent mechanic who can superintend a business."[22]

J. K. Mitchell captured the central argument for uniting liberal and technical learning. His closing address to his winter lecture series of 1833–34 at the Franklin Institute—"Some of the Means of Elevating the Character of the Working Classes"—began with the common observation that there was no "necessary connexion between manual labor and degradation" nor "any essential disjunction of the work of the hands from that of the head." Most of his lecture, however, was a defense of liberal learning for mechanics. He argued that liberal (classical) learning contributed to the moral culture of the mechanic, thus elevating his character, and that it gave him the respectability he needed to improve his status. Liberal learning also developed the mental discipline of the mechanic, Mitchell said. Through liberal learning the great political revolution of 1776 would become the social revolution of the nineteenth century, breaking down those "artificial barriers of society, instituted in Europe."[23]

Mitchell argued that the source of the American mechanic's relatively low status lay with his decision to forgo the mental discipline developed through the study of "classical and elegant literature." "There *is* time" for polite literature in the busy world of the artisan, said Mitchell. "If such an education were usual with mechanics it would afford them a new and elegant recreation, without diminishing their zeal for their art." His hope was that "*our mechanics* will be entitled, *in the very best sense of the word*, to the name of *gentlemen*."[24]

Mitchell then addressed the problem of integrating the study of science with instruction in a trade. Like Walter Johnson of the Franklin Institute, who believed that the study of science exerted a liberalizing influence on mechanics, Mitchell thought that the lessons of science transcended particular trades. They could make the mechanic respectable. In his closing remarks he charged his audience to elevate the character of a future generation of mechanics. "Let the mechanics of one generation be, as they should be, philosophically educated, and, in America at least, such an education will become forever indispensable."[25]

The mission of mechanics' institutes incorporated two great domains of knowledge: moral philosophy and natural philosophy. Johnson clearly placed moral philosophy first in order of importance. "Of all the departments of human knowledge," said Johnson, "those which treat of man himself—his character, relations, duties, and destinies—are unquestionably the most important." Next in order of importance, said Johnson, were the arts and their related sciences.[26]

Johnson walked a fine line between theory and practice, allowing that it was not necessary for the artisan to "waste his time in attempts to follow the philosophers through all the mazes of speculation" but rather to begin labors "where theirs have ended." Nonetheless, it was Johnson's conviction that innovation and invention should be based on science and that the abstractions of science should be translated into practice.[27]

For Johnson, the moral and scientific ends of education were wedded in a view of the "industrious citizen," one who understood the "scientific principles of his employment," who was rational, orderly, and morally pure. In the workshops of virtuous and rational mechanics, minds were not distracted by trivia or folly. Here curiosity, ingenuity, and rationality were fused in creative behavior. Here, also, was a climate of cooperative learning and emulation. In this situation, said Johnson, lay the opportunity to know the art of others and to improve one's own.[28]

SCHOOLS AND LECTURES

Providing schools and lecture series was one of two major educational functions of mechanics' institutes and associations. The other included providing reading rooms and libraries. Annual fairs and exhibitions were educational as well, though their main purpose was to provide a showcase for manufacturers and inventors. And the evaluation of inventions and proposed patents was educational in a broad sense as committees formed for that purpose discussed and analyzed inventions on display.

Courses of study operated at several levels. Charitable associations ran schools for the orphaned and indigent. They also sponsored lecture series, both in the popular lyceum mode and in the academically serious. Institutes like the Franklin Institute developed an advanced system of instruction. The capability of an institute to offer instruction often rested on its financial viability. Plans were made and not carried through; lecture series were begun but frequently discontinued because of lack of interest and financial exigency. Still, the schools and lecture series of these organizations persisted and were central features of their educational purpose.

The General Society of Mechanics and Tradesmen of the City of New York and the Mechanics' Institute of the City of New York Social and educational uplift was part of a broad goal of achieving political and intellectual enlightenment that was endorsed early on by the General Society of Mechanics and Tradesmen of the City of New York. As part of its mission the General Society established a school for the "gratuitous education of the children of indigent or deceased members." This mission later expanded to include children whose parents could pay modest tuition.[29] In rhetoric and spirit typical of the late-eighteenth-century enlightenment, George Clinton, Jr., celebrated the close relation between democratic institutions and a virtuous and knowledgeable people. "To arrive at a just sense of our duties, learning and instruction are necessary," said Clinton, and a "free people . . . will ever be studious of cultivating useful knowledge." In this spirit the association promoted education as a means to social improvement, ran a school for indigent families and apprentices, subsidized an apprentice library association, and took an active interest in providing instruction for its members.[30]

The school of the General Society of Mechanics and Tradesmen existed from 1820 to 1858. As early as 1822, when there were eighty-six pupils enrolled (fifty of deceased or impoverished members of the society) under the tutelage of Charles Starr, apprentices of members were offered English language instruction in the evenings. Literature and labor commingled as master mechanics and apprentices devoted their evenings to self-improvement. The success of the school led to a more liberal policy that allowed children of nonmembers to attend for a modest sum. In 1851 there were 270 male and female students enrolled.[31] These were "chiefly children and wards of members of the Institute" who were admitted on "reduced terms." In the new quarters at Division Street and the Bowery there were also classes being held in modeling. In 1859 a Free Evening School was established. Its curriculum, offered four evenings a week, included freehand drawing, mechanical and architectural drafting, design, and modeling.[32]

Lectures on science were the mainstay of self-improvement programs offered by mechanics' institutes.[33] The reception of science, however, was mixed if we are to judge by M. M. Noah's address to the General Society of Mechanics and Tradesmen of New York in 1822. He was "not partial to any system which imposes too much on the mind of an apprentice," Noah remarked, adding that he "would rather see them men of sense than men of science." Still, he concluded, "it is not alone sufficient to know how to complete a piece of work, it is proper to know the causes that lead to its completion."[34]

In 1831, when the lecture series began at the Mechanics' Institute of New York, there were 413 members. The first course, delivered in the winter of 1831–32, consisted of thirty lectures on natural philosophy and chemistry. E. J. Webb delivered a lecture series on architecture, and the next year there were forty lectures on mechanical philosophy and chemistry and another lecture on mathematics delivered gratuitously. In the same year, there were also lectures on anatomy and physiology. It was noted that the expenses for this series were paid through the sale of tickets.[35]

The first lecture in the 1833 series was given by Professor James Renwick on "Natural Philosophy." Two others followed: one on American literature and the other on the "Importance of Industrious Habits to Young Men."[36] The series, sponsored by the institute, was apparently successful, but advice was needed. In 1835, L. S. Gale—corresponding secretary for the institute, a lecturer in chemistry at New York City College, and a lecturer in geology at University of the City of New York—wrote to Professor J. K. Mitchell of Philadelphia to ask for details of the lectures given at the Franklin Institute. Such correspondence was not unusual, and it often focused on fees and organization. The questions he asked in this letter, however, give a good indication of what was on the minds of those instructing mechanics. Gale wished to know the number, duration, and rotation of courses, whether practical chemistry was taught, the condition of lecture rooms and apparatus, and whether the mechanics or the lecturer was primarily responsible for arousing interest in the meetings of the organization.[37]

Clearly Gale was concerned with what was pedagogically sound, but the question of audience interest apparently lay heaviest on his mind. In the same letter Gale noted that the lectures on natural philosophy had failed to attract mechanics, and he offered the explanation that "the mechanics as a body have not enough of [illegible] to render a scientific subject interesting: it may be more owing perhaps to another cause namely the fact that they as a class have little leisure to attend to subjects of a scientific nature."[38]

Lack of interest was apparently taking its toll. Even though the institute had three thousand members by 1836, the lecture series had moved away from natural philosophy and was attempting to appeal to more people by including lectures on "Precious Stones," "Silver Looking Glasses," "Coloring and Marbling Papers," and "A Chemical Analysis of the Stomachs of 2 Individuals Supposed to Have Been Poisoned by Arsenic." Science had not disappeared, as evidenced by such lectures as "Specific Gravity of Liquids and Solids," but clearly diversity was needed to keep the series self-supporting.[39]

The Massachusetts Charitable Mechanic Association Like the General Society of Mechanics and Tradesmen of the City of New York, the Massachusetts Charitable Mechanic Association (founded in 1795) operated schools and sponsored lecture series. Along with the New York City association it was one of the oldest benevolent societies in the new republic. It spent its money on annual festivals, banking, support for widows of indigent members, support of an apprentice library, lecture series, exhibitions, and frequent social occasions typically featuring a dinner, many toasts, songs, and prayer. Its primary function at inception was to extend "the practice of benevolence," and its activities showed that it promoted the mechanics' arts in a comprehensive way.

Concern with the education of apprentices seems to have begun in 1819 when William Jackson, the superintendent of a soap and candle manufactory, proposed a lecture series, and a committee inquired into the possibility of employing someone to "deliver a course of lectures on chemistry, architecture, or mechanics at some future period."[40] Desire apparently was difficult to turn into commitment, however. After eight months of deliberation and debate, part of which revealed an antiscience disposition among some mechanics, the committee did issue a favorable report on the proposal. Still, the report was tabled indefinitely. "Mindless parochialism" was the enemy, said the committee, for it prevented access to new ideas and impeded innovation. The real test of progressive knowledge was the marketplace, and those workmen who failed that test paid a high price indeed.[41]

Failure to implement the lecture series did not deter its proponents. At the triennial festival in 1824, Alpheus Cary, the keynote speaker and a stonecutter by trade, inspired his audience with examples of the scientific learning occurring in institutes in London, New York, and Philadelphia. Lectures, he noted, were more effective than books. When supplemented by suitable "experimental apparatus," he predicted, lectures would engage the audience.[42]

The winter of 1826 to 1827 was pivotal for proponents of the lecture series. Timothy Claxton, a philosophical instrument maker and veteran of the mechanics' institute in London, arrived in Boston to find the city without a society to offer scientific and practical lectures to mechanics. With Claxton's initiative and the support of several members of the Massachusetts Charitable Mechanic Association, the Boston Mechanics' Institution was founded in January 1827. In that year a course of lectures on mechanical philosophy was initiated. In deference to those lacking elementary education, instruction was delivered in a "plain, intelligible manner, divested as far as practicable of technical phraseology and such terms as tend to discourage rather than promote a love of science."[43]

Presumably under pressure and perhaps with some embarrassment, the Massachusetts Charitable Mechanic Association responded by appointing a special committee to reconsider holding a lecture series. The committee recommended a "twelve part series, including lectures on astronomy, electricity, hydrostatics, matter, machines, and pneumatics." The plan was approved "without dissent," and the series was so successful over the next ten years that it caused the demise of the education activities of the Boston Mechanics' Institute. The lecture series of the MCMA ended in 1842 when the association changed its priorities to exhibitions.[44]

The Massachusetts Charitable Mechanic Association opened a school in 1829, offering writing and arithmetic. Bookkeeping and drawing were added in 1831 and 1837, respectively. The writing course was discontinued in 1842, but drawing was immensely successful. The School Committee observed that those who attended "were young men who had arrived at an age to appreciate such instruction and they felt while there that they were as much pursuing a branch of their several professions as if in the Employer[s'] workshops."[45] In 1850 a school was established that offered drawing, mathematics, surveying, and mechanical and civil engineering. Classes were held every evening; tuition was six dollars for thirty-six lessons and four dollars for eighteen lessons.[46]

The Mechanics Apprentices' Library Association was long associated with but operated independently of the Massachusetts Charitable Mechanic Association. Moreover, its activities went beyond caring for the library. The early 1820s were a time of expanded and spirited educational activities. The *Proceedings* and *Transactions* of the association show vigorous leadership in offering lecture series on chemistry, physics, biology, astronomy, acoustics, geography, geology, and elocution. There were also frequent debates on issues of broad civic interest. The minutes record that in 1832 Josiah Holbrook, the famous organizer of the lyceum movement, gave a "valuable donation of Geometrical Apparatus" to the association. In 1845 the elocution class issued the *Mechanic Apprentice*.[47]

Because the Mechanics Apprentices' Library Association had a meager budget, it relied on members to develop most of the lectures. The group's minutes show that there was considerable frustration in getting members to prepare lectures. In fact, the Committee on Lectures in 1832 reported that it was utterly impossible to obtain good lectures for free.

The subjects of greatest importance were mechanics and chemistry, according to the Committee on Lectures. This plan, it was argued, would "promote the mechanic arts," improve business, and elevate mechanics above "low pursuits."[48] Apparently the committee's recommendations caused some tension within the association, for the minutes of 4 March 1834 record the president's attempt to convince members that science not be underrated even though apprenticeship focused on studies of vocational utility. Other subjects drawn from history and biography deserved great attention, he said, as they "teach us to perform the *noblest* duties of life" (emphasis in original). Apprentices were urged to reject the belief that science was the one path through the "desert" of life and to avoid the error of supposing that the only object of existence is to become conversant with knowledge that "strictly relates to one's trade."[49]

In spite of the frustrations that the president was apparently feeling, numerous lectures were delivered. And as might be expected from the liberal leanings of those who argued for greater breadth of knowledge, scientific lectures dominated. Thus we find such lectures as "Mechanical Powers with Illustrations," "Chemistry—the Powers and Properties of Calorie," "Steam and Steam Engines Illustrated by Working Models and Other Apparatus."[50]

With most of the lectures given over to scientific topics, it was left to another committee (and probably the elocution class) to deal with American social, political, and economic issues. The questions for debate were similar to those debated by the many library clubs and lyceums that dotted the United States in this period. Added to the national issues of slavery, tariff, and capital punishment, however, were those concerning mechanics as a group: merit and social mobility, the lyceum plan of instruction, and the impact of new technology on the welfare of mechanics.[51]

In addition to offering lecture series and debates, the Massachusetts Charitable Mechanic Association opened a school. In the early 1840s a committee appointed to take charge of the schools established schools of writing, arithmetic, and drawing. James French was in charge of writing,

William Rogers of arithmetic, and S. F. Durivage of the "art of drawing." Interest was great, judging by the 136 students enrolled in the writing school and the forty-seven enrolled in the drawing school. In the sober judgment of the committee, however, the schools in arithmetic and writing did not succeed because of the lack of a "suitable schoolroom" and because of the sixty-eight scholars who "violated the rules of the schools." The committee consequently recommended abandoning the schools for writing and arithmetic unless a "proper schoolroom was obtained." The drawing school met with greater enthusiasm from the committee, which noted that at the end of the term twenty-eight of the pupils "exhibited over two hundred specimens of drawing, many of which were highly creditable, and gave evidence of a knowledge of the art."[52]

In spite of the difficulties, the writing and arithmetic schools were continued, perhaps more with hope than success. In 1844 the offerings of the school were greatly extended through the patronage of a "gentleman of this city" who donated $20,000 to the association with the stipulations that another $20,000 be raised by the association and that a school free to mechanics' apprentices be kept open for at least five months per year. The school was to offer instruction in the "laws of motion, the principles of construction, the properties of matter, chemistry as connected with the arts and manufactures, drawing [and] other branches" as seen essential to the education of mechanics' apprentices.[53]

THE FRANKLIN INSTITUTE

More than any other attempt, the activities launched by the founding of the Franklin Institute in 1824 helped set a standard and define the educational mission of mechanics' institutes in the early nineteenth century. During its first year the Institute hosted lectures on "water," "perpetual motion," "architecture," "patent rights," "bookkeeping," and "time." The Committee on Lectures recommended professorships in natural philosophy, applied chemistry and mineralogy, architecture, and mechanics.[54] Lectures on chemistry were given Saturday; lectures on mechanics and architecture began at seven o'clock on alternate Mondays. Admission was open to women and young children, and between 1831 and 1833 one hundred ninety-four tickets were sold to "ladies."[55]

The motivations of the women who attended lectures probably varied, like those of men, from a desire to participate in a social event in the guise of intellectual stimulation to a desire to be on the expanding front of scientific knowledge. We do know, though, how one lecturer on chemistry—J. K.

Mitchell, a physician—perceived their attendance. He put the presence of women into the broader perspective of their traditional roles of nurturing and childrearing. He "exulted" in their presence and its likely influence on the character of their children. The mother, said Mitchell, taught by example. In the critical period of early childhood, a "discipline of thought" and "flexibility of . . . mind" are developed. These were part of a larger moral sentiment that included "the love of labor, and the taste for learning." Here, indeed, future Newtons and Franklins were nurtured, but only if the mother were able to satisfy the child's curiosity without destroying his "eager thirst after knowledge" by "impatient ignorance." In this manner Mitchell brought together the traditional role of womanhood and the progress of scientific and technical thought. No matter that the future Newtons and Franklins were male infants; it was enough that the knowledge on which scientific and technical thought rested also supported the new republic and that the home provided a place in which the intelligent mother would nurture future scientists.[56]

Sinclair has written that the lecture series posed the Franklin Institute with one of its first problems involving the mission and audience for its programs. It was, as the Board of Managers found out, difficult to balance instruction with entertainment. Moreover, the cost of hiring professors to lecture instead of using volunteers was an expense that had to be offset by large and usually diverse audiences.[57] Apparently the effort succeeded, for we find the *Saturday Evening Post* reporting in 1829 that "the style adopted by the professors is easy and familiar, and the demonstrations are so conducted as to be intelligible to all."[58]

In May 1824 the Committee on Instruction at the Franklin Institute proposed professorships in natural philosophy, architecture, mechanics, and chemistry and mineralogy, each connected with the arts and manufactures.[59] Between 1824 and 1826 the institute's offerings expanded on several fronts, including drawing and mathematics. The successes of the drawing and mathematics schools over the next several years were widely divergent. The initial enrollment of fifty students in the drawing school was promising, and by 1829 the school was overcrowded, with "numerous applications for admission refused." In 1832 the drawing school had thirty-nine students.[60]

The fortunes of the mathematics school were noticeably different. The school offered arithmetic, algebra, geometry, mensuration, navigation, and surveying, but by 1831 the Committee on Instruction had acknowledged its failure. The school had struggled for six years to fill a gap in elementary mathematics instruction, but it seemed that its curriculum had not been "adapted to the wants of those for whose benefit it was intended." It was replaced by an English school. "Its miscalculation," Sinclair has noted, "was in limiting [its] mathematical . . . scope and thus its potential as a mechanism for social mobility."[61]

Amid its continuing commitment to evening lectures and basic instruction in English, mathematics, and drawing, the Franklin Institute also took ambitious steps to establish a high school department. Lectures, as Walter R. Johnson later observed, were subsidiary to, not substitutes for lessons, recitations, examinations, and that "system of responsibilities by which the talents of the teacher are made to act on the mind of the pupil."[62]

As with other educational activities, the intent of the high school, said the Committee on Instruction, was to allow for social mobility for those "sons of our tradesmen and other citizens in moderate circumstances." Social mobility was conceived generally in terms of access to those studies that had been the prerogative of "children of the rich." The committee argued that its school should not assume that pupils would become mechanics or manufacturers or that "their prospects in future life [would be] confined within the walls of their workshops."[63]

The high school curriculum retained the language-centeredness of the traditional Latin grammar school, but it did allow for modern languages and selected courses in such practical subjects as bookkeeping, mechanics, natural philosophy, and natural history. The retention of classical learning in the high school should not disguise the dispute that was brewing within the Institute over liberal versus practical studies. An alternative proposal to the classical high school was made by Peter Browne, who argued for a school without Greek and Latin, which he believed were a waste of time for mechanics. The Board of Managers, however, insisted that those "odious monopolies of knowledge" be abolished by offering three years of Greek and Latin and modern language studies as the foundations for respectability. The Committee on Instruction opted for educational tradition to enhance mechanics' prospects for social mobility, as Philadelphia's Central High School would later do.[64]

The study of language laid the foundation for social respectability. Next to language, the most important areas of study at the Franklin Institute High School were mathematics and drawing. Over a three-year period the student proceeded from the study of arithmetic, using Colburn's familiar text, to algebra and then to geometry and trigonometry. Mensuration of heights, distance, surfaces, and solids was also offered. Drawing was studied daily as well, beginning with linear drawing, proceeding to drawing in perspective, and moving through the drawing of mechanical implements, maps, landscapes, models and machinery, objects from nature, and finally to architectural drawing.

Science was an important subject at the institute but not nearly as conspicuous as language and mathematics. The study of natural philosophy was a weekly exercise during the second year; chemistry was offered in the third year. Mechanical philosophy, the explanation of the structure and uses of machinery, was a weekly exercise for one quarter. Of the sciences, only astronomy was offered for two quarters during the second year. Other subjects of immediate utility were scattered throughout the master curriculum plan.

To be admitted to the high school, students had to "spell correctly, read plain English prose with fluency, write a fair hand, perform arithmetical operations, at least in the fundamental rules, and parse easy sentences in the English language." The fee was seven dollars per quarter. The Committee on Instruction was realistic about the completion rate, however, noting that only "scholars of the very best capacity and most exemplary diligence" would be able to complete the course of studies in the allotted time. Therefore students who had completed at least one year were given a certificate "specifying the time employed, the branches studied, and the deportment exhibited during [their] connexion with the school."[65]

The success of the high school department seems to have been immediate. There were, in 1826, one hundred student monitors who assisted younger students. Of the 304 pupils in various subjects, virtually all took English, elocution, and mathematics. More than two-thirds took geography and linear drawing, one-half took French, and a little over one-third took Latin. Only 10 to 15 percent of the students took one of the remaining subjects: Greek, Spanish, German, and chemistry.[66]

In 1828 Walter Johnson, principal and lecturer in natural philosophy, began a series of essays on education in the *Journal of the Franklin Institute*. These essays, like those published earlier in the *Commonwealth*, were remarkable for their insights and sensitivity to the art and organization of instruction, the physical environment for learning, and the motivation of students. They bear the marks of Pestalozzian thought and of the teachings of Maria Edgeworth, as well as a concern for efficiency evident in the use of the monitorial method of instruction.

Johnson long had been interested in the training of teachers, believing that they required special instruction. In his "Observations on the Improvement of Seminaries of Learning in the United States: With Suggestions for Its Accomplishment" (1825) he recognized that "every man is not by nature an instructor." Many, said Johnson, believed that teaching could proceed with no "definite ideas of the peculiar duties and difficulties of employment," and much "disappointment and mortification" has resulted from men having "presumed to be qualified to *teach* from the moment that they passed the period of ordinary pupilage." Though it came before the development of most normal schools in the United States, his proposal was founded on the same tenets.[67]

Johnson's essays, which were carried in the *Journal of the Franklin Institute,* provide a comprehensive view of the theory of instruction used at the institute. Like those of other reformers of his generation and the next, Johnson's ideas reflect a new awareness of the environmental factors affecting learning and instruction. His remarks make it clear that he saw method and environment as mutually supportive elements in a larger system of schooling. Method and system were inextricably wedded, but as Johnson warned, the relation of part (method) to whole (system) was not automatic. "A method," he observed, "may often be executed by one who possesses little power of combination, and who would be wholly unfit to direct a system." With this brief and insightful comment, Johnson captured the meaning of education for both workman and teacher. The person who sees the necessary functional combination of parts forming the system was, it would seem, a good manager of both education and industrial endeavors.[68]

Because Johnson was sensitive to the physical environment for education, we have a detailed description of the facilities for the high school. From his explanation and measurements we see the standard pattern for monitorial instruction: the great study hall with extensions at both ends (shaped as an uppercase "I") for recitation and English studies, the master's elevated seat overseeing all, and the semicircular benches, small tables, and blackboards for recitation. Here the large group was under the watchful eye of the master while small group instruction was offered by the monitors.[69]

Johnson recognized the tedium of endlessly repeated lessons and the difficulty of motivating students. For this reason he believed that the "mechanical parts of teaching" should be turned over to the young monitors "for whom they still wear the charm of novelty, and to whom they afford excellent opportunities for increasing their expertness." The master was thus relieved of "irksome teaching" and left to address those aspects of teaching requiring "much elucidation."[70] He also oversaw and instructed tutors and monitors, preserved order, prescribed methods, heard appeals from discontented scholars, and examined scholars.[71]

Physical resources played a key part in the education of young mechanics. Though modest in number, texts and apparatus were well selected. An open bookcase in the study room held various dictionaries—Greek, Latin, French, German, and English. There were a few collections of speeches and compositions for use by students enrolled in elocution. Among the works on teaching were French normal school journals and the works of Bacon, Comenius, Locke, Dumarsais, Knox, and Rollin, which could be used "for general hints, or for practical illustrations of the methods of teaching in the several departments."[72]

Johnson was obviously pleased with the institute's acquisition of apparatus. The holdings in natural philosophy and chemistry he called "respectable," and the "electrical machines, batteries, and other apparatus [were] believed to be inferior to few collections in the country." The pneumatic apparatus was "excellent," he noted, but the electromagnetic instruments, mechanical powers, and astronomical instruments were less than satisfactory. There were two each of nine-inch, eighteen-inch, and twenty-four-inch terrestrial globes. Large maps of the world, the United States, Pennsylvania, the western states, South America, and other subdivisions were used, as were sixty small maps on pasteboards, a general school atlas, and Worcester's Gazetteer.[73]

For classes in linear drawing, students used thirty original patterns made by Mr. W. Mason. The patterns were done in India ink on large map paper and included "some class of tools, implements, furniture, or utensils, represented in bold lines, easily distinguished at the distance of 50 or 60 feet." One hundred and twenty patterns, each twelve by eight inches, were used for studying the "elements of landscape and figure drawing." Johnson hoped that patterns for the study of natural history and architecture would be added.[74]

Models and apparatus for machine drawing were abundant, said Johnson, though he did not list them. We can, however, get an idea of what was available for study from the catalog of the Committee on Models. Many of the models mentioned by the committee were patent models, but there were also ones to illustrate "Euclid's Problems" and an "Inclined Plane." Other generic models included a chimney, dry dock, bridge, saw, and hammer. Students could also observe patentable ideas in the models of a cooking stove, steam engine boiler, cast-iron waterwheel, flying shuttle, and brass screw press.[75]

A PLAN FOR THE FUTURE

Slightly ten years after the founding of the Franklin Institute plans were laid to develop a polytechnic institute. The plans were never implemented but are interesting because they embodied virtually every educational experiment at the institute in the previous ten years and anticipated developments under the later land grant college movement.

A series of documents—including Walter Johnson's address to the American Institute of Instruction and memorials by the Board of Managers of the Franklin Institute and citizens of the city and county of Philadelphia—give us the specifics of the proposal for a School of the Arts. Those who supported the proposal envisioned a state-supported school "connected with the Franklin Institute," a school working in collaboration with "every workshop, laboratory, mill, and manufacturing establishment in the city and its neighborhood" to bring "useful and practical knowledge" to artisans and farmers.[76]

When Johnson put forward his proposal in 1835, he opened his talk by reciting what was to become a familiar litany of reasons for establishing such schools. The initiatives of France, Russia, England, and Germany were rehearsed, as was the necessity for the United States to remain competitive. Far more important for Johnson, however, was the "elevation of character" produced by rational and organized thought, the "worthy employment [of] thoughts during leisure time, and the reduction in the "painfulness of manual labor" that would free the artisan for study leading to greater productivity and more "purified" thoughts. In freeing the imagination, such a school would be "no less important in a civilized community than one for literature or abstract science."[77]

Johnson saw a natural union of schools "advancing general science" with those "promoting the arts." Like others familiar with the historical development of the arts, he avoided suggesting that the arts were merely applied sciences. In many cases, he reminded his audience, art "obeyed [the] laws of nature before science had discovered or announced their existence." For Johnson, science, mathematics, and practice were a whole system of inquiry, not simply elements in a trade school. Allowing for practical modifications of mathematical laws, the experimenter—duly adept at "devising, combining, and adjusting apparatus" and constructing models for his experiment—brought nature and art together. Here he formed the habits of mind necessary to progressive science.[78]

As Johnson's plan took shape over the next two years, his supporters drew heavily on the instructional precedents established at the Franklin Institute. They reiterated the powerful message that instruction in science was necessary for overcoming the abysmal state of ignorance that prevailed among Pennsylvania farmers. This situation, they said, was untenable. The lack of instruction in the common schools, it was feared, opened the way to "peddling about various different models of ploughs which, like patent medicines, are puffed off as superior to all others ever invented." A lucky farmer lost only his purse from such bad advice.[79]

The plan proposed by the Board of Managers of the Franklin Institute for a School of Arts (1837) suggested six departments: mechanical science and mechanical arts; chemistry and chemical arts; mathematics and related arts; geology, mineralogy, and mining; civil engineering and architecture; and agriculture and rural economy. The general model for all instruction was one in which the principles of physical science were taught and applied "by detailed practical lessons, and especially by actual *discipline* in the workshop."[80]

Education in the workshop was to take a variety of forms. For the mechanic arts, a department of model-making would supply students with "models of machinery [and] structures . . . which the student should be taught to imitate with his own hands." In chemistry laboratories the student would learn "all the minutia of manipulation by conducting experiments and performing analyses." Further practical application was to take place in workshops and manufactures. In the department of mathematics, the drawing school was the center of hands-on activities. Here the student would learn to apply the principles of perspective and descriptive geometry, sketching, linear drawing, architectural and machine drawing, and topographical drawing. Other departments followed a similar pattern of laboratory and hands-on learning.[81]

The plans for a school of arts, like later developments in agricultural and mechanical colleges, attempted to maintain the delicate balance between theory and practice. Science was clearly necessary to the development of the arts, yet science not appropriated for the utility of the arts had its enemies. Those enemies, who had a similar distrust of the classics, were suspicious of studies that had no practical effect. The machinist was to move beyond a general knowledge of mechanic powers, motion, and forces to familiarity with the "great variety of combinations" of machinery. He needed to grasp the "advantages of the minutest modification of the parts," to be "perfectly at home in regard to every point in the construction," to be "prepared at any time to reduce his plans to an exact form on paper, or to [m]ake accurate copies of the models he is investigating."[82]

It was likewise with the application of chemistry to dye making and calico printing; soil analysis and husbandry for the farmer; and mineralogy for the miner. Knowledge was to be conveyed "experimentally," the net result being a mastery of the details of application and a general habit of mind characterized by disciplined accuracy and analysis. With this, memorialists for the proposal said, the "young mechanic, artizan, or manufacturer" would secure the "respect of his fellow citizens."[83]

LIBRARIES AND READING ROOMS

Like the schools of mechanics' institutes, libraries and reading rooms were extensions of the formal process of education. Accessibility was their key structural feature, and all attempted to collect those books and periodicals thought necessary to their broad educational mission.

The Mechanic Apprentices' Library of Boston (later the Mechanic Apprentices' Library Association) began with about fifteen hundred books donated by William Wood, a Boston merchant and later the founder of libraries in several other cities, who had given the books to the Massachusetts Charitable Mechanic Association. Wood asked that the books be made available to apprentices, and the association established rules for their circulation. There were apparently 763 apprentices who were potential members of the library at the time it was founded.[84]

The purposes of the library were citizenship education and the moral elevation of mechanics. In his address at the founding of the Apprentice Library Association in 1820, Theodore Lyman, Jr., urged apprentices never to let the "traveller or the stranger come among us, and find our mechanics unacquainted with the History, laws and interests of their Country." Such self-conscious nationalism was part of the larger moral education of the apprentices. "Above all," said Lyman, "read the books which relate to the history of your country."[85]

The library grew modestly, reporting 2,000 volumes in 1830 and 2,113 in 1832. In the latter year there were only sixty members compared with one hundred members in 1830. The number of volumes decreased to 1,920 volumes in 1835 but rose to 3,000 volumes in 1844, with two hundred members reported in the same year. By 1859 there were 4,493 volumes, and current newspapers were available.[86] In 1832 these numbered twenty, including several general ones from Boston, such as the *Boston Daily Globe* and *Boston Telegraph*, and regional papers, such as the *New England Galaxy* and *New England Artisan*. Other magazines were also available, including *Youth's Companion*, *Christian Watchman*, and *Masonic Mirror*.[87]

Information on the holdings of some other mechanic association libraries is more detailed. The most impressive feature of the General Society of Tradesmen and Mechanics (New York) was its commitment to reading rooms and apprentice libraries. Most of the volumes probably were donated, but monies were spent on new books and periodicals and on the repair of old books. The apprentice library linked to the General Society operated in conjunction with the school and opened in 1820 with slightly fewer than four hundred volumes. The apprentice library of the New York Mechanics' Institute numbered six thousand volumes by 1822, and between 1820 and 1822 about nineteen hundred apprentices used the library.[88] These figures had increased dramatically by the 1860s when readership averaged about fifty-eight hundred and the volumes circulated numbered about 92,400. By this time the library functioned as a public library, though apprentices still accounted for about 58 percent of the borrowers. Other readership categories reported included gratuitous female readers (32 percent), accounting for 24 percent of the volumes borrowed; pay readers (7 percent), borrowing 9 percent of the volumes; and members of the Society (3 percent), borrowing 3 percent of the volumes.[89]

Catalogs for the Apprentices' Library associated with the General Society give a good description of the reading fare available to apprentices and others who used the library. In 1839 there were 1,925 books available for borrowers and readers. The subject matter ranged from agriculture and gardening to belles lettres to history, law, logic, mechanics, natural and moral philosophy, and theology. Unlike previous catalogs, the catalog for this year listed books in thirty-six categories. Theology, civil history, biography, travels, and belles lettres accounted for 58 percent of the holdings. Natural and moral philosophy, law, politics, and geography were next with fifteen percent. Chemistry, astronomy, botany, electricity, geology, natural history, and medicine made up less than 10 percent of the holdings, while technology—including mechanics, military, and navigation—constituted less than 5 percent. Books on mathematics made up less than 1 percent of the holdings.[90] This general pattern of distribution persisted into the late 1850s, judging from the 1855 catalog. Of the fifteen thousand volumes in the Apprentices' Library (not including the De Milt Reference Library) in New York, a little more than 4 percent were in the natural sciences, mathematics, and technology.[91] This distribution probably reflected the tastes of the donors, but the collection satisfied the apprentices and provided reference works for serious study. Still, the holdings reflect the time-honored tradition of providing a liberal education for mechanics.

In Cincinnati, the Apprentices' Library was organized in 1821. It merged with the library of the Ohio Mechanics' Institute in 1852, but in 1837 it had purchased the Circulating Library Society.[92] The minutes of the annual meeting of subscribers to the library in 1823 recorded that there were "1,127 volumes of valuable books and that 180 to 200 of these volumes are in use weekly." By 1843 the number of volumes in the library was 2,639.[93]

The library holdings were not noticeably different from those of the General Society in New York City. Catalogs from 1840 and 1849 show the bulk of the works were histories, literature (particularly British), belles lettres, narrations of adventures, and biographies. Works on the various sciences were well represented but not numerous. These included books on surveying, natural history, geology, astronomy, agriculture, and physiology. There were a few works on psychology and geometry as well. The catalogs also list forty periodicals, including the *Journal of the Franklin Institute*, *London Mechanics Magazine*, *Western Literary Journal*, *Knickerbocker*, *Democratic Review*, *Cincinnati Quarterly Journal and Review*, and *Harbinger*, published by the Brook Farm Phalanx.[94]

Registers of the library kept from 1834 to 1840 provide insights into how the library was used. They show, for example, that literature and belles lettres were most frequently borrowed (38 percent), while history and periodicals each constituted 15 percent of the types of books borrowed. The periodical most frequently borrowed was *Mechanics Magazine*. Orations and science each composed 10 percent of the borrowing, and religious materials, biographies, travels, lectures, and philosophy made up between 1 and 3 percent.[95]

The 1836–38 register is unusual because it contains both the number of volumes borrowed by each user and, for sixty-eight of the 411 books borrowed, the user's occupation and address. The titles of the books borrowed were not listed in the 1836 register. Of the sixty-eight books for whom a user and occupation were recorded, a wide range of occupations was represented. Three carpenters borrowed ten books; two saddlers, six books; four shoemakers, four books; one storekeeper, six books; one blacksmith, three books; and one cabinetmaker, three books. The Ohio Mechanics' Institute librarian checked out two books, as did a confectioner, chairmaker, printer, and butcher. One book each was issued to a millwright, coachmaker, cooper, teacher, tanner, attorney, excavator, umbrella maker, seamstress, physician, potter, brush maker, book binder, founder, sash maker, silver plater, tinner, machinist, bookstore operator, bricklayer, shoe store employee, gunsmith, silversmith, tailor, and lawyer.[96] Judging from this small sample, most users apparently borrowed only one book during the year. Only a carpenter, saddler, and storekeeper exceeded three books.

The 1836–38 library record of the Ohio Mechanics' Institute is the only document of the institute listing the occupations of users. The OMI library records from 1848 reveal that 889 volumes were used by members and that 905 volumes were checked out by 109 minors, 106 by teachers, and 56 by twenty-seven "ladies."[97] A library register for 1842 to 1856 shows vigorous reading habits among women. Some borrowed close to three hundred books over a decade. A schoolteacher named Angelina Farley borrowed two to five books each month. The titles of the volumes were not recorded in this register.[98]

EXHIBITIONS

Mechanics' institutes and associations and inventors' organizations, such as the American Institute, sponsored annual fairs and exhibitions. Their immediate purpose was to promote local and regional manufactures by exhibiting their products. "Many excellent workmen, have become better known," announced a circular of 1833, "who while *they* have been better served, have at the same time rewarded and stimulated American skill and industry."[99]

Larger exhibitions drew products from several states. Their broader purposes were to encourage the values of inventiveness, high-quality workmanship, and competition in the name of scientific and technological progress and national prosperity. Exhibitions thus served both ideological and business purposes. They were, moreover, educational for the general public, apprentices, and of course manufacturers.

Following precedents set by British and French manufactures and governments, the Franklin Institute of Philadelphia began its exhibitions in 1824 and soon became a model for other cities. The benefits and rules for competitions were described by William Grierson in his "Observations on Competitions Among Working Tradesmen." Grierson's major concern was lack of participation by apprentices and journeymen. Apprentices, he recommended, should be assigned to a "separate class of competitors" so that awards might be placed within their reach. Grierson also spoke to the problem of low participation by journeymen. His solution lay in incentives, on the one hand, and opportunity to connect workshop production to public exhibitions on the other. The problem of misspent leisure time—a perennial complaint by educators and employers—was addressed by encouraging scientific study related to the workshop and preparation of public exhibitions.[100]

Organizers of exhibitions in Philadelphia and other cities soon learned that special themes and operating mechanisms were crowd pleasers. At the second exhibition of the Franklin Institute, for example, all gold medals were reserved for those who demonstrated improvements in the coal and iron industries of Pennsylvania. The institute even reserved a gold medal for anyone who could produce a sample of blister steel "superior to any imported." As Sinclair has pointed out, the institute attempted to define both markets and production standards. In this way it helped establish the domain of American manufacturers and raise the level of technical skills in manufacturing.[101]

The Massachusetts Charitable Mechanic Association's interest in public exhibitions began in 1818 when it sponsored annual competitions for young mechanics in selected trades. According to Kornblith, however, these attracted little public attention. The appointment of a special committee prompted renewed interest in 1832, but it was not until 1836 that a committee proposed an annual exhibition to promote competition and encourage ingenuity.[102]

The first exhibition opened at Faneuil Hall and Quincy Hall on 18 September 1837. If later exhibitions are any guide, the order of opening exercises began with an anthem, followed by a prayer, an ode, an address, and a hymn. The address at the first exhibition was given by Governor Edward Everett, who announced that the "mechanician, not the magician, is now the master of life." The exhibition was attended by seventy thousand people, who saw displays ranging from penmanship to jewelry, brass clocks to stoves, boots to musical instruments, and jellies to screw cutters and steam engines. Four years later, at the 1841 exhibition, speaker and hardware dealer Stephen Fairbanks placed the exhibitions in a philosophic context when he declared that the products displayed were testimony to the "triumph of mind over matter" and mechanical skill informed by science.[103]

Fairbanks' rhetoric seems exaggerated today, but it highlights the important educational message of the exhibitions, namely that they were object lessons in inventiveness and creativity brought before the public in a way that appealed to understanding through immediate sensory impact. This surely was part of the reasoning behind the (New York) Mechanics' Institute's permanent "polytechnic" exhibition at its new quarters, which opened in 1851 at the corner of Division Street and the Bowery. The plan, an attempt to imitate the polytechnic institute in London, used about half of the four-floor building for permanent public exhibitions of such objects as steam engines, machinery, and working models.[104]

Sponsors of fairs and their advocates, like *Scientific American*, clearly saw both the financial and educational benefits of exhibits. *Scientific American* put it well in a short scenario just prior to the opening of the Crystal Palace Exhibition (World's Fair) in 1853: "Some visitors go to Industrial Fairs for pleasure, such as to see the curious and pretty things, but a large number of all classes go to see what is new, and pick up what is useful. 'There,' said an inventor [with]in our hearing, 'is the very thing that has bothered my head for years; it always baffled me, and here it is, and so simple, too.' He really felt some relief, and was the gainer by coming to the Fair." [105]

The culmination of three decades of annual fairs and exhibits by numerous mechanics' institutes, agricultural societies, and trade associations in the United States was the Crystal Palace Exhibition. *Scientific American,* always the promoter of inventions and watchdog of inventors, devoted several columns to educating potential fairgoers. Sensing the public's lack of education, it set out to give a comparative analysis of new inventions on both sides of the Atlantic, along with updated information about which improvements were superior to others. [106]

Scientific American also offered advice on how to observe at the fair. "Great pleasure [could be] derived in seeing beautiful machinery operate even without understanding how its various motions are produced," said a columnist, but a "higher" pleasure was possible through understanding. Mechanics visiting the exhibition were encouraged to move beyond the "mere pleasure derived from seeing the machinery in motion" and attempt to understand its causes. Otherwise, it was observed, they would be unable to profit from their observations. Moreover, said the columnist, the mechanic should not confine his observation to his trade only. The rationale was simple: "the majority of the most important inventions which have been produced, were by men whose occupations in their nature, were very far removed from the inventions which they produced." Finally, mechanics were advised to "keep notebooks, in which to record their observations, and take sketches, if required." Memory was no substitute for writing when attempting to recollect "complicated machinery with its various motions." [107]

CONCLUSION

The educational activities of mechanics' institutes and associations were guided by a profound belief in the power of education and progressive science to shape a new nation in which the interests of that broad class of workmen called mechanics would be acknowledged and their role as productive, republican citizens rewarded. Skilled labor was their contribution to national welfare, and they expected a nation to respond by opening doors to upward socioeconomic mobility. In their quest for inclusion they sought to democratize knowledge that was once the prerogative of a few college faculty members and their students. Their mission was at once moral, political, and economic. They defined both political and economic citizenship as their moral right, just as they defined their right to valued knowledge within the context of a morality of aspiration.

The Franklinesque mission of these associations inspired attempts to wed the technical and the liberal. Thus the premise that the value of knowledge should be judged by its occupational utility was placed beside the concern that adults and apprentices master that knowledge which was socially and culturally honored. Nowhere was this more evident than in apprentice libraries and the curriculum of the high school department at the Franklin Institute.

Classes offered by these associations were a mix of pedagogical and curricular experiment and tradition. Frequently they were inspired by Pestalozzian pedagogy and a preference for hands-on and visual techniques. Just as often, however, there was a reluctance by collegiate lecturers to abandon the time-honored emphasis upon classification and formal definitions. In natural philosophy and applied mechanics, lecturers also faced the dilemma of having to explain concepts without mathematics, a teaching practice made necessary by the poor mathematical background of their students.

The utility of science and mathematics for both mental discipline and technical application seemed obvious to those who taught it. In practice, however, it was a different matter as the verbalism of traditional lecture and text was often incongruous with the experiential background of masters, journeymen, and apprentices. The divorce of subjects from utility and the empiricism of technical application was viewed with suspicion, even though the theoretical was a badge of gentlemanly status. In all, instruction in mechanics' associations and institutes was a compromise born out of the need to maintain academic legitimacy while demonstrating the utility of science and mathematics to those who, in shops and manufactures, had often worked out the implications of theory long before having studied it.

7

SCIENCE FOR WOMEN:
THE TROY FEMALE SEMINARY

Mechanics' institutes and associations served a special but broad class of workers who shared the goal of upward socioeconomic mobility through participation in the technological and industrial future of the United States. They generally were mutual welfare societies with a special concern for the educational advancement of adult members, children, and apprentices. They served the larger public as popularizers of science and technology. The Troy Female Seminary served a much narrower clientele, though it was a leader in scientific study for women. Emma Willard, its founder, was a pedagogical pioneer in the study of science and a crusader for scientific learning at a time when a small elite controlled access to scientific knowledge in American colleges. Like the mechanics' institutes, the Troy Female Seminary opened the secrets of science to new audiences.[1]

Before founding the Troy Female Seminary in 1821, Emma Hart Willard had acquired a great deal of teaching experience. She began teaching at age seventeen in a village school near the Hartford and New Haven turnpike in Connecticut. During the summer she taught at a "select school for older boys and girls" in her father's house, and during the winter she taught at the school she had attended as a youngster. She also attended school herself in Hartford during the spring and autumn terms. At age twenty she became a teaching assistant at Westfield Academy, but within a few months she took a position at Middlebury Female Academy in Middlebury, Vermont, where she had more control of the classes she taught. Here she introduced dancing as a way to keep students warm in the frigid class-room. (Dancing later became one of the unusual features of the curriculum at the Troy Female Seminary.) At Middlebury she was courted by Dr. John Willard, a physician, and they married in the summer of 1809.[2]

Willard's entrepreneurial spirit, her desire to improve upon the women's academies with which she was familiar, and her attempt to overcome her husband's financial reverses led her to found the Middlebury Female Seminary in the spring of 1814. The school was a success, with seventy pupils enrolled, forty of them boarders. It was difficult for Willard to introduce "higher" subjects because she could not afford to hire professors from Middlebury College, and the college refused to allow her pupils to sit in on selected classes. Her solution was simple but demanding: she would learn the subjects, teach them herself, and devise new methods of teaching. At Middlebury Female Seminary she improved the teaching of geography and moral and mental philosophy. She taught herself mathematics and then taught others. To demonstrate that females had the mental discipline necessary for mathematical study she held "public examinations" and invited professors at Middlebury College and prominent citizens to attend.[3]

From her experience at Middlebury, Willard drafted a "Plan for Improving Female Education," which found its way to General Van Schoonhoven and De Witt Clinton, governor of New York. On the basis of "The Plan," as it came to be known, combined with the good graces of her student contacts in Waterford, New York, and the recommendation of Clinton, the legislature granted a charter to the Waterford Academy for Young Ladies. The prospect of receiving financial aid from the state's literary fund created high hopes for the venture. It quickly became apparent, however, that the legislature would not grant the requested funds. The Board of Regents decided against using the literary fund to subsidize the operations of the academy.[4]

Waterford Academy could not be sustained without state funds and subsidies from the town's residents. But the citizens of Troy, a few miles to the north, thought differently. With a population of five thousand in 1821 and prosperous manufactories that included cotton mills, a nail factory, a paper mill, a soap factory, tanneries, and potteries, Troy could afford a female seminary. Moreover, the construction of the Erie Canal promised new commerce with the connection to westward settlement. It was here that Willard established the Troy Female Seminary, with ninety pupils enrolled, twenty-nine of them residents of Troy.[5]

Between 1810 and 1840 the life cycle of women in the United States was undergoing substantial change that would affect both the perceptions and reality of the intellectual role women would play in the new republic. Allmendinger has stressed the role of population growth, increasing family size, declining availability of land, and overcrowding in that transformation. Rural families in New York and New England began to "plan" the lives of their daughters in the event of deferred marriage while they taught.[6]

At the time of the founding of the Troy Female Seminary, collegiate education for most women (ladies) was devoted to polite learning—knowledge associated with traditional domestic roles—and provided the accoutrements for getting along in polite society. Mathematics and science instruction was neglected, despite the protests of those who recognized the necessity for a new republican woman in a new nation. Algebra and geometry, if taught at all, were defended on the grounds of their contribution to mental discipline, since they had little immediate utility for women. Almira Hart Lincoln Phelps, Emma Willard's sister, defended mental discipline and the strengthening of reasoning powers on grounds that they were necessary counterweights to the restrictive habits of domesticity and the "lively imaginations" of women. Though mental discipline was not a major educational objective for women, it could be justified on moral grounds and hence was a necessary correlate to moral discipline.[7] When Willard's Waterford Female Academy planned to offer geometry, logic, and natural philosophy, it was an unusual and daring venture.

The lack of adequate financial support to continue Waterford Academy, combined with the interest and support shown by the citizens of Troy in establishing a female seminary, led to the founding of the Troy Female Seminary. During the years that followed, the school became a leading light in scientific study for women, and science education for women grew more popular. The curriculum was similar to that of men's collegiate institutions. Deborah Warner and Nathan Reingold have pointed out that women were encouraged to be "cultivators" of science, not necessarily "practitioners." The Troy Female Seminary offered a curriculum similar to that in men's collegiate institutions but was not alone in advocating science for women. In the three decades after its founding, other precedents for teaching science were being set at Mount Holyoke Seminary, the Young Ladies' High School in Boston, the Seminary for Female Teachers at Ipswich, Massachusetts, and the Brooklyn Female Academy. By the late 1850s, scientific apparatus was common in female academies and colleges.[8]

Graduates of Troy and other institutions for women established a broad network of women who bore testimony to intellectual respectability through the study of science. They were members of what Barbara Solomon calls a "new American type: the educated woman." Anne Fiore Scott has emphasized the importance of the Troy school in establishing this network of former pupils—which ranged from Troy to western New York to Maryland, Georgia, and Alabama—who perpetuated Willard's belief that women were as intellectually capable as men.[9]

For all the promotion of scientific study for women, however, their domestic and reproductive roles still limited their achievements. Even proponents of more rigorous education for women, such as Mrs. Townshend Stith, still acceded that the study of mathematics and science belonged primarily to men, even though she advocated mental discipline as a chief goal of the new women's education. Such discipline, she argued, was preparation for further learning, regardless of the subjects studied.[10]

The natural sciences made slow headway in female education. The engaging enthusiasm of Lucy Goodale when she spoke of the "castle of science" at Mount Holyoke in 1841 does not seem to have captured everyone's imagination. Catharine McKeen of the same institution observed in her "Mental Education of Woman" (1856), that the "natural sciences ought to take a more prominent place than they have usually occupied" in the education of women. McKeen agreed with Stith that mental discipline was necessary for further serious study, a position that fit well with her argument that "the degree of woman's cultivation ought . . . to be measured only by the *extent of her capabilities*."[11]

The Troy Female Seminary

The key document in the founding of the Troy Female Seminary was Willard's Plan, which was remarkable for both its substance and style. Its brevity and formal organization was designed for a legislature tending to other business and unlikely to give much attention to Willard's appeal for public funds.[12]

The first section of The Plan argued that denying public funds to female education was unfair because it led to the instability of the institution. Having too few teachers for the number of students was not only pedagogically unsound, but it also created a preoccupation with making ends meet. Public funds, Willard argued, would solve both problems.

In the remainder of The Plan Willard argued that female education ought not be based on the precepts of a finishing school, which was "too exclusively directed, to fit [females] for displaying to advantage the charms of youth and beauty." Rather, said Willard, it ought to take adornment less seriously and devote more attention to preparation "for the serious duties of maturer years": "though [it is] well to decorate the blossom, it is far better to prepare for the harvest." Female education, she said, should not exist merely to prepare women "to please the other [sex]," even though obedience to the other sex was the price of the benefits of "support and protection." Yet, in general, subservience was appropriate only to God, and it was he to whom "education [should] be directed." Men ought not be the "standard for the formation of the female character," said Willard, for a system of education ought not be founded on the approbation of "imperfect and erring" human beings. Willard, however, made certain the legislature did not misinterpret her plan as proposing a "masculine education" for females. She simply argued that for the public purse a female institution ought to "possess the respectability, permanency, and uniformity of operation of those appropriated to males."[13]

Willard's "Sketch of a Female Seminary" included buildings with large rooms for lodging and recitation, scientific apparatus, a "domestic department," a library that contained musical instruments, good paintings, maps, globes, and a "small collection of philosophical apparatus." The school should have a "judicious board of trust" and provide instruction in four areas: religious and moral, literary, domestic, and ornamental.[14]

The emphasis on science was evident in the original plan for the Troy Female Seminary. Willard forcefully argued that instruction in science and philosophy required state assistance. More important, however, science was part of a "course of study," belonging with languages, literature, history, and geography.[15] Females should not be kept in "ignorance of the great machinery of nature," said Willard. They, like males, should therefore study natural philosophy, which was "calculated to heighten the moral taste, by bringing to view the majesty and beauty of order and design; and to enliven piety, by enabling the mind more clearly to perceive, throughout the manifold works of God, that wisdom, in which he hath made them all."[16] In this way Willard combined the ideal of Republican Motherhood—the mother as nurturer of the nation—with the study of science, giving credibility to the idea that women could be mainstays of domesticity, nurturers of their children's intellectual development, and intellectual companions to their husbands.[17]

Domestic studies were justified by their usefulness in helping women "regulate the internal concerns of every family." Propriety and utility were combined in a moral vision of domesticity that included wife, homemaker, and mother. "Drawing, painting, elegant penmanship, music, and the grace of motion" were the ornamental studies. These, however, were optional. Needlework was a low priority. Drawing was studied for its contribution to both recreation and physical well-being.[18]

Willard described the benefits of publicly supported female seminaries but was careful to link support to public education in general. Seminaries "would constitute a grade of public instruction" and would also furnish "instructresses, initiated in their modes of teaching, and imbued with their maxims." They would be beneficial to common schools in general, she argued, by supplying well-prepared teachers. Willard invoked the common but inspired argument that former republican governments had failed because of greed and its effect on "morals and manners." This, she said, could be prevented through education for public virtue. Thus women, through teaching, became the preservers of republican government, a message that had not been lost on Benjamin Rush nor would be lost on Horace Mann, both of whom proclaimed a new civic view of womanhood for a new republic.[19]

When Willard opened her Troy Female Seminary there were 217 students, a figure that grew rapidly and peaked in 1838 at 418. Enrollments decreased to a low of 153 in 1844 and stabilized at about two hundred students until 1852. The decline in the early 1840s was not entirely "real," however; 93 to 172 students were not "claimed" on official reports because they were enrolled in "insufficient studies." We do not know the ages of students before 1839, but from that date to 1852 the average age varied from 16.1 to 17 years. Over a fourteen-year period, the ages of students ranged from eight to forty.[20]

Teachers at the Troy Female Seminary were as diverse as the students. The average age was about thirty-one, but they ranged from nineteen to seventy-one. Salaries ranged between $350.00 and $450.00, but the variation did not correlate with age or subject taught. The average teacher had ten years of experience. Many assignments were broad, as was characteristic of a period in which specialization had not come of age. Thus, for example, a teacher might teach only English grammar and reading, another mental philosophy, optics, and hydrostatics, while yet another arithmetic, history, natural theology, and geometry. One of the more complicated assignments included rhetoric, history, arithmetic, English grammar, French grammar, physiology, and geography of the heavens. The most specialized assignments were in music and drawing, for which a teacher would teach only oil painting, piano and signing, or drawing and painting.[21]

Teachers faced the recurrent problem of compensating for deficiencies in their students' earlier education. Perhaps this problem was far greater in a school that reached out in new directions and demanded for women the same academic background as for men. "Additional Remarks," appended to an 1841 report to the New York State Regents, dwells on academic deficiencies among students. "As heretofore," it was noted, "we have found it necessary to instruct most of our pupils in the elementary studies; even the most advanced, at their entrance, have been deficient in Spelling, Reading, Grammar, and Arithmetic." And again: "We are much hindered in our attempts to produce such a plan as will be for the ultimate benefit of the individuals, by the defects in their early training. . . . Defects in early education, compel us to spend the time at first principles and elementary studies which should be devoted to advancing higher departments of study, to the culture of the higher powers of the intellect." [22]

The report also documents the steps taken to deal with student deficiencies. One day per week was devoted to composition and the related studies of grammar, rhetoric, and literary styles. Weekly, every student wrote an essay or letter and made corrections, the purpose of which, said the report, was "to qualify our pupils to write with accuracy and readiness, a business or friendly letter." [23]

The method for correcting compositions was probably that established by Emma Willard as early as 1823. Each week Willard corrected and read some of the compositions aloud without knowing who wrote them. Said one student: "The teachers tear the names from the compositions before they are handed to her and she never knows who's [sic] she reads and therefore criticises upon them." [24] Every class was expected to attend to pronunciation and elocution, and separate lectures on these subjects were also given. In daily recitations, "conversational lectures and a critical examination in the textbooks" were combined. In short, it seems that instruction in all courses attempted to address deficiencies in the basics. [25]

Attempts to deal with academic deficiencies were guided by broad principles that underlay the philosophy of instruction at Troy Female Seminary. Perhaps most important was the protoprogressive, Pestalozzian principle that there should be a "regular gradation of study, adapted to the growing capacities of the pupils." This principle was combined with the belief that academic studies should "exercise" the student's "powers of accurate and ready observation" and "vigorous and sound judgment." Mental discipline thus remained a traditional educational objective, and each branch of study exercised "different faculties of the mind." [26]

Like the principles that guided instruction, teaching techniques were a mix of traditional and modern. On the one hand, traditional lectures and recitations were common. Yet development of the skills of "thinking" and "investigation" probably stretched and frequently broke the tether of recitation and memorization. In keeping with the laboratory method of instruction, philosophic apparatus and a cabinet of minerals were used for study of the natural sciences. There was "extensive use of blackboards, maps, globes, philosophical apparatus and specimens in the natural sciences."[27] In fact, investment in and donations of classroom materials increased steadily with the increase in enrollment. In 1829 Union College lent some of its philosophical apparatus to aid lectures, and Emma Willard's husband spent about $1,000.00 on books for the departments of science and literature. Chemical apparatus was purchased from the Troy Lyceum.[28] In 1839 there were 288 books valued at $250.05. This rose to 915 books valued at $1,389.43 in 1846 and 915 books valued at $1384.28 in 1852. The purchase and value of apparatus rose correspondingly. Apparatus was valued at only $570.78 in 1839, growing to $1732.14 in 1852.[29]

ATTEMPTS AT A NEW PEDAGOGY

Field work and the subjects of drawing and geometry taught at Troy Female Seminary demanded visual-spatial skills frequently excluded from the formal education of young women. The immediate utility of both algebra and geometry was not evident for most women, and Willard had to teach herself mathematics. Emma Willard's acute spatial sense and powers of observation shaped both the curriculum and the pedagogy at the Troy Female Seminary. Margaret Rossiter has observed that the syllogistic argument made to the New York State Legislature in behalf of state financial support in fact reflected Willard's love of plane geometry.[30]

Willard's journal and letters from France and Great Britain show a disciplined eye for detail and geometric configuration. One is struck, for example, by her geometric descriptions as she wrote from Le Havre to her sister Almira Hart in 1833. As she entered the parlor and dining room of the home she was visiting, she noted the "parallelograms of oaken plank, about the width and twice the length of a brick, and laid like bricks in a pavement." Apparently Willard entered the room, proceeded to the center, and turned methodically to each side of the room in order to take its measure: "The room we find is about twenty feet square. . . . Three large panes of glass, one above the other, fill each of the two moveable sashes. . . . Now let us turn to the left. . . . Now let us wheel around, and examine the part of the room opposite the windows. . . . We have now inspected three sides of the room. . . . The fourth has nothing worthy of note, but the door, which leads into a corridor."[31]

Willard then looked from the window and noted the dimensions of the street, the building materials used in the houses, and the styles of the buildings. As she "rang[ed] about the house" she noted the construction of the stairs—"each flight . . . being exactly above the others"—commenting, in addition, that in "massy buildings the main partitions must of course be carried up, on account of the strength of the edifice." Her aesthetic sense was evident in her observations on the black roofs of houses and the smoking chimneys. From Paris, the same detailed observations are part of her letter of 10 November 1830, in which she observed from her hotel the "large parallelogram of buildings" extending from the "rear of the palace," a "quarter of a mile to the north."[32]

Other parts of the journal reinforce our impressions that Willard had a discerning and geometric eye. When taking a train to Liverpool she records information about the difficulties in constructing the railroad. Passing through a deep cut she notes the "effect of perspective": "The rocks on each side, lie in horizontal strata; and as we traced them to a distance, by the gas lights, they would, to an eye at rest, appear to converge to the distant point of sight; but by the unwonted rapidity of motion these lines seemed every moment opening, and diverging before us."[33]

Willard's teaching methods at the Troy Female Seminary bear a special relation to her self-education and to her talent for spatial relations as evidenced in her other writings. Her teaching methods, particularly those used in her geography texts, have been studied by Daniel Calhoun, who points out that Willard's accomplishments lay along two dimensions: finding new ways to teach women and finding new ways to teach geography. Thus her attempts at pedagogical innovation spanned both the social and the cognitive. "Willard," says Calhoun, "was ready for methods that would make the conceptual landscape equally accessible to others." Her visual imagery, he continues, allowed any student to begin in the secure comfort of familiarity and move "into [the] rich, tapestried background" of more sophisticated understanding. In the final analysis, however, Calhoun finds Willard's attempts to visualize history "too complex to be effective," noting that she did not provide students with the "cognitive clues" needed to move from the "domestic present" to an understanding of the past.[34] It may be that the practiced eye of a geometric mind was at odds with the linearity of historical thought at the time.

Science Education Willard's fascination with spatial relations, her own experiments with visualization in the teaching of geography, and her commitment to teaching science to women were brought together in the plan for science education at Troy. The extent to which her students participated in the science, mathematics, and drawing curriculum is shown in table 7.1.

Table 7.1. Percentage of Students Enrolled in Mathematics, Drawing, and Science at Troy Female Seminary, 1839 and 1850

	Date	
Subject	1839	1850
Arithmetic	—	21.9
Algebra	14.3	27.4
Geometry	15.2	13.7
Trigonometry	—	4.1
Natural philosophy	6.7	12.3
Mechanics	6.7	4.1
Optics	6.7	8.2
Hydrostatics	6.7	9.6
Chemistry	9.5	6.8
Botany	12.3	10.9
Geology	2.0	0
Astronomy	12.3	4.1
Physical geography	6.7	2.7
Drawing	24.8	30.1

Source: Trustees Reports, Troy Female Seminary, 1839, 1850. Special Collections, Emma Willard School, Troy, New York. A 25 percent sample was taken using every fourth page of the student rolls. The sample size for 1839 was 105; for 1850, seventy-three. Of those in the 1839 sample, 64 percent were enrolled in at least one of the above courses. The corresponding figure in the 1850 sample was 88 percent.

The rates in the table do not tell us the probability that a student at the seminary would have participated, but they do provide a view of the activity at the seminary in these subject areas.

In general, enrollments in science and mathematics increased between 1839 and 1850. In the former year 64 percent of the students were enrolled in at least one course in science, mathematics, or drawing; by 1850, the figure was 88 percent. In the sciences the increase between 1839 and 1850 is most noticeable in natural philosophy, with only minor increases in optics and hydrostatics. Participation actually declined slightly in mechanics, chemistry, botany, and geology. Larger drops in enrollment occurred in astronomy and physical geography. Twenty-two percent of the students were enrolled in arithmetic in 1850, though no comparable data is available for 1839. A major jump in enrollment occurred in algebra, where enrollment almost doubled from 14 to 27 percent, perhaps reflecting a higher level of preparation for entering students. In geometry enrollments changed little, dropping only slightly from 15 to 14 percent between 1839 and 1850. Enrollments in drawing shifted from 25 percent in 1839 to 30 percent in 1850.

Student responses to science teaching indicate that natural science was frequently taught in the context of technology and was accompanied by instruction in moral philosophy and natural theology. Thus one encounters student notes that combine the applications of science to technology, the study of science as a form of mental discipline, and scientific learning as a means to understanding God's handiwork. In 1840 Caroline Wills, a student, recorded various applications of science to mining and medicine, noting that a knowledge of magnetism helped to improve the quality of air in English needle manufacturing. Six months later she recorded in her diary the applications of coal to heating and "propelling" locomotives and the use of iron in building machinery. Wills concludes in her notes of 22 January that scientific research "establishes the mind in the truths of religion, and teaches us that our own bodies which are food for worms are but compositions of a few simple elements." On several occasions Wills' notes reflect the theme of order that was apparently a mainstay of instruction in science. She records that "the principle of order, is not yet very deeply implanted in my mind," and she notes later that we should look for regularity and order in nature.[35]

Other diaries and copybooks reinforce our impression that order was an important theme in science teaching at Troy Female Seminary and that it cut across various subjects. This was, no doubt, testimony to the synthesis of moral and natural philosophy in both curriculum and instruction. In addition to the "facts" of chemistry, biology, optics, hydrostatics, steam engines, magnetism, and acoustics and the biographical information on famous scientists, one encounters references to the design and order of the universe in "the relations which different parts [of] nature bear to each other."[36]

Emma Willard's goal of spreading scientific literacy among women was aided immensely by the work of Amos Eaton of Rensselaer Institute. Eaton, long a proponent of science education for women, was directly involved with Troy Female Seminary as a mentor to Willard and her sister Almira, and as a lecturer.[37] Eaton was apparently well liked, though perhaps none knew of his characteristically immodest assessment of the role he played at Troy Female Seminary: "I made Mrs. Willard's School all that it is (she now clears $10,000 per year). I supported all the schools here, and many in New England, by supplying them with everything which gave them character for Science."[38]

Whatever role pride or envy played in his involvement with the Troy Female Seminary, Eaton was nonetheless known by Willard as the "Republican Philosopher," a label appropriate for one who, in the fall of 1841, was offering courses in eleven subjects. As early as 1821 Eaton had altered his lecture schedule to accommodate the women under Willard's care. This accommodation apparently continued, for we find the same in 1823 for lectures in mineralogy and zoology given at the Troy lyceum.[39]

Second only to Eaton's in importance (though probably more important as science teaching developed at Troy Female Seminary and elsewhere) was the science instruction provided by Almira Lincoln. Lincoln owed a great deal to Eaton's encouragement, writing to him that "indeed I have often said that whatever success I have met with as a writer, is wholly owing to your encouragement, at the outset." This acknowledgment probably referred to Eaton's encouragement of her translation of the *Chemical Dictionary*.[40]

Like many teachers at Troy Female Seminary, Almira Lincoln served an apprenticeship with Emma Willard and taught elementary courses while preparing to teach more advanced offerings. From Eaton she learned the value of laboratory instruction in chemistry, field trips in botany, and clear prose in textbooks. As her facility with apparatus developed, her students observed her experiments when they accompanied lectures.[41]

In general, Lincoln applied the Pestalozzian methods that were a part of Eaton's own work and were advocated by reform-minded educators in common school journals of the day. Lincoln seems also to have been influenced by Rousseau's *Letters on the Elements of Botany*, the plan of which was evident in her own *Familiar Lectures on Botany* (1829). The antiverbalism conspicuous in Rousseau's work on education was also evident in Lincoln's observation that "botany is not merely a science of words, which only exercises the memory, and teaches the names of plants." Rather she embraced an instrumental view of language, stressing its symbolic function but always relating the words of science to real objects and insisting that her students not be "passive receivers of instruction."[42] Lincoln's developmental view of learning recognized that students do not learn "perfectly" and that their minds need to be strengthened gradually. Borrowing liberally from Lockean epistemology, which emphasized the origin of ideas in sense impressions, she proceeded to deduce a pedagogy that stressed careful observation and the use of texts that helped the student generalize from first-hand impressions. Her *Familiar Lectures* guided the teacher through a method that eschewed abstraction and introduced technical terms only in the context of immediate observations.[43]

Lincoln adapted her method for teaching botany to chemistry and natural philosophy. Here, according to Bolzau, she followed the lead of Eaton at Rensselaer, requiring her students to perform experiments and to give lectures to other students. Drawings were substituted when apparatus was insufficient. Each student was examined publicly on an assigned topic.[44]

Lincoln's views on the language of science seem to have been more conventional than Eaton's. She was less confident in the power of experiments to clarify basic scientific concepts, arguing that learning the language of science was a necessary prerequisite to learning its principles. Said Lincoln in her *Chemistry for Beginners:* "A brilliant course of experiments is often of as little use to the beginner as the sight of an exhibition of fire-works, or the ascension of a balloon. They show, indeed the skill and knowledge of the experimenter, but rather confuse, than assist the ignorant pupil. Thus it is that many a college student graduates, without having profited by the elaborate and elegant lectures with which he may have been favored, because he was ignorant of the language and first principles of science."[45]

Teaching natural philosophy to young children offered perhaps the best test of Lincoln's commitment to Pestalozzian methods. The subject provided the teacher with an opportunity to use innovative methods, since it had been generally neglected in public schools. With natural philosophy, the "incessant curiosity" of the child could be combined with the stimulation of sensory perception to promote a lifelong habit of careful observation. In addition, the concept of causation and its theological implications could be taught naturally, using the child's questions about his or her natural environment. "The accelerated motion of a stone rolling down hill, the gliding of a sled upon ice, the rebounding of an elastic ball, the action of the common bellows, or the spinning of a top" are excellent opportunities for instruction in natural philosophy, said Lincoln. In turn they demonstrate the "grand truth" of religion—the hierarchy of causation to which "we ascend to the *one, great, First cause.*"[46]

The study of technology, natural philosophy, and moral philosophy were mutually reinforcing, for the skills and habits of mind needed to understand each were similar. There was in her argument a hint that the student of science should not mistakenly cultivate an attitude of intellectual superiority. The mechanic's shop, she explained, allowed students to "examine the implements, machinery, or mode of operation, with a view to the application of [their] theoretical knowledge." "Do not scorn to listen to the most simple account of mechanical operations," warned Lincoln. Those operations are based on principles found in textbooks that "the mechanic, though ignorant of science, understands practically."[47]

CONCLUSION

The experiment at Troy Female Seminary was an early step in the emancipation of women from the stigma of intellectual inferiority and the cultural reluctance to admit their capability for mental discipline. Yet it was more than that. It was an attempt to induct American women into the new culture of science and technology and thus transcend the culturally prescribed limits of domesticity with its restrictions on mental discipline and acceptable work roles. Education at Troy Female Seminary, however, was never intended to remove women from the role of homemaker and helpmate. Rather, it sought to unite the moral and scientific in a vision of the new republican woman who would help to perpetuate republican society with its commitment to progress through science and technology.

At Troy Female Seminary women were introduced to the study of science as a part of a larger moral vision and as a means to mental discipline. In the case of the latter, the approach shared the concern at Rensselaer with the development of men and women who could understand science in its relation to technological advance. Even more important, however, was the role of science in developing the skills of careful and precise observation— generic skills that could, presumably, be carried over to other studies. The study of science was thus allied with visual-spatial skills and strong doses of antiverbalism and hands-on instruction. The use of scientific apparatus by women, for example, was not common even in institutions that professed to teach young ladies something of natural philosophy. Nor was it common to teach perspective geometry and drawing that emphasized mechanical precision.

Emma Willard's own background and the influence of Amos Eaton on teachers at Troy Female Seminary assured that students would understand the significance of visual-spatial skills and skills of observation for the study of science as well as the relation of science to technological progress. Troy Female Seminary thus took on an institutional significance beyond that of popularizing scientific study for women. It aimed, rather, to integrate its women into a moral and technological vision of progress— a vision that altered only moderately their occupational futures but which offered them more than the role of observers. Women at Troy were not destined to be operatives, nor were they to be foremen and superintendents in manufacturing. They were, however, to become teachers and mothers who could help to actively perpetuate the vision of scientific and technological progress to new generations.

A Precedent for Technological Education: The Rensselaer School

The Rensselaer School and the Troy Female Seminary appeared within three years of each other near the future confluence of the Hudson River and Erie Canal. The career of Amos Eaton before the founding of the new school by Stephen Van Rensselaer is well documented.[1] Before his leadership at the Rensselaer School, Eaton encountered professional success and failure, dedication and regret, and his career spanned law, business, science, and education. His law career began in 1802, when he was a land agent for John Livingston, and it extended to some ill-conceived financial exploits and imprisonment following a guilty verdict on charges of forgery. Eaton was given a conditional pardon in 1815 and a full pardon in 1817.[2]

His scientific and teaching careers fared better. His early education included working with a blacksmith named Russell Beebe, pursuing his interest in surveying, taking a classical course under Richard Everett at New Britain, and studying science and the arts under David Porter of Hillsdale, New York. He wrote, at age seventeen, a small volume on surveying that was published in 1800. Its title spoke bluntly of the need for plain English in science and mathematics: *Art Without Science; or the Art of Surveying, Unshackled with the terms and sciences of Mathematics. Designed for Farmers' Boys*. Science became a lifelong love for Eaton, but he apparently understood very early the obstacles of language that lay in the path of scientific knowledge. Eaton began attending Williams College in 1795, where he studied Latin, Greek, geography, logic, natural philosophy, and mathematics. He graduated in 1799. Between 1795 and 1799 Eaton's attendance at Williams was irregular. He taught at country schools, sometimes without pay, and developed an early interest in school architecture. In fact, he agreed to teach in his "native parish" free of charge, providing "that the school-house should be built upon a plan which [he] proposed."[3]

Eaton's work as an attorney and land agent was but a long hiatus in his real vocation as scientist and educator. Within six months of his pardon he began the study of mineralogy and chemistry under Benjamin Silliman at Yale. He also studied botany under Professor Eli Ives and worked with John Torrey on botanical classification. He prepared and published *A Botanical Dictionary*. This book along with the influence of Professor Day at Williams College, probably gained him an appointment to lecture on mineralogy and botany at Williams College. Here he was caught up in the study of natural history carried on by Ebenezer Kellogg and Chester Dewey.[4]

Between 1817 and 1824 Eaton "wandered through the New England states and New York like a religious evangelist." As an itinerant and very successful lecturer he spread his own enthusiasm for natural science while continuing his investigations, including "geometrical surveys" used in constructing geological maps. The key to his success as a lecturer in botany, chemistry, mineralogy, and geology was described by Eaton in a letter to John Torrey: "I will tell you, I am perfectly acquainted with this sort of people. 'I become all things to all men.' Silliman, McNeven, Griscom or Davy would do nothing here. I turn everything in science into common talk. I illustrate the most abstruse parts by a dish-kettle, a warming-pan, a bread-tray, a tea-pot, a soap bowl or a cheese press."[5]

Amos Eaton was the ultimate popularizer of science: affable, well-spoken, and knowledgeable, with a propensity for plain talk. His presence probably never commanded the public attention that Silliman later received at his lectures before the Lowell Institute, and certainly he did not become an apparatus entrepreneur, as did Josiah Holbrook. Yet his efforts were pioneering.[6] There is a tone of anti-intellectualism in his correspondence, but his serious study of the biological sciences, geology, and chemistry went unabated during his days of itinerant lecturing.

Eaton made his reputation on both the popular and the academic fronts of science. He prided himself as one of "three or four" who, in the first decade of the nineteenth century, "endeavored to keep pace with the modern sciences of Europe." At the same time, he popularized botany in a small elementary treatise titled *The Young Botanist's Tablet of Memory* (1810).

This volume was revised and issued as his *Manual of Botany* (1817), which sold one thousand copies in six months.[7]

Eaton's study of mineralogy was characteristically the same as his study of botany. He placed great emphasis on fieldwork, popularized his findings in lecture and text, and contributed frequently to such academic publications as Silliman's *Journal*. In geology, his efforts were prodigious. He took every opportunity for observation, published the *Index to the Geology of the Northern States* (1818), conducted geological surveys, and delivered lectures.[8]

The combination of the erudite and practical was also evident in Eaton's work in chemistry. He was particularly interested in agricultural chemistry, as is evidenced by his geological surveys of New York state. He wrote in 1821 the *Chemical Note-Book for the Country Class Room, (Containing Memoranda of Principles To Be Illustrated By Short Courses of Experiments in Country Villages)* (1821), and in 1822 he wrote *Chemical Instructor, Presenting a Familiar Method of Teaching the Chemical Principles and Operations of the Most Practical Utility to Farmers, Mechanics, Housekeepers and Physicians; and Most Interesting to Clergymen and Lawyers Intended for Academies and for the Popular Classroom*.[9]

Eaton's commitment to the study of chemistry, along with his belief in its utility, is apparent in the organization and content of instruction at Rensselaer. In August 1824 he announced a course of lectures titled "Operative Chemists" that would be delivered in Troy. He emphasized the practical focus of his experiments but reassured his audience that he was not one of those "travelling chemists, who amuse with isolated experiments, selected merely to dazzle the eyes of the ignorant." His was not a "puppet show," he explained. The unique feature of the series was its requirement that students perform the experiments under the immediate direction of the teacher. Both ladies and gentlemen were welcome, he announced, the former being "accommodated in a manner which shall be agreeable to them." Those not attending the day class to perform the experiments were allowed to attend the evening lecture series. In this way the "Rensselaerean system" was born in Troy.[10]

THE RENSSELAER SCHOOL

The constitution and bylaws of the Rensselaer School note that the school (later to become Rensselaer Polytechnic Institute) was a place for "instructing persons, who may choose to apply themselves, in the *application of science to the common purposes of life*."[11] This goal was defined by

Stephen Van Rensselaer in a letter dated 5 November 1824 that itself became part of the constitution. (It is commonly accepted that Amos Eaton was Van Rensselaer's ghostwriter and that Eaton formulated the plan for the school.)

One of the aims of the Rensselaer School was to "qualify teachers for instructing the sons and daughters of Farmers and Mechanics, by lectures or otherwise, in the application of experimental chemistry, philosophy, and natural history, to agriculture, domestic economy, the arts and manufactures." The thrust of the proposal was to supply instructors to many school districts rather than to endow a single public institution that would be accessible only to a few "whose parents are able and willing to send their children from home." By establishing a rotating schedule of lectures every two to three years in each public school district, Rensselaer believed that the school could avoid the risks of centralization and bring scientific knowledge to common school pupils.[12]

Rensselaer's draft of the bylaws specified the progressive pedagogy that became the identifying characteristic of the Rensselaer School. He appointed Amos Eaton to the "senior professorship" in "Chemistry and Experimental Philosophy," and named him a "Lecturer in Geology, Land surveying, and the laws regulating town officers and jurors." Eaton came to personify the Rensselaerean system of education.[13]

Under the system, students were divided into sections of five or fewer for instruction. The students delivered lectures and performed experiments themselves. Activity, not passivity, was the Rensselaerean trademark. In this way, it was thought, students would learn "like apprentices to a trade" and "become operative chemists." Grading was based on student performance in and explanations of the experiments. Degrees were awarded after the student gave a course of lectures, which constituted a public examination. No degrees were awarded before the student turned sixteen.[14]

The bylaws of 1825 closely follow Rensselaer's draft and are remarkable for their specificity in pedagogical matters. During the summer session, students attended lectures on chemistry, experimental philosophy, astronomy, geology, mineralogy, botany, zoology, and "so much mathematics as is necessary for land surveying." Hands-on experience was provided for natural history, and students became "familiar with every important subject of natural history, and every manipulation." Students visited nearby farms that had agreements with the school. They kept journals on the "progress of vegetation" and analyzed "all the kinds of soils and manures, used by the cultivators of the school farms, with a view to become acquainted with the causes of success and failure." The activities were specified in great detail in the constitution and included "the art of inoculating and engrafting trees, transplanting by roots, cutting and . . . pruning trees, surveying farms, calculating height and distances, measuring corded wood, scantling and boards, and the solid contents of timber, gauging casks, taking measures, and calculating the velocity and pressure of rivers, water race-ways, aqueducts, &c. collecting and preserving plants and minerals." Students also visited manufacturers and workshops connected with the school and were "taught the application of science to all the most important operations of the artist."[15]

During the winter term students gave their "experimental and demonstrative lectures" on the lessons learned during the summer sessions. In the evenings they attended a course of lectures on each subject. Professors could require that students lecture before other students or before a popular audience. In the winter term students also worked in the workshop in the school building, using small tools. The purpose of these activities was to teach the student enough to make small repairs. This would avert the "delay and expense" involved in contacting a "distant mechanic" when no special tools were required. In this way the student became a general handyman and acquired the basic information and skills qualifying him for entry into a detailed study of any trade.[16]

The principles enunciated in the constitution and bylaws were summarized in the 1827 catalog of the school as "The Three Distinctive Characteristics of the School." In most schools and colleges, it was written, the teacher "improves *himself* more than he does his *pupils*." It followed that the best way to improve knowledge was to have students "learn by giving experimental and demonstrative lectures, with experiments and specimens." The second principle of Rensselaer education stated that "in every branch of learning, the pupil begins with its practical application; and is introduced to a knowledge of elementary principles, from time to time as his progress requires." Thus, for example, the student would observe a bleaching factory, a tannery, or millstones and then go on to produce choline gas in the laboratory, make an "insoluble precipitate of tannin and animal gel," or remove the water from gypsum "to observe the effect of retention." The final principle combined physical and mental labor. Field trips to survey, collect specimens, and examine workshops and factories were good exercise but avoided the "vulgarisms" of running, jumping, scuffling, and climbing that detracted from that "dignity of deportment and carriage, which becomes a man of science."[17] The curriculum thus aimed to integrate technology, science, and moral philosophy.

THE CURRICULUM AT RENSSELAER

Table 8.1 summarizes the schedule and courses in the first few years after the founding of the Rensselaer School. The integration of lectures, field trips, and student experiments is its conspicuous feature.

The schedule at Rensselaer was efficient, using a system of rotated classes. Formal lectures, laboratory exercises, and student projects reinforced one another daily. Student lectures offered both the lecturer and listener "critical" involvement in the teaching process.[18] Moreover, there was little free time for students, a fact that reflected a typical concern of early-nineteenth-century colleges and academies with the proper use of leisure time. It was said that leisure time bred unproductive habits and was the seedbed of moral degradation. Finally, the concern for citizenship education was evident in the parliamentary activities on Friday and Saturday. Nothing was left to chance, it seems. Yet, at the same time, the school was student-oriented in the sense that it emphasized the activity of the student as the key to efficient learning.

The details of subject matter at Rensselaer may be gathered from published catalogs, student notebooks, and drafts of lectures. As would be expected, the curriculum evolved, but many of the unique features remained until the reorganization in 1849 and 1850. Before then, important but less comprehensive changes occurred. In 1832 the classical department was added, offering trigonometry, mechanics, mensuration, English, etymology, and composition in the winter term. In the summer term the department offered mechanics, land surveying, extemporaneous speaking, bookkeeping, elementary mathematics, botany, geological and chronological history, and the natural history of astronomy. Languages could be added with the approval of the Prudential Committee.[19]

The course in civil engineering began at Rensselaer Institute in 1835 when the school was authorized by the state legislature to establish a department of mathematical arts offering instruction in "Engineering and Technology." Eaton, however, had begun preparing for this change in organization as early as 1830, when he initiated a series of lectures on technology lasting four months, with two ninety-minute lectures per week.[20] Both the bachelor of natural sciences and "Degree of Civil Engineer" were offered.[21]

We know in detail the subjects that students in mathematics (1834–35) (figure 8.1) and engineering (1841–42) at Rensselaer Institute were expected to know (see appendix). In the latter year they were to be "familiar" with laying out roads, railroads, and canals with a compass and making

Table 8.1. Daily Schedule and Curriculum of Rensselaer School, 1827–1829

25 minutes after sunrise	*Fall term:* Monday, one-hour exam on moral and mental philosophy. Tuesday through Friday, students appear for examinations on previous exercises. *Winter term:* Same. *Spring term:* Same.
9:00 A.M.	*Fall term:* Lecture on botany by professor. *Winter term:* Lecture by professor. *Spring term:* Review of fall term, including experiments for six weeks.
10:00 A.M.– 1:00 P.M.	*Fall term:* Officer of the day, a student, gives lecture with professor present. Students give critique of lecture. Students are divided into four divisions using four different rooms: natural history, common laboratory, natural philosophy, assay. Students rotate to new room at end of each sub term. Each student gives extemporaneous lecture. Each day students reconvene to criticize all lectures. *Winter term:* Same, but subjects are rhetoric, geography, history, logic, etymology. Science as in fall term. *Spring term:* Last nine weeks used for practical application of science, as in fall term.
1:00 P.M.	Dinner
1:30–4:00 P.M. (flexible)	*Fall term:* If not lecturing, students prepare for following day's experiments and lectures. *Winter term:* Activities, determined by weather, include use of sextant, compass, blowpipe, telescope and other optical instruments, and maps. *Spring term:* Field trips for observing plants, minerals; trips to locks, aqueducts, mills, ice factories; cultivating experimental garden.
Midafternoon	*Fall term:* Visits to workshops, factories, or field trips to collect and observe various natural phenomena.
Friday and Saturday evenings	*Fall term:* Parliamentary exercises simulated as representative Congress.
Saturday	Every other Saturday, students at liberty. Alternate Saturdays given over to parliamentary exercises.

Table 8.1. Continued

Sunday	One-hour examination on sacred history. Attendance at religious workshop required (no denomination specified).

Note: For students under 17, there was a preparatory branch in the "elementary parts" of the various subjects. Branch instruction was offered in botany, geology, chemistry, natural philosophy, rhetoric, geography, mathematics, and logic, but without "expensive apparatus."

Source: Rensselaer School Exercises in Fall, Winter, and Spring Terms, including those of the Preparation and District Branches, 1827, pp. 38–46; and "Rensselaer School Extended," Bulletin, 1829. Rensselaer Polytechnic Institute, Archives and Special Collections.

calculations for embankments and excavations. Students were expected to use and understand the principles of tables of "versed sines." They were also required to make calculations for "filling and emptying locks," specific gravity, waterways and raceways, millstones, air pressure, pumps, lightning rods, and latitude and longitude by lunar elevations and eclipses. Other applications of mathematics were required for measuring heights of hills and their profiles, fixing a transit line, and topographical surveys. Finally, students were to be practical geologists, botanists, and architects and draftsmen.[22]

The next major shift in curriculum occurred in 1850 with the reorganization of the school. The new direction had been taking shape since 1847 with the appointment of Benjamin Franklin Greene as senior professor. Greene had come to Rensselaer as a student in 1841 and graduated in 1842. A letter to Amos Eaton in October 1841 inquiring into the adequacy of his preparation to study at Rensselaer reveals something of the background of this bright student and his level of accomplishment, especially in mathematics and to some extent in the sciences: "I will now state to you the progress which I have up to this time made in my several studies.—Have been through with Day's Algebra pretty carefully two years since.—Have also been through with Davies' Legendres' Geometry excepting the section upon spherical Trigonometry.—Have also attended somewhat to Davies' Surveying and Leveling.—Have had and studied to some extent, Chemistry, Nat. Philosophy, Geology and Mineralogy.—And I think I may *safely* say, that I am *very fond* of them."[23]

In 1847 Greene began calling the institute a polytechnic school even though it was not legalized as such until 1861.[24] The institute, in any case, was organized into a General School and Technical Schools, the latter di-

MATHEMATICS.

Synopsis of the Mathematical Course of Instruction at Rensselaer Institute, from Nov. 19, 1834, to Feb. 11, 1835.

All Instruments are furnished by the Institution, excepting, that each Student provides himself a Scale, Protractor, and Dividers. The whole School is occupied with practical Mathematics only, for 12 weeks. Other Sciences are noticed, as far as the course of Mathematics requires—particularly Mechanical Philosophy.

I. Arithmetic.

Rule of proportion.
Decimals.
Duo-decimals.
Square-root.
A knowledge of these rules implies sufficient knowledge *of Arithmetic for the course.*

II. Names of Instruments to be learned *by inspection.*

1. Dividers.
2. Protractor.
3. Scale.
4. Compass.
5. Level.
6. Chain.
7. Chain-tallies.
8. Mile-tallies.
9. Quadrant.
10. Sextant.
11. Barometer.
12. Thermometer.
13. Hydrometer.
14. Hygrometer.
15. Pluviometer.
16. Hydrostatic bellows.
17. Hydrostatic cylinders.
18. Siphon, Tantalus.
19. Common pump.
20. Lever.
21. Wheel and Axle.
22. Pully.
23. Inclined plane.
24. Wedge.
25. Screw.
26. Funicular and Genicular power.
27. Terestrial globe.
28. Stand-horizon.
29. Liquid-horizon.
30. Glass-horizon.
31. Brass-horizon.

III. Names of Solids to be learned by *inspecting models.*

32. Cube.
33. Parallelopiped.
34. Rhomb.
35. Pyramid.
36. Cone.
37. Sphere.
38. Oblate spheroid.
39. Elongated spheroid.
40. Cylinder.
41. Frustrum of cone.
42. Triangular section.
43. Circular section.
44. Elliptical section.
45. Parabolic section.
46. Hyperbolic section.
47. Polyhedron, (tetrahedron—pentahedron—hexa—hepta—octa—ennea—deca—endeca—dodecaedron, &c.)
48. Hemisphere.
49. Segment of a sphere.
50. Sector of a sphere, (or a triangular pyramid.)

IV. Names of Figures by lines and superficies; to be learned by inspection.

☞ Each Student must draw every figure.
51. Right line.
52. Curved line.
53. Perpendicular line.
54. Horizontal line.
55. Diagonal line.
56. Right angle.
57. Obtuse angle.
58. Acute angle.
59. Right-angled triangle.
60. Obtuse-angled triangle.
61. Acute-angled triangle.
62. Equilateral triangle.
63. Isosceles triangle.
64. Scalene triangle.
65. Parallelogram.
66. Square.
67. Rhomb.
68. Trapezium.
69. Trapezoid.
70. Polygon, (pentagon—hexa—hepta—octa—ennea—deca—endeca—dodecagon.)
71. Circle.
72. Periphery.
73. Arc.
74. Diameter.
75. Radius.
76. Chord line.
77. Tangent line.
78. Semi-circle.
79. Segment.
80. Sector.
81. Ellipse.
82. Focus.
83. Conjugate diameter.
84. Transverse diameter.
85. Parallel lines.

V. Trigonometry, geometrically.

86. Distance, and
87. Height, *by quadrant.*
88. Distance, and
89. Height, *by a compass.*
90. Distance, and
91. Height, *by a pole or rope.*
92. Distance, and
93. Height, *by a plane table.*

VI. Trigonometry, Arithmetically.

94 By rule of proportion, thus: as one angle is to its opposite side, so is any other angle to its opposite side.
95. Natural sines of degrees, substituted for degrees.
96 Geometrical exhibition of Natural sines.
97. Distances, and
98. Heights.

VII. Mensuration of Superficies.

99. Square.
100. Parallelogram.
101. Rhomb.
102. Rhomboid.
103. Equal triangles on equal bases between parallel lines.
104. Circles. [See Text-book, p. 12 to p. 14.]

VIII. Mensuration of Solids.

[See Text-book, p. 14 to p. 16.]

IX. Land Surveying.

[See Text-book, p. 17 to p. 52.]

X. Engineering.

[See Text-Book, p. 52 to 86.]

XI. Cords and Bushels.

[See Text-Book—p. 90 to 91.]

XII. Water Pressure and Supply.

[See Text-Book—p. 91 to 92.]

XIII. Navigation.

[See Bowditch.]

Female Mathematicians.

The waste of time in many female schools, by the fashionable mummery of Algebra, half learned and never applied, has caused many to ascribe the failure in mathematics to the perversion of female genius, when it is drawn from elegant literature, music, painting, &c., to the severe sciences. The true cause is to be found in parsimony, which excludes competent teachers, badly selected subjects, and wretchedly compiled text-books. Our country is inundated with wild schemes of learning; while the speculating book-sellers are sending their harpie-like pedlars, to rob our youth of the last fragments of common sense.

The teachers of the Institute are desirous to make the experiment with a small class of ladies at the school in Walnut-Grove. Their immediate superintendent will be a lady of respectability; but they will be taught by the most experienced teachers of the Institute. A pleasant upper room, separate from those occupied by the students, will be furnished with full suits of instruments, &c. They will have every advantage of regular students; but, for the sake of the trial, they shall pay but half the fees, for the ensuing term.

N. B. All students will meet in the Natural History room at 10 A. M., daily, to hear the lecture of a Professor, accompanied with demonstrations.

AMOS EATON, *Agent.*

Students will be received until Dec. 1.

vided into General Studies and Special Studies. The General School offered courses in mathematics (higher algebra, analytical trigonometry, analytical geometry, and differential and integral calculus), mechanics, physics (magnetism, electricity, acoustics, and optics), chemistry (inorganic and organic), natural history, geology, cosmography, including physical geography, literature (English composition, elocution, criticism, French, German), and graphic arts (descriptive geometry, linear perspective and geometrical drawing, topographical drawing, and free drawing).

The General Studies division of the Technical Schools included practical mechanics, construction drawing, machine drawing, topographical drawing, engineering geodesy, metrical arithmetic, practical geology, practical mineralogy, graphics of carpentry and stone cutting, industrial physics, general constructions, theory of machines, transformation of motion, prime movers, and construction of machines. As of 1851, only one group of Special Studies for Technical Schools at Rensselaer existed—the School of Civil Engineering.[25] The relative emphases of the courses of lectures in the General Studies section of the Technical Schools division may be gathered from the number of lectures offered in each subject, as shown in table 8.2. Algebra, analytic trigonometry, geometry, differential and integral calculus, and analytic mechanics received the most attention. Next in order of priority were chemistry, magnetism, electricity, light, heat, chain and compass surveying, trigonometry, topography, and hydrography. These were followed by elementary mechanics, and, next in order, mineralogy, geology, descriptive geometry, chemistry, physics, engineering fieldwork, and construction materials. Other subjects of lesser importance were mensuration, botany, mechanical and hydraulic engineering, steam engines, practical astronomy, and the use of field instruments. Clearly the shift in curriculum by midcentury was toward more sophisticated mathematics and the foundations of science. Hands-on subjects were beginning to take a back seat as Rensselaer became a polytechnic institution.

By 1851 the curriculum evolved toward greater specialization with an expanding scientific base, necessitating, also, a greater sophistication in mathematics. Unlike the traditional curriculum of classical studies, "subjects rather than authors" were emphasized. The changing curriculum also attempted to give a broader course of studies that prepared the student for the language and communications skills needed in his roles as engineer and scientist. Greene, as Eaton before him, understood the utility of a moral foundation for mathematical and scientific study. "The developing of habits among its members, in consonance with their destined position as men of science, and their relations to society as men of action," he said, was im-

Table 8.2. Summary of Courses of Lectures at the Rensselaer Polytechnic Institute, 1851

Number of Lectures	Titles	Subjects
40	Analysis	Algebra, analytical trigonometry, analytical geometry, differential and integral calculus.
20	Practical geometry	Mensuration of lines, surfaces, and solids.
12	Practical trigonometry	Mensuration of heights and distances.
20	Elementary mechanics	Mechanics of solids and fluids— explanatory and descriptive.
25	Elementary chemistry	Chemistry of nonmetallic and metallic elements.
12	Structural and physiological botany	Descriptive and geographical botany.
15	Mineralogy and geology	Descriptive and systematic geology and physical geography.
40	Rational mechanics	General analytical mechanics.
8	Equilibrium	Walls, arches, roofs, bridges, etc.
10	Machines	Mechanical engineering.
10	Hydraulic works	Hydraulic engineering.
8	Steam engine	Hydraulic engineering.
25	Experimental physics	Magnetism, electricity, light, heat.
15	Descriptive geometry	Projections, shades, shadows, perspective.
25	General geodesy	Chain and compass surveying, trigonometry, topography, and hydrography.
10	Practical astronomy	Problems, etc., time, latitude, and longitude.
15	Technical chemistry and physics	As before.
15	Engineering fieldwork	Instrumental operations, generally, in the surveys, location and construction of public works.
15	Materials used in construction	Their origin, strength, durability, preparation, preservation, etc.

Table 8.2. Continued

Number of Lectures	Titles	Subjects
12	Nature and use of field instruments	Theory, construction, use, adjustments, tests, etc., of compass, theodolite, transit, level barometer, sextant, etc.

Source: "Programme, Etc., of the Rensselaer Institute; A Polytechnic Institution at the City of Troy," February 1851, 2–3.

perative. The skills of critical observation were accompanied by rhetorical skills in an attempt to cultivate socially conscious and technically able engineers. Habits of "minute and critical observation, of accuracy and discrimination," were to be accompanied by the *"ready* ability to give a clear and forcible expression to a view or opinion, whether written or oral, adapted to the ready apprehension of other intelligent minds."[26]

INSTRUCTION AT RENSSELAER

Published courses of study are valuable guides to the scope and sequence of topics that students were expected to master. They do not, however, give a micro view of instruction. In fact, such a view is difficult to recapture, as few student notebooks and faculty lectures survive. Some records, however, do allow a partial reconstruction of the lectures at Rensselaer.

From the notes of Robert McManus, a student at Rensselaer, we see the details of one of Amos Eaton's lectures on natural philosophy. The lecture, given 6 October 1828, was probably the first of a series, judging from the concern with definition and classification. Historical information on the evolution of the scope of natural philosophy was given, with Eaton noting that the French philosophes reduced it to mechanical philosophy and astronomy. Eaton, however, followed Biot's scheme, which also included optics, electricity, and magnetism.[27]

As with natural philosophy, Eaton was equally careful to provide the proper classification and definition of mechanical philosophy. Examples illustrating statics and dynamics were drawn from the working of bellows, levers, and wheel and axle. Newton's laws were introduced, as was the concept of gravitation. Eaton also covered the concepts of motion, weight, velocity, and momentum. Eaton explained the practical application of momentum by noting that when power is applied to a body, it must be applied to the center of gravity.[28]

The McManus papers also include notes on Eaton's engineering lectures given in the same autumn term. So that the student might understand the reason for study, Eaton's lecture did not begin with the usual comments on materials—for example, stone, timber, iron, and mortar—but with actual constructions, such as canals. Eaton then considered those factors which the civil engineer must consider before construction: wind, soil, stagnant water, fields under cultivation. "An engineer," recorded McManus, "should always observe the health of the inhabitants near the Canal." Following this general advice and justification for study were lectures on building materials, geology, mineralogy, and chemistry, including John Finch's atomic theory of chemistry.[29]

Judging from other papers left by students and from examination questions, studies ranged from the basics to the theoretical to application. George Cook, a student who became a district school teacher, civil engineer for railroads, manufacturer of glass, professor, state geologist and member of the American Association for the Advancement of Science, left his notebook of chemistry lectures he delivered at Rensselaer in the winter of 1844–45. He began his course of study with three lectures on "imponderable agents," including heat, light, galvanism, and electricity. Lecture four was on the concept of affinity, and lectures five through fourteen were on various nonmetallic elements. These were followed by lectures on metalloids and metals and concluded with lecture twenty-one, on organic chemistry. Throughout, Cook emphasized the application of chemistry to the study and practice of agriculture.[30]

Cook also left a diary for 1838–39 while he was a student and an assistant at Rensselaer. Along with observations on student conduct, he recorded the activities of students calculating pressure under "different heads," conducting surveys, and "lecturing round." He noted that student lectures on mechanical powers were "not good." The opening to a series of lectures on natural philosophy by an unnamed professor were "very clear to all," however. Cook records his own activities, including collecting botanical specimens ("botanizing"), taking measurements for excavations and embankments, listening to Eaton's lecture on sacred history (a "medley of questions, answer[s] [and] illustrations"), listening to explanations of a method for "calculating . . . triurating surfaces of millstones," "finding the power with which gravitation acts on the moon," listening to lectures on circulation of the blood and on optics, and attending sermons.[31]

Visits to nearby rivers, mills, and construction sites were important to instruction at Rensselaer. Cook records in his diary on 29 May 1839 that the class "measure[d] a trunk [branch] of the Poestenkill." Another student, Reed Bontecou, who became a physician, records in 1842 that his class visited the Poestenkill Mills. The trip also included a visit to the Marshall Mills and the inspection of a tunnel that had been dug for a raceway to the mills. On another day the class "went over to the Troy and Schenectady railroad cut to witness the operation of the new steam excavator."[32]

Two examinations given at Rensselaer detail the type and level of mastery expected of students. Several of the fifty-two questions on mathematics, surveying, and mensuration from an 1835 examination are listed below. They represent a relatively simple level of mathematical knowledge, especially compared to that demanded at midcentury, when Rensselaer became a polytechnic institution:

- Apply the rule of proportions in finding the distance across a river, by an isosceles triangle without any mathematical instruments.
- Apply scale and dividers in the taking of chains and links from a diagonal scale.
- Apply compass in taking course and bearings.
- Apply the sextant in taking angular distance between bodies.
- Apply hygrometer in taking moisture.
- Cast the contents of a field, by trapezoids extended to a meridian.
- Exhibit the radius, sine and cosine.
- Cast the solid contents of a cone.
- Exhibit the sector and segment of a sphere, by models.
- Cast the measure of water pressure at any height of head.[33]

The subjects in which students were examined in 1842 were similar: extracting cube roots, applying the Pythagorean theorem, calculating volume, surveying and calculating areas, measuring specific gravity, determining latitude and longitude, applying the concepts of mechanical powers, calculating velocity and its application to water flow, and "taking the height of the atmosphere when it ceases to be dense enough to reflect light."[34]

Records from the late 1840s and the 1850s give us a more complete view of instruction at Rensselaer. They indicate, moreover, instruction of greater depth and breadth. The letters of Edward Allen show a picture of the demanding daily schedule. Allen, a student and lecturer, was responsible, along with another student, for two sections each of ten students. His lectures on surveying and chemistry were thirty minutes, followed by criticisms. Students then repeated his lectures in small sections. The remaining class time was spent attending lectures on mechanics and geometry, and he was enrolled in a drawing class.[35]

We know from Allen's diary that the student body at Rensselaer was diverse, as his characterizations of a few of the students indicate: Barnard of Worcester, who "stands among the first here"; Davis of Templeton was "not so advanced, having never before studied Geometry much"; Morton, "a normalite from Plymouth," was a "very good scholar, rather slow but solid"; Chum Ware was "good in mathematics"; King of Florida was "not in good health, sallow, but [a] good-hearted fellow, not so good a mathematician as the others"; and Tweedale was a "rough, solid, shrewd strong man, of energy, but miserably unneat, making queer figures for diagrams on the black board, fond of discussion, and promising well."[36]

Both student notebooks and faculty lecture notes give us detailed information on courses in mechanics, civil engineering, mathematics, and drawing. Dascom Greene lectured on civil engineering. His topics on strength of materials included deflection of transverse stresses, tensile and compressing strains, strength under transverse strains, forces of torsion, formulae for flecture and rupture by transverse strains, and longitudinal stress. Eight other lectures on construction materials also related to civil engineering. Advantages and disadvantages of various materials were explained. Problems with foundations were addressed, as were basic principles for dealing with settling. The lectures ranged over the construction of pilings, dams, joints for beams, bridge centers, railway curves, grades, and traction.[37]

Greene's lectures also covered the basic theory of machines, the concept of work, and prime movers, including hydraulic motors and steam engines. Various types of machines were explained. Students were taught that work equaled the unit of "force space" divided by time. Types of motion and friction were included, as were equations for balance. Theories of cranks, flywheels, governors, and pile driving followed (fig. 8.2). Six lectures on steam engines explained the relations among pressure, temperature, and volume of steam, the velocity of an engine in relation to its load, optimum temperatures, the features of low- and high-pressure steam engines, and maximum load and pressure using tables and formulae. Four lectures on hydraulic motors covered horizontal and vertical waterwheels. The theories of turbines, pressure, and reaction wheels were explained, as was the time-honored overshot waterwheel, including measures of radius, velocity, depth and width of crown, number of buckets, form of buckets, velocity of water jet, and settings on the sluice.[38]

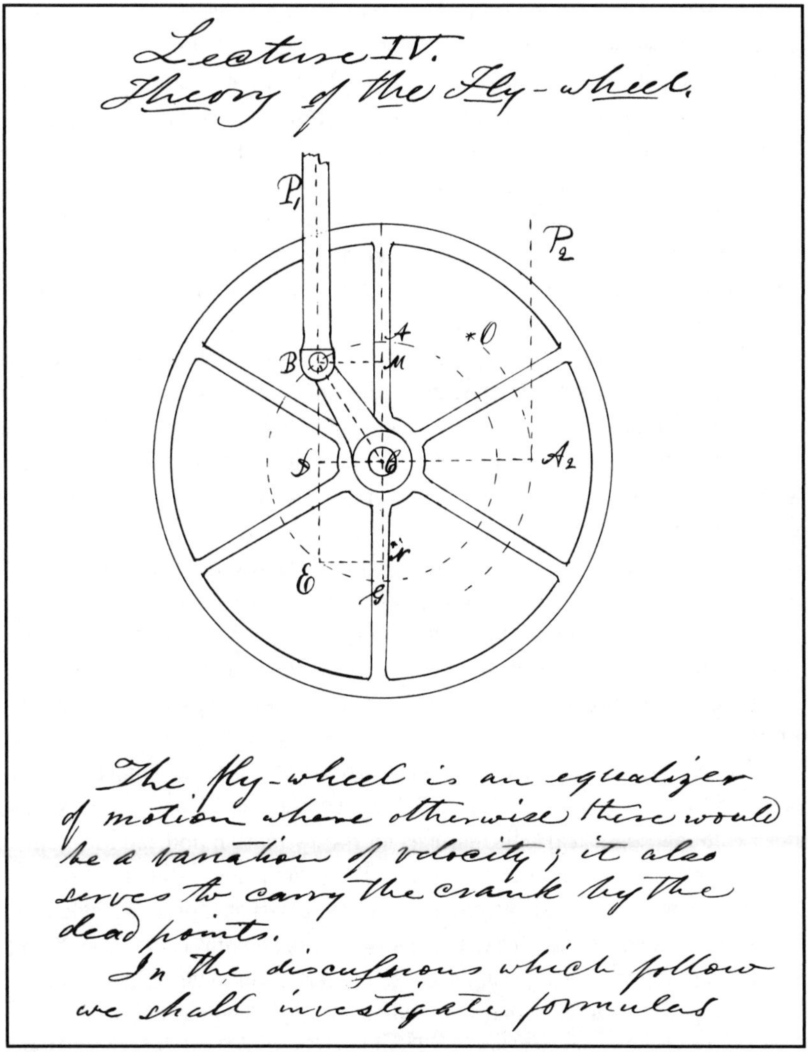

Lecture IV.
Theory of the Fly-wheel.

The fly-wheel is an equalizer of motion where otherwise there would be a variation of velocity; it also serves to carry the crank by the dead points.

In the discussions which follow we shall investigate formulas

Fig. 8.2. Lecture notes. From Dascom Greene Papers, 1852. Archives and Special Collections, Rensselaer Polytechnic Institute. Photo courtesy Rensselaer Polytechnic Institute.

The notebook of Theodore Cooper, a student, shows that fairly sophisticated courses were offered on "rational mechanics" and "mechanics of solids," each of which required calculus. The courses were highly mathematized, in keeping with Rensselaer's move toward becoming a truly polytechnic institute. Rational mechanics began with the usual definitions of space, time, matter, motion, velocity, and volume and moved quickly to integrals. The "resultants" for compound forces were calculated, as were "equalibrating" forces. Translatory and rotary motion and various problems on the center of gravity, volume, rectilinear motion, and the equilibrium of a free point followed. Page after page of equations on the mechanics of fluids were included subsequent to the discussion of general mechanics. These included formulae for pressure, discharge, and flotation of spheres. The theory of machines treated friction and its measurement, velocity of a shaft, uniform motion, pendulums, balance wheels, governors, flywheels, and angular velocities. Formulae for high- and low-pressure steam engines, engine resistances, and adhesion followed. The set of lectures also included formulae for "constructions," primarily matters for civil engineering. Among these were the stability of retaining walls, prism of greatest pressure, theory of the arch, moments of thrust, noncentral arches, polycentral arches, stability of an arch, abutments and framed structures, girder bridges, bracing, suspension bridges, piers, and piping systems for water.[39]

Charles Downe's notebook on his lectures on physical mechanics covered some of the same topics as Cooper's, though the course of study was not nearly so mathematical. His lectures on rotary motion and the mechanics of fluids were nearly identical to Cooper's student notes, but the opening twenty lectures stressed astronomy, friction, elasticity, prisms, molecular forces and displacement, torsion, tensive strains, compression, transverse strains, and tangential stress. Discussions were replete with formulae, but verbal explanations were more in evidence than in Cooper's notes.[40]

Finally, the student notebook of Thaddeus Sanford Smith gives us a view of what Rensselaer students learned of descriptive geometry and drawing. The basic definitions and principles were presented, and then the course was organized around problems. As part of the study of cycloid, epicycloidal, hypercycloid, and involute curves, for example, the student began with the elementary principle that "the tangent to a circle is perpendicular to [the] radius at [the] point of tangency." It logically followed, then, that "any point of these curves is describing a momentary circular arc about the point of contact of the moving and base lines as a momentary centre." Thus, "the tangent to any of these curves at any point, is perpendicular to the line joining that point with the common point of contact of the moving and base line."[41]

The "Course for Shades and Shadows" began with such "first principles" as the following: "shadow given by its boundary," "sine of shade = contact of an opaque body with a tangent cylinder of rays," and "a plane, which shall be a plane of rays, may be drawn through any line in space." The student then proceeded to "shades," learning, for example, that to "find the element of shade on a cylinder cone" a plane was passed "parallel to a given line and tangent to the Cyl. or Cone, *the line being a ray*." The student was then referred to the appropriate problems. General and special methods for shadows were explained and illustrated: shades and shadows on curved and double curved surfaces, for instance, and the shadow of a screw. Overall, the sequence followed Davies' text, with general methods being introduced first, followed by special methods and then problems from the text.[42]

Both instruction and curriculum at Rensselaer reflected an increasingly agreed-upon core of knowledge requisite for the making of an engineer. Civil engineering was the forte of the school, but the curriculum covered all engineering studies. The presentation of studies became more mathematized, but verbal and quantitative studies were still in balance, and the visual-tactile dimensions of learning still played a major role in the Rensselaerean method of instruction in 1850. Yet change was imminent as theory and mathematics assumed a stronger role in professionalizing engineering studies.

Educating Women at Rensselaer Education at Rensselaer was dominated by male interests and an emerging engineering culture that was the prerogative of males. Yet from the outset Rensselaer accommodated, not simply tolerated, women in its classrooms. Amos Eaton's commitment to the education of women in science, technology, and mathematics began early in his lecturing career. In a letter to John Torrey in October 1817 he noted that his lectures at Northhampton were attended by fifty-five ladies in an occupationally diverse audience. At Rensselaer he later allowed women to present courses of lectures, which were attended mainly by students enrolled at the Troy Female Seminary.[43] Eaton, moreover, was a strong advocate of coeducation, and by 1825 we know that young women and men sat together to hear Eaton's "philosophical lectures." Though the occasion was serious, it had its lighter moments, if we are to judge by one female student's response: "I have been to the Rensselaer School, to attend the philosophical lectures. They are delivered by the celebrated Mr. Eaton, who has several students, young gentlemen. I hope they will not lose their hearts among twenty or thirty pretty girls. For my part, I kept my eyes fixed as fast as might be upon the good old lecturer, as I am of the opinion, that he is the best possible safeguard, with his philosophy and his apparatus; for you know philosophy and love are sworn enemies!"[44]

Eaton was convinced that women were as capable as men of passing examinations in science and mathematics. Though women were not recognized formally as degree students at Rensselaer, Eaton set out to prove his point by petitioning the Board of Examiners at Rensselaer Institute to test them. In 1835 Eaton asked that eight young ladies be questioned so that a "fair comparison" might be drawn "between the study of speculative geometry and algebra as generally practiced in female seminaries, and this mode of applying mathematics to the essential calculations of Geography, Astronomy, Meteorology, necessary admeasurements, etc." Whether Eaton's primary motivation was to prove the superiority of his method or the intellectual equality of women is unknown, but in any case three examiners proceeded with the experiment. The results were gratifying for Eaton and no doubt flattering for the young ladies. "This trial," it was reported, "sufficiently demonstrates the superiority of practical mathematics, over the mere unapplied elements," and "its superior interest gives it the advantage."[45]

Eaton's experiment with giving women examinations in science and mathematics was but a means to making a case for his broader view that schooling for women be restructured to fit the changing role of women in the new republic. He reflected in 1830 upon the dismal state of women's education. "The waste of time in many female schools, by the fashionable mummery of algebra, half learned and never applied," said Eaton, "has caused many to ascribe the failure in mathematics to the perversion of the female genius, when it is drawn from elegant literature, music, painting, etc., to the severe sciences."[46]

Five years later he included women's education in his ruminations on technological advance. Responding to changing demands in the labor force, Eaton wrote that *"the education of all girls should be adopted to some useful employment. . . .* After our factories had driven girls from the spinning wheel, and thereby put an end to two-thirds of their labor, the important question occurred: what employment shall be substituted?" Before the question could be settled, the result, he observed, was to idle one-third of the nation's youth.[47]

Eaton's solution was a plan whereby women made the transition from technological unemployment to permanent places in the American socio-economic hierarchy. Eaton retained a belief in the traditional family role of women, but he attempted to place that role in the context of production. Women were to "perform all the light and cleanly operations required in the manufactories," and they "should be the sole operators with the needle in the conversion of all manufactured stuffs, cotton, woollen, silk, and linen, into wearing apparel . . . from the coarsest coat to the most delicate article of the milliner's shop." In addition, said Eaton, "they should conduct all the in-door business of the dairy and of the kitchen." Finally, he recommended that women be the "only teachers" of children under twelve years old. This, he said, would give the proper moral sentiment to teaching and elevate the status of "common school-masters."[48]

Translated into matters of curriculum and pedagogy it followed that the education of girls in the mechanical arts "should never be neglected." Included also were the study of geology, physical geography, botany, zoology, and chemistry, especially as they related to domestic operations of health and economy, and moral philosophy and communication.[49]

Eaton's pedagogical conclusions followed from his belief that women should be the moral mainstays of families while assisting their husbands in the conduct of business. He was clearly not proposing the liberation of women from their central position in the family. Yet his solution to the problem of wasting human resources also envisioned the wife and mother as an important participant in the economic life of the family: "Girls should be taught like boys," he noted, because "the interest of men and women of a family [was] the same," and "women ought to be acquainted with the business part of the education of men." Women were a resource, Eaton said, "valuable at home," not "worthless as a fungus."[50]

CONCLUSION

Amos Eaton's Rensselaerean plan began as a vocationally oriented, pedagogically innovative hands-on training for adults and youth who sought to become engineers during a period when engineering had not yet emerged as a profession. The plan itself was part of Eaton's vision to shape society through the teaching of science and technology. Eaton himself was the ultimate popularizer of science in the best sense—a serious student with missionary zeal and a penchant for pedagogical innovation. He recognized the need to disseminate scientific knowledge in an efficient way. Both his plan for training science teachers for the public schools and his pedagogy were necessary extensions of the broader purpose of promoting scientific literacy for technological advance.

Generic skills belonging to the visual-spatial domain of learning and hands-on application were taught side by side with theory and intermediate mathematics in the early years at Rensselaer. Tradesmen, would-be engineers, and women from nearby Troy Female Seminary studied in the same classrooms, though the latter never acquired full membership in the Rensselaerean community.

Rensselaer gradually moved toward the polytechnic model of instruction, expanding from a one-year school to a three-year polytechnic model and offering subjects essential to the education of engineers. Theory and mathematics grew in importance in both curriculum and instruction. Utility remained the byword at Rensselaer, however, though critics decried its vocationalism.

Under Benjamin F. Greene, Rensselaer pursued a vision different from Eaton's. The popularization of science grew less important and the training of professional engineers moreso. Greene's plans for a true polytechic institute were not fulfilled under his direction, but they "provided a blueprint for subsequent realization, [though] not in its actual detail, but as a stimulus and objective."[51] This was the case, also, with Eaton. Though the latter's accomplishments fell far short when viewed from the standpoint of creating a true polytechnic institute, they were conspicuous and exceptional for their time.

APPENDIX: SUBJECTS CONSTITUTING THE COURSE ON CIVIL ENGINEERING AT RENSSELAER INSTITUTE

This material is from the *Catalog of Rensselaer Institute*, 1841–42, pp. 4–5, Archives and Special Collections, Rensselaer Polytechnic Institute.

1. He must be familiar with the use of the level and compass in laying out roads, McAdam roads, rail-roads, canals, etc.
2. He must be perfectly familiar with running courses, staking out, and calculating for excavations and embankments.
3. He must be familiar with casting and constructing tables of versed sines; also the principles on which tables of natural sines are calculated, constructed and used.
4. He must be familiar by practice with the calculations for filling and emptying locks, the supply of water by weight and measure which any stream will afford per second as a feeder or for any hydraulic purpose.
5. He must be familiar with taking specific gravity of materials for construction.
6. He must be familiar by practice in calculating the power which any stream of water will give per second to propelling mills, factories, or other machinery by measuring a trunk of it and its descents.

7. He must be familiar by practice in calculating for water-works; whether conveyed in pipes, boxes, or open raceways.

8. He must be familiar with statics and dynamics, hydrostatics, and hydrodynamics, so far as respects application in flumes, undershots and overshots, and descending raceways; also the velocity and efficient powers of spouting fluids, applied to driving machinery.

9. He must be familiar with the calculations of the quantity of grain ground by the rubbing areas of millstones, per minute or second.

10. He must be familiar with calculating the height of the atmosphere, (as far as density will reflect) and its pressure on liquids in cases of pumps, and in all other cases where its pressure influences mechanical operations.

11. He must be familiar with casting the heights of nimbose clouds by lightning, also of the cirrose and cirrocumulose by two stations, when the fitting of lightening rods, etc. are concerned.

12. He must be perfectly familiar taking and calculating latitude, by the sun, moon, and north star.

13. He must be familiar with taking longitude by lunar elevations, by eclipses of the sun and moon and by eclipse of Jupiter's satellites.

14. He must be perfectly familiar with taking the heights of hills and mountains, with the barometer; also with taking extemporaneous surveys and profiles with the barometer and triangular spans.

15. He must be qualified by practice to fix a transit line whenever required.

16. He must be qualified by practice to determine the variation of the needle at any time and place, and very nearly.

17. He must be qualified by practice to make a topographical survey of a State, County, &c., by fixing a base line on the [?] of a lake, river, or a natural plane of earth; also to extend surveys from the base line to the required points by triangular spans.

18. He must be qualified to change spherical areas of large districts, taken by latitude and longitude, into rectangular areas, by Mercator's method.

19. He must be a practical land surveyor, in theory and practice.

20. He must be a practical geologist, so far as to be able to make a correct report of the rocky and earthy deposits, through which he lays a canal, rail-road, &c.; also so far as to enable him to judge of inorganic materials for construction.

21. He must be so far a Botanist and botanical physiologist as to be able to judge of timer, earthy mould, &c., which [having once been organized] are subject to chemical decomposition, consequently dissolution.

22. He must be so far versed in architecture, as to be enabled to direct the construction of bridges and other works of engineering, in a comely style.

23. He must be so far familiar in plotting and business drafting as to perform all ordinary operations required in engineering. The most finished perspectives and ornamental drawings are not required of the Engineer; but are very desirable.

CONCLUSION

In the seven decades preceding the Civil War an emergent technical literacy set the stage for the rapid development of technical and scientific learning that would follow the war. This immensely creative and experimental period made it possible for educators in the postbellum period to sort, select, and apply elements of technical literacy in land grant colleges, technical institutes, and industrial schools.

Technical literacy drew heavily on Enlightenment ideals that emphasized progress through scientific learning and technological advance. Implicit in this broad view of progress were the ideals of invention and innovation, which were seen as requirements for the success of the growing manufacturing sector in the American economy. The large-scale capital investment needed to establish expanding markets was one factor in success, but that success could not be achieved without the mastery of the skills and knowledge necessary to new production techniques and new ways of organizing labor. The factory itself was a machine to organize both production and labor. Interchangeable parts, vertical integration of production stages, technological convergence, and improved power technologies all shaped the requirements for a new literacy. As metal and steam replaced wood and water, the roles of blacksmith and millwright were transformed into machinist and engineer.

As technology helped to shape both curriculum and pedagogy in mechanics' institutes and new, experimental collegiate institutions, so educator-essayists in scientific and technical journals and authors of textbooks helped to promote the values of this new literacy. Moreover, they worked to translate technical content into nontechnical, nonmathematical language, thus appealing to many more people, both male and female. Despite their noble efforts at popularization, however, educators were hampered by widespread ignorance of basic skills among their students. Many for whom their writings were intended probably remained outside their sphere of influence.

Much of the educational activity accompanying the growth of technical literacy was directed toward a broad class of workers called mechanics. The desire for upward mobility among this class shaped decisions about what skills and knowledge were needed to separate them from manufacturing operatives and to transform artisans into businessmen. In this way the issue of generic versus special skills, which was forced on educators by technological convergence, became part of debates over curriculum. Likewise, debates over the proper balance of the liberal and the technical were rooted in the aim to emulate gentlemanly learning while remaining anchored in a world of experience and hands-on learning. The tension between the liberal and the vocational continued throughout the first half of the nineteenth century.

The new world of machines which fascinated early-nineteenth-century observers of technology and advocates of mechanized labor became the object of study by serious scholars, popular lecturers, and workmen who believed that an understanding of machines was a means to upward occupational mobility. All surely understood the machine as a metaphor for progress, yet the world of machines was not accessible through traditional language skills. While adequate for descriptive purposes, verbal skills could not explain the grammar of the machine nor represent machine designs in a way that allowed mechanics to build, maintain, and repair them. Spatial thinking, the "language" of drawing, the construction of models, and the study of perspective geometry, on the other hand, helped to bridge the gap between theory and experience, between the linearity of traditional language and the nonlinearity of machines in motion. Using the skills of drawing and graphic representation, the grammar of the machine could be made accessible in a way that aided those who worked with machinery daily.

For some, the language of drawing went beyond immediate utility in the workshop or manufactory. Its language was a form of artistic expression; its utility lay in its aid to creativity and in its contribution to innovation, mechanical or otherwise. Apparatus and working models were popular for lecture demonstrations and public exhibitions and a requirement for many patent applications. More important, they allowed mechanics and inventors to compare, with an eye to improvement, their own work with that of others. Innovation was the lifeblood of technology, and the use of models was a way to share the products of new ideas.

The pedagogical innovations that paralleled technological advance in the early nineteenth century helped to set the stage for an assault on academic traditions jealously guarded by collegiate institutions. Educators in mechanics' associations and institutes and at Rensselaer Polytechnic Institute and Troy Female Seminary, for example, drew heavily on the work of Pestalozzi, as did some textbook reformers like Warren Colburn and those who advocated teaching more science in the common schools. Their challenge, however, was not simply to popularize the mysteries of science and mathematics and to make a place for technology in the revered halls of gentlemanly education. Rather, they faced the tasks of dealing with the epistemological difficulties of nineteenth-century science and making a place for the inductive methods of science alongside the deductive methods predominant in traditional language learning.

Pure deduction was ill-suited to grasping the practical significance of technological advance. Ironically, it was the basis for much of the mathematics (less so in perspective and projective geometry) that was the foundation for machine design and machine tooling. Newtonian physics had settled the issue of qualitative versus quantitative methods in natural philosophy, but it did not stop the debate over geometric versus algebraic expression. Baconian science had made the case for the utility of science, but the crude empiricism practiced by many who attacked speculative philosophy and embraced the Baconian spirit made a mockery of serious attempts to unite science using mathematics. These unresolved tensions were evident in attempts to teach science and mathematics and their technical applications.

The result of these unresolved disputes over the teaching of science and mathematics was a continuing tension in pedagogical reform itself. The hands-on pedagogy of Pestalozzi, combined with the method of induction, made a powerful case for establishing a new pedagogy based on problem solving within the context of familiar experience. The use of apparatus, including models, also helped to transfer unfamiliar, abstract knowledge into the familiar world of the visual and tactile. It was this approach that enabled educators to overcome the poor preparation in reading and mathematics under which many students labored. The catechetical format of many texts attempted to place the unfamiliar and difficult in a familiar setting while reinforcing the authority of the instructor.

The predominance of text-driven instruction in most schools probably resulted far too often in the mindless repetition of definitions and formulae. Yet this was not inevitable if texts were accompanied by practical application and field work. More difficult to overcome were the potentially incompatible objectives of mental discipline on the one hand and utility on the other. Mathematics and the study of ancient languages had long been favorite tools for developing mental discipline, though the former suffered because of poor elementary instruction. Language study was in the enviable position of being recognized as the mark of education for gentlemen.

The difficulty of uniting utility with mental discipline paralleled the tensions in pedagogical reform itself. When set side by side, Euclidean proofs and practical applications of drawing in perspective, for example, begged for some synthesis. The best that most textbook authors could offer, however, was to claim the utility of both and hope that instructors could convince skeptics that a true education embraced the eye, hand, and head. Innovative educators like Emma Willard, Amos Eaton, and Walter Johnson responded to the challenge of uniting the tactile, visual, and mental—of bridging experience and theory. They did this by promoting "active" student learning, by placing the study of science and mathematics in a technological context, and by insisting that the goals of education span the liberal and the technical.

The key to bridging the technical and liberal in the education of both men and women, however, lay only partly in the protoprogressive pedagogical reforms that recognized the developmental nature of learning. These reforms could help unite the "process" of teaching with the mastery of knowledge that was the product of instruction. Yet pedagogical reform had limits that could be overcome only by the unifying moral nature of education itself. This, indeed, was the element that made the synthesis of competing elements in technical literacy possible.

The Franklinesque mission of mechanics' associations and institutes made them an ideal setting for uniting the technical, liberal, and moral in education. The praxis of science, craft, and art was easily subsumed under the purpose of upward occupational mobility. The morality of aspiration, the spirit of emulation, and the importance of innovation to technological progress all were wedded to the ideals of a more inclusive citizenship that paid tribute to progress and democracy.

Certainly the new vision of citizenship that incorporated both old elements of the craft tradition and the new role of artisan-entrepreneur was a male prerogative in most instances. The message of citizenship to women who attended evening lectures was limited by their traditional occupational and social roles. As mothers of sons who would eventually participate in the political and economic progress that would result from technological advance, they played important moral and nurturing roles. But only in this restricted sense were they participants in a community that defined itself, in part, by a mastery of technical knowledge.

At both Rensselaer Polytechnic Institute and Troy Female Seminary women were part of the new community. Their role was defined and limited by traditional occupational roles and a gender-based social division of labor. Like their counterparts who attended evening lectures, they possessed a knowledge that was qualitatively different from that acquired by manufacturing operatives. At Rensselaer and Troy Female Seminary, however, the level of mastery of technical, scientific, and mathematical knowledge was probably far greater than that of those who relied on evening lectures. At both institutions it was clear that women were seen as partners in business enterprise. The partnerships were not equal, to be sure, but they were premised on the assumption that women were capable of mental discipline and could understand the practical, technical consequences of studying science and mathematics.

Technical literacy spanned the two great domains of knowledge in nineteenth-century America: natural and moral philosophy. It belonged *to* them in the sense that part of its knowledge was rooted in their precepts and laws. From natural philosophy and mathematics technical literacy borrowed an understanding of the secrets of nature and the special notational systems needed to express them. From moral philosophy and from the thematic content of natural philosophy it borrowed a conception of natural law that included God's will and a vision of man's nature that was essentially moral. It transcended natural and moral philosophy, however, in both scope and practice. The recognition of the different languages and their associated grammars allowed for a synthesis of different academic disciplines. This is not to say that the synthesis was entirely successful. It was experimental, and the problems were monumental. Yet in the pedagogy and curriculum of new institutions, experiments to unite liberal and technical learning were carried out successfully. Moreover, these same experiments set important precedents for the great institution building that followed the Civil War.

It was in the moral domain of knowledge that the recognition and achievement of technical literacy made its most lasting impact. The mastery of scientific, mathematical, technical, and moral knowledge envisioned by advocates of technical literacy helped to buttress and perpetuate the cultural predispositions rooted in late-eighteenth-century Enlightenment thought. These included the view that progress was both a technical and moral matter; that is, technological advance was both a moral and intellectual obligation. The justification for these new obligations lay in the concept of progress itself. The widely shared view of progress as a moral certainty in the nineteenth century was the answer of the new democracy to its skeptics. It was a moral certainty that cut across both the political and economic dimensions of American society. Progress as a moral certainty did not, of course, prevent labor strife on the horizon, nor the regional conflicts that would erupt with the Civil War. Yet this vision of progress was so comprehensive, so compelling, and so firmly tied to technological advance that it assured the triumph of a vision that linked moral certainty to the fortunes of democracy and technology.

Notes

Introduction

1. See Arthur A. Ekrich, Jr., *The Idea of Progress in America, 1815–1860* (New York: Columbia University Press, 1944).

2. Myron C. Tuman, *A Preface to Literacy: An Inquiry into Pedagogy, Practice and Progress* (Tuscaloosa: University of Alabama Press, 1987), 172.

3. Daniel Resnick, "What Does It Mean to Be Literate?" (paper presented at the Pittsburgh Symposium: First Biennial Conference on Social History, 10–11 May 1988, Pittsburgh).

4. John Craig, "An Address Delivered at a Meeting of the Citizens of Cincinnati Convened for the Purpose of Forming a Mechanics' Institute" (Cincinnati: Ohio Mechanics' Institute, 1829), 17.

5. Hugo A. Meier, "Technology and Democracy, 1800–1860," *Mississippi Valley Historical Review* 43, no. 4 (June 1956): 619.

6. Edwin Layton, Jr., "Technology as Knowledge," *Technology and Culture* 15 (January 1974): 37; and Eugene Ferguson, "Elegant Inventions: The Artistic Component of Technology," *Technology and Culture* 19 (July 1978): 460.

7. George H. Daniels, *Science in American Society; A Social History* (New York: Knopf, 1971), 157.

8. John B. Rae, "The 'Know-How' Tradition: Technology in American History," *Technology and Culture* 1 (Spring 1960): 142. Modeling the historical relation of technology to science was the topic of a group of essays in *Technology and Culture* 6 (Fall 1965): 547–620.

Chapter 1: Empirical Foundations for Technical Literacy

1. Douglas C. North, *The Economic Growth of the United States, 1790–1860* (New York: W. W. Norton, 1966), 189, 197–98, 208.

2. Ibid., 172.

3. This is so despite Ferguson's objection that it was the ironmonger, not the millwright, who was the predecessor of the engineer (Eugene S. Ferguson, "The Origins of the Steam Engine," *Scientific American*, January 1964, 101).

4. Louis C. Hunter, *A History of Industrial Power in the United States, 1780–1930*, vol. 1: *Waterpower in the Century of the Steam Engine* (Charlottesville: University Press of Virginia, 1979), 92, 93, 160–63, 167. This method of trial and error, used by many millwrights, may be contrasted with that of the French (most notably Poncelet, Burdin, Morin, and Fourneyron), whose studies of water power always remained closely allied with French academics, particularly the Ecole Polytechnique, which provided college education for engineers. See Edwin T. Layton, Jr., "Millwrights and Engineers, Science, Social Roles, and the Evolution of the Turbine in America," in *The Dynamics of Science and Technology, Social Values, Technical Norms and Scientific Criteria in the Development of Knowledge*, ed. Wolfgang Krohn, Edwin T. Layton, Jr., and Peter Weingart (Dordrecht: D. Reidel, 1978), 64. According to Hunter, "wheel efficiency in using the available supply of water; higher rotating speeds; adaptability of a wheel to use with a wide range of heads; and ability to operate submerged" were critical improvements in wheel design (293).

5. Ibid., 95.

6. Ibid., 95–96.

7. Oliver Evans, *The Young-Millwright and Miller's Guide* (reprint, New York: Arno Press, 1972), 23, 29.

8. Layton, "Millwrights and Engineers," 67.

9. Layton used the case study of the Parker Brothers to illustrate the different conceptualization of how reaction wheels (turbines) operate. The French, including Fourneyron, tried to achieve "shockless" entry of the water into the wheel. American millwrights, on the other hand, focused on the impulse of the water; for them the object in constructing efficient waterwheels was not to reduce but to increase the impulse of the water as it hit the wheel. Thus the French and Americans came to opposite conclusions about the "proper" entry of water into the reaction wheel. For the French "the essence of the problem was that the effective angle of tangent varied with the speed of the wheel." Once the speed of the wheel was known, the angle could be calculated (Layton, "Millwrights and Engineers," 65–66).

10. Hunter, *Waterpower in the Century of the Steam Engine*, 303–6.

11. Ibid., 313–22. See also Robert V. Bruce, *The Launching of Modern American Science, 1846–1876* (Ithaca, N.Y.: Cornell University Press, 1987), 156. Reports of the Fourneyron turbine appeared in the *Journal of the Franklin Institute* in 1831.

12. The extent of the Lowell project was immense. See Patrick M. Malone, *Canals and Industry: Engineering in Lowell, 1821–1880* (Lowell, Mass.: Lowell Museum, 1983), 5–10.

13. Among those who developed their ideas were Asa Swain, James Leffel, and John B. McCormick (Layton, "Millwrights and Engineers," 79, 82).

14. Louis C. Hunter, *A History of Industrial Power in the United States, 1780–1930*, vol. 2: *Steam Power* (Charlottesville: University Press of Virginia, 1985), 169–70, 173.

15. Ibid., 246–47. For the external factors influencing the use of the stationary steam engine and regional economies see *Steam Power*, 60–61, 84, 92.

16. Ibid., 252.

17. Ibid., 19, 21, 26.

18. Henry Voight to William Thornton, 29 June 1809. Quoted from Thompson West-cott, *The Life of John Fitch, the Inventor of the Steamboat* (Philadelphia, 1857), 306, in Carroll W. Purcell, Jr., *Early Stationary Steam Engines in America; A Study in the Migration of a Technology* (Washington, D.C.: Smithsonian Institution Press, 1969), 20–21.

19. Hunter, *Steam Power*, 127.

20. Ibid., 81–82.

21. Ibid., 83–84, 126, 176, 186, 201–10.

22. H. W. Dickinson, *A Short History of the Steam Engine* (New York: Augustius M. Kelley, 1966), 92. The conventional mill engine used a small diameter cylinder with a long stroke. The beams that had long served to balance the movement of the engine were replaced by a direct connection (connecting rod) between crosshead and crank, and cutoffs that could make use of the "expansive" steam were employed in a limited way. From 1850 to 1880 the automatic valve cutoff engine was pioneered, most notably by Corliss and by Charles T. Porter and John F. Allen. Allen invented the Porter-Allen engine, which was characterized by greater efficiency, fuel economy, and uniformity of motion (Hunter, *Steam Power*, 123–24, 130.)

23. Ibid., 125–26, 152–55.

24. Ibid., 151, 263.

25. Carroll W. Purcell, Jr., *Early Stationary Steam Engines in America; A Study in the Migration of a Technology* (Washington, D.C.: Smithsonian Institution Press, 1969), 94–95, 107.

26. Edwin T. Freedley, *Philadelphia and Its Manufactures: A Hand Book Exhibiting the Development, Variety, and Statistics of the Manufacturing Industry of Philadelphia in 1857; together with Sketches of Remarkable Manufactories; and a List of Articles Now Made in Philadelphia* (Philadelphia: Edward Young, 1858), 30–31.

27. Bruce Sinclair, *Philadelphia's Philosopher Mechanics; A History of the Franklin Institute, 1824–1865* (Baltimore: Johns Hopkins University Press, 1974), 172.

28. David J. Jeremy, "Innovation in American Textile Technology During the Early Nineteenth Century," *Technology and Culture* 14, no. 1 (January 1973): 46, 74. Jeremy has focused on the nature of technology as a determinant of the direction of innovation. See also H. J. Habakkuk, *American and British Technology in the Nineteenth Century; The Search for Labor-Saving Inventions* (Cambridge: Cambridge University Press, 1967), 24–26, 31.

29. Jeremy, "Innovation in American Textile Technology," 57. See also David J. Jeremy, *Transatlantic Industrial Revolution: The Diffusion of Textile Technologies Between Britain and America, 1790–1830s* (Oxford: Basil Blackwell, 1981), 180, 253.

30. Nathan Rosenberg, *Perspectives on Technology* (Cambridge: Cambridge University Press, 1976), 54. Perhaps the most famous example of American vertical integration occurred in woolen manufacturing with the adoption of the ring condenser that solved the problem of producing a "continuous sliver from the end of the carding machine" (56).

31. George Sweet Gibb, *The Saco-Lowell Shops: Textile Machinery Building in New England, 1813–1949* (Cambridge: Harvard University Press, 1950), 10–12.

32. Ibid., 168–69, 171.

33. Gibb, *Saco-Lowell Shops*, 35.

34. Ibid.

35. Ibid., 36–37, 39.

36. *The Manufactories and Manufacturers of Pennsylvania of the Nineteenth Century* (Philadelphia: Galaxy, 1875), 6–9, 16.

37. See Paul Uselding, "Measuring Techniques and Manufacturing," in *Yankee Enterprise: The Rise of the American System of Manufactures*, ed. Otto Mayr and Robert C. Post (Washington, D.C.: Smithsonian Institution Press, 1984), 105.

38. Rosenberg, *Perspectives on Technology*, 12.

39. Ibid., 15–16.

40. Nathan Rosenberg, "Why in America?" in Mayr and Post, *Yankee Enterprise*, 57–59.

41. For analyses see Robert S. Woodbury, "History of the Milling Machine," in Woodbury, *Studies in the History of Machine Tools* (Cambridge: MIT Press, 1972); and Rosenberg, *Perspectives on Technology*, 17, 19–20.

42. On the gradual decline of the apprenticeship system see W. J. Rorabaugh, *The Craft Apprentice: From Franklin to the Machine Age in America* (New York: Oxford University Press, 1986). Rorabaugh analyzes the effects of economic dislocation following the Revolutionary War, the broad dissemination of printed technical information, and the cash wage on the apprenticeship system.

43. Anthony F. G. Wallace, *Rockdale: The Growth of an American Village in the Early Industrial Revolution* (New York: W. W. Norton, 1978), 150.

44. Ibid., 147–48.

45. Eugene S. Ferguson, ed., *Early Engineering Reminiscences (1815–40) of George Escol Sellers* (Washington, D.C.: Smithsonian Institution Press, 1965), 27.

46. Ibid., 48.

47. For the essential design features of the lathe in the nineteenth century see Robert S. Woodbury, *History of the Lathe to 1850; A Study in the Growth of a Technical Element of an Industrial Economy*, Monograph Series no. 1 (Cleveland: Society for the History of Technology, 1961), 58–60. See also F. N. Zagorski, *An Outline of the History of Metal Cutting Machines to the Middle of the Nineteenth Century*, trans. and ed. Edwin A. Battison (New Delhi: Amerind Publishing, 1982), 255; and David Wilkinson, "Reminiscences," in Carroll W. Purcell, Jr., *Readings in Technology and American Life* (New York: Oxford University Press, 1969), 46.

48. Robert S. Woodbury, "History of the Gearcutting Machine," in Woodbury, *Studies in the History of Machine Tools* (Cambridge: MIT Press, 1972), 3.

49. Penrose R. Hoopes, *Connecticut Clockmakers of the Eighteenth Century* (Hartford: Edwin Valentine Mitchell, 1930), 4, 23, 25; Chauncey Jerome, *History of the American Clock Business* (New Haven: F. C. Dayton, Jr., 1860); and Penrose R. Hoopes, ed., *Shop Records of Daniel Burnap, Clockmaker* (Hartford: Connecticut Historical Society, 1958), 109.

50. L. T. C. Rolt, *Tools for the Job: A History of Machine Tools to 1950* (London: Her Majesty's Stationery Office, 1986), 136.

51. David A. Hounshell, *From the American System to Mass Production, 1800–1932: The Development of Manufacturing Technology in the United States* (Baltimore: Johns Hopkins University Press, 1984), 26.

52. Merritt Roe Smith, *Harpers Ferry Armory and the New Technology* (Ithaca, N.Y.: Cornell University Press, 1977), 106–7.

53. On the history of the American system see Nathan Rosenberg, *The American System of Manufactures* (Edinburgh: Edinburgh University Press, 1969); David A. Hounshell, "From the American System to Mass Production: The Development of Manufacturing Technology in the United States, 1850–1920" (Ph.D. diss., University of Delaware, 1978); and Hounshell, *American System*. An excellent bibliography on the American system is in Mayr and Post, *Yankee Enterprise*.

54. Smith, *Harpers Ferry Armory*, 105–7, 207; L. T. C. Rolt, *Tools for the Job*, 151; R. S. Woodbury, "The Legend of Eli Whitney," *Technology and Culture* 1, no. 3 (1960). On the degree of interchangeability see Charles H. Fitch, "Report on the Manufactures of Interchangeable Mechanism, 1. The Manufacture of Fire Arms," *Report on the Manufactures of the United States at the Tenth Census* (1880), vol. 2 (Washington: Government Printing Office, 1883).

55. Donald Hoke, *Ingenious Yankees: The Rise of the American System of Manufactures in the Private Sector* (New York: Columbia University Press, 1990), 12.

56. Ibid., 12, 45. Hounshell maintains that "the degree of precision in wooden clock-making is so far removed from that required in small arms production that the two cannot be compared" (56, 60).

57. Hounshell, *American System*, 25–29, 42, 157–59.

58. Ibid., 41–42.

59. Interchangeability was primitive by twentieth-century standards, and the "roughness of interchangeability" was a concept well understood by nineteenth-century manufacturers. Adjustments were expected in the finished product, and the more complex the item, the more adjustments were needed (Hoke, *Ingenious Yankees*, 31, 33). In the late-eighteenth and early-nineteenth centuries, uniformity meant a tolerance of one thirty-second of an inch, whereas in 1880 it meant a tolerance of a thousandth of an inch (Fitch, "Report on the Manufactures of Interchangeable Mechanism, 1. The Manufacture of Fire Arms," 2, 6). Fitch's retrospective assessment is a necessary correction of the unfettered enthusiasm of men like John Hall.

60. For a comprehensive treatment of the later managerial revolution in American manufacturing, transportation, and communication see Alfred D. Chandler, *The Visible Hand: The Managerial Revolution in American Business* (Cambridge: Harvard University Press, 1977).

61. For definitional problems of the American system see Eugene S. Ferguson, "History and Historiography," in Mayr and Post, *Yankee Enterprise*. On the social basis of the American system see John E. Sawyer, "The Social Basis of the American System of Manufacturing," *Journal of Economic History* 14 (1954): 361–79; and David Pye, *The Nature and Aesthetics of Design* (London: Barrie and Jenkins, 1978), 33.

62. Smith, *Harpers Ferry Armory*, 240–41.

63. Susan E. Hirsch, *The Roots of the American Working Class: The Industrialization of Crafts in Newark, 1800–1860* (Philadelphia: University of Pennsylvania Press, 1978), 11, 21–22.

64. Robert F. Seybolt, *Apprenticeship and Apprenticeship Education in Colonial New England and New York* (New York: Columbia University, Teachers College Press, 1917), 96–98.

65. W. J. Rorabaugh, *The Craft Apprentice: From Franklin to the Machine Age in America* (New York: Oxford University Press, 1986), 136–39; and Lee Soltow and

Edward Stevens, *The Rise of Literacy and the Common School in the United States: A Socioeconomic Analysis to 1870* (Chicago: University of Chicago Press, 1981), 70–74, 136.

66. Ibid., 158–61.

67. Rex Burns, *Success in America: The Yeoman Dream and the Industrial Revolution* (Amherst: University of Massachusetts, 1976), 93.

68. Kornblith, *Artisans to Businessmen*, 133.

69. Rorabaugh, *Craft Apprentice*, 33–36.

70. Ibid., 63.

71. Ibid., 151.

72. Ibid., 144.

73. Barbara Mayer Wertheimer, *We Were There: The Story of Working Women in America* (New York: Pantheon Books, 1977), 85–86.

74. Mary H. Blewett, *Men, Women, and Work, Class, Gender, and Protest in the New England Shoe Industry, 1780–1910* (Urbana: University of Illinois Press, 1988), 70; Mary H. Blewett, "The Sexual Division of Labor and the Artisan Tradition in Early Industrial Capitalism: The Case of New England Shoemaking, 1780–1860," in Carol Groneman and Mary Beth Norton, eds., *To Toil the Livelong Day, America's Women at Work, 1780–1980* (Ithaca, N.Y.: Cornell University Press, 1987), 37–39.

75. For the experience of young women outside Waltham and Lowell see Barbara Mayer Wertheimer, *We Were There*, 53–54; and Louise Lamphere, *From Working Daughters to Working Mothers: Immigrant Women in a New England Industrial Community* (Ithaca, N.Y.: Cornell University Press, 1987), 53–54.

76. Harriet H. Robinson, *Loom and Spindle, or Life Among the Early Mill Girls* (Kailua, Hawaii: Press Pacifica, 1976), 8–9.

77. Lamphere, *From Working Daughters to Working Mothers*, 58.

78. Carl Siracusa, *A Mechanical People, Perceptions of the Industrial Order in Massachusetts, 1815–1880* (Middletown, Conn.: Wesleyan University Press, 1979), 69.

79. *Lowell Offering*, series 1, no. 2 (October 1840–March 1841): 25.

80. Robinson, *Loom and Spindle*, 26.

81. Ibid., 146.

82. Julianna, "The Evils of Factory Life," in *Factory Tracts, Factory Life as It Is* (Lowell, Mass.: Female Labor Reform Association, 1845; reprint, Lowell Publishing Co., 1982), no. 1 (October 1845): 4.

Chapter 2: The Content and Pedagogy for Spatial Thinking

1. John A. Kouwenhoven, "American Studies: Words or Things?" in *Material Culture Studies in America*, ed. Thomas J. Schlereth (Nashville: American Association for State and Local History, 1982), 84; Peter Caws, "Praxis and Technē," in *The History and Philosophy of Technology*, ed. George Bugliarello and Dean B. Doner (Urbana: University of Illinois Press, 1979), 227. See also Doblin, quoted in Charles L. Owen, "Technology, Literacy, and Graphic Systems," in *Toward a New Understanding of Literacy*, ed. Merald E. Wrolsted and Dennis F. Fisher (New York: Praeger, 1986), 167.

2. Olson and Bialystok remind us that "meanings represent the intentions, purposes, and goals of the perceiver, [as perhaps communicated in traditional verbal form,] while the structural descriptions of objects reflect the properties appropriate to assigning the

object . . . meaning" (David R. Olson and Ellen Bialystok, *Spatial Cognition: The Structure and Development of Mental Representations of Spatial Relations* [Hillsdale, N.J.: Lawrence Erlbaum, 1983], 21).

3. Doblin, quoted in Owen, "Technology, Literacy, and Graphic Systems," 167.

4. Eugene S. Ferguson, "The Mind's Eye: Nonverbal Thought in Technology," *Science* 197 (26 August 1977): 827–28.

5. Hindle notes that in the late eighteenth century "most mechanics lacked an extended verbal education; their craft heritage encouraged secrecy; and their work was primarily a series of exercises in spatial thinking, not talking." Good machine design, like portrait painting, says Hindle, required a "sense of overall spatial design" (Brooke Hindle, *Emulation and Invention* [New York: New York University Press, 1981], 34, 83, 138).

6. Ibid., 133.

7. David Pye, *The Nature and Aesthetics of Design* (London: Barrie and Jenkins, 1978), 27, 33, 37.

8. The importance of spatial thinking to others involved with the evolution of the steam engine and the science of kinematics is also well documented. See Eugene S. Ferguson, *Kinematics of Mechanisms from the Time of Watt, Contributions from the Museum of History and Technology*, no. 27, bull. 228 (Washington, D.C.: Smithsonian Institution, 1962).

9. Ibid., 191, 195, 197–98. Watt was aware of Matthew Wasbrough's crank patent (which actually used "racks with teeth" and a system of wheels and pulleys) but "remained unconvinced of the superiority of the crank over other devices and did not immediately appreciate the regulating ability of a flywheel" (192; see Henry W. Dickinson and Rhys Jenkins, *James Watt and the Steam Engine* [Oxford: Clarendon, 1927], 150, 154).

10. Watt's parallel motion linkage was the first of many four-bar linkages developed during the next one hundred years (Ferguson, *Kinematics of Mechanism*, 199). R. S. Hartenberg's discussion of the vectorial representation of complex numbers and its application to calculating the angular velocity and acceleration in four-bar linkages is technical but helpful even for the nonengineer. The calculations are beyond the skills of the uninitiated, but his explanation and drawings clearly demonstrate the kinematics of the four-bar linkage (R. S. Hartenberg, "Complex Numbers and Four-Bar Linkages," *Machine Design* 30 [20 March 1958]: 156–63). For an interesting technical but not mathematically sophisticated account on linkages used to "describe" a straight line see A. B. Kempe, "How to Draw a Straight Line; A Lecture on Linkages" (1877) in *Squaring the Circle and Other Monographs* (New York: Chelsea Publishing, 1953).

11. Ferguson, *Kinematics of Mechanisms*, 209.

12. Hachette's classification included the elementary motions of continuous circular, alternating circular, continuous rectilinear, and alternating rectilinear motions. These elementary motions could be combined to produce complex motions. Others filled the gaps and modified Hachette's scheme—Lanz and Betancourt by adding continuous and alternating curvilinear motion; Borgnis by classifying machine elements into classes. Borgnis' six orders of machine elements are "recepteurs (receivers of motion from the prime mover), comunicateurs, modificateurs (modifiers of velocity), supports (for example, bearings), regulateurs [governors], and operateurs (which produced the final effect)" (Ferguson, *Kinematics of Mechanisms*, 209–11).

13. Robert Willis was Jacksonian Professor of natural and experimental philosophy

and author of *Principles of Mechanism* (1841). He was convinced that the designer of machines could be more efficient if he understood the mathematics of motion and reduced motion to general formulae (Ferguson, *Kinematics of Mechanisms*, 212–13). William Rankine was professor of civil engineering at the University of Glasgow; he published *Manual of Machinery and Millwork* in 1869. He extended Willis' analysis and applied the concept of "instant centers" to velocity analysis. See Gernot Bohme et al., "The Scientification of Technology," in *The Dynamics of Science and Technology, Social Values, Technical Norms and Scientific Criteria in the Development of Knowledge*, ed. Wolfgang Krohn, Edwin T. Layton, Jr., and Peter Weingart (Dordrecht, Netherlands: D. Reidel, 1978).

14. Ferguson, *Kinematics of Mechanisms*, 216.

15. Eugene Ferguson, "On the Origin and Development of American Mechanical Know-How," *Midcontinent American Studies Journal* 3 (Fall 1962): 8, 10.

16. Peter Jeffrey Booker, *A History of Engineering Drawing* (London: Chatto and Windus, 1963), 140.

17. The implications of the spatial-visual component of vernacular expression for aesthetic theory appeared in Horatio Greenough, *The Travels, Observations, and Experience of a Yankee Stonecutter* (1852). Greenough linked the functional forms admired by mechanics and engineers to a metaphysics and theology that celebrated one truth in art. His was, notes Kouwenhoven, the "first reasoned defense of the vernacular in the arts" (John A. Kouwenhoven, *Made in America: The Arts in Modern Civilization* [Newton Centre, Mass.: Charles T. Branford, 1948], 108).

18. "Mechanism," *Scientific American* 7, no. 5 (18 October 1851): 38.

19. "Artist of the Ideal and Real; or Poets and Inventors," *Scientific American* 4, no. 14 (23 December 1848): 107.

20. Anthony Wallace, *Rockdale: The Growth of an American Village in the Early Industrial Revolution* (New York: Knopf, 1978), 238–39.

21. Ibid., 189, 238.

22. Kouwenhoven, "American Studies," 83.

23. Ibid., 84.

24. David R. Olson and Jerome S. Bruner, "Learning Through Experience and Learning Through Media," in *Media and Symbols: The Forms of Expression, Communication, and Education*, 73rd yearbook of the National Society for the Study of Education, ed. David R. Olson (Chicago: University of Chicago Press, 1974), 126.

25. Edwin T. Layton, Jr., "Technology as Knowledge," *Technology and Culture* 15 (January 1974): 32.

26. Harley Parker, "The Beholder's Share and the Problem of Literacy," in *Media and Symbols*, pt. 1, 94.

27. Caws, "Praxis and Technē," 227.

28. Ibid., 231.

29. Ferguson, *Reminiscences*, 40. See also Eugene Ferguson, "On the Origin and Development of American Mechanical Know-How," *Midcontinent American Studies Journal* 3 (Fall 1962): 8, 10.

30. Ferguson, *Reminiscences*, 49.

31. Ibid., 169, 170–71.

32. Ibid., 169.

33. Ibid., 170.

34. Ibid.

35. Ibid.

36. Ibid., 170–71.

37. Carroll W. Purcell, Jr., *Early Stationary Steam Engines in America; A Study of the Migration of a Technology* (Washington, D.C.: Smithsonian Institution Press, 1969), 126.

38. "On the Importance of Drawing to Mechanics," *Journal of the Franklin Institute* 2 (September 1826): 190.

39. Ibid.

40. "On the Rise and Progress of the Franklin Institute," *Franklin Journal and American Mechanics' Magazine* 1 (March 1826): 131.

41. Walter R. Johnson, "On the Utility of Visible Illustrations," *American Annals of Education and Instruction* 3, no. 3 (March 1833): 101, 103, 111.

42. T. D. S., "How to Study a Drawing," *Greenough's American Polytechnic Journal* 3 (January–June 1854): 77; and J. J. G. [J. J. Greenough], "Book Notice," *Greenough's American Polytechnic Journal* 2 (July–December 1853): 240.

43. "Plan of Study and Instruction in the State Normal School at Bridgewater, Massachusetts," *Nineteenth Annual Report of Education of Massachusetts* (1856), 18–19.

44. "Instruction in Drawing," *American Journal of Education* 4 (1857): 230.

45. *American Journal of Education* 1 (1826): 87, 91.

46. *Common School Journal* 1 (15 January 1839): 18–21.

47. J. S. Buckingham, "On the Principles, Means, and Ends of Education," *Common School Assistant* 3 (May 1838): 59; and J. S. Buckingham, "Drawing," *Common School Assistant* 3 (August 1838): 34.

48. "Writing and Drawing," *Common School Journal* 6 (15 April 1844): 133.

49. Buckingham borrowed many of his ideas from Cousin's *Report on Common School Education in Holland*. Buckingham, "On the Principles, Means, and Ends of Education," 59; J. S. Buckingham, "Drawing," 34.

50. *Common School Assistant* 3 (May 1838): 34. See also *Common School Assistant* 3 (August 1838): 59; and *Common School Assistant* 4 (July 1839): 49–50.

51. *Common School Journal* 6 (15 April 1844): 133. On the techniques of teaching drawing see "Drawing," *Common School Journal* 6 (15 June 1844): 198–200.

52. [Horace Mann], "Writing and Drawing," *Common School Journal* 6 (15 April 1844): 134.

53. R. Dagley, *A Compendium of the Theory and Practice of Drawing and Painting*, 2nd ed. (London: G. and W. B. Whittaker, 1822), xi. (When two dates follow titles in text, as they do here, the earliest edition is listed first, followed by the edition used for citation.)

54. Baron Charles Dupin, *Mathematics Practically Applied to the Useful and Fine Arts*, adapted by George Birkbeck (London: Charles and William Tait, 1827), i, ii, v, vi.

55. Ibid., xv.

56. William J. Whitaker, *A Progressive Course of Inventive Drawing on the Principles of Pestalozzi* (Boston: William J. Whitaker, 1851), 6.

57. A. Cornu, *Course of Linear Drawing, Applied to the Drawing of Machinery and Other Constructions* (Philadelphia: J. Dobson, 1842), 7.

58. *American Journal of Education* 4, no. 2 (March–April 1829): 97–107.

59. "General Education," *Mechanics' Magazine and Register of Inventions and Improvements* 1 (May 1833): 241.

60. Maria Edgeworth and R. L. Edgeworth, *Essays on Practical Education, A New*

Edition in Two Volumes, vol. 1 (London: R. Hunter, 1815). My comments on the chapter titled "Toys" are based on the 1815 edition. Comments on mechanics are based on the 1835 edition.

61. J. R. Edgeworth, "Description of a Cheap, Simple, and Portable Instrument for Determining the Positions of Objects in Taking a Picture from the Life," *Emporium of Arts and Sciences* 2 (February 1813): 259–61.

62. M. Francoeur, *An Introduction to Linear Drawing,* trans. William B. Fowle (Boston: Hilliard, Gray, Little, and Wilkins, 1828), iv.

63. Rembrandt Peale, *Graphics; A Popular System of Drawing and Writing for the Use of Schools and Families* (Philadelphia: C. Sherman, 1841), 8–9, 12.

64. Ibid., 13.

65. Ibid., 22–23.

66. Ibid., 12, 16, 31.

67. *Common School Drawing Master, Containing Schmid's Practical Perspective* (Boston: E. P. Peabody, 1846), iii. The review of Schmid's work is found in *Common School Journal* 5 (15 August 1843): 241. The last name is spelled "Schmidt" in the review.

68. Schmid, *Common School Drawing Master,* 7–8.

69. Ibid.

70. "Instruction in Drawing," 229–32.

71. *Journal of the Franklin Institute* 20 (August 1837): 148.

72. "Young Mechanics—The Way to Rise," *Scientific American* 6 (24 May 1851): 285.

73. For statutory requirements see *United States Statutes at Large* 1 (1793): 318–22; *United States Statutes at Large* 5 (1836): 117–25; *United States Statutes at Large* 12 (1861): 246–49. See also Bruce W. Bugbee, *Genesis of American Patent and Copyright Law* (Washington, D.C.: Public Affairs Press, 1967); Robert C. Post, "'Liberalizers' versus 'Scientific Men' in the Antebellum Patent Office," *Technology and Culture* 17, no. 1 (January 1976): 24–54; Christopher Baer, *Little Machines: Patent Models in the Nineteenth Century* (Greensville, Del.: Hagley Museum, 1979); Daniel Preston, "The Administration and Reform of the U.S. Patent Office, 1790–1836," *Journal of the Early Republic* 5 (Fall 1985): 331–53. For examples of the use of models by inventors and experimenters see John Banks, *A Treatise on Mills, in Four Parts* (London: W. Richardson, 1795); Greville Bache and Dorothy Bache, *Oliver Evans, A Chronicle of Early American Engineering* (Philadelphia: Historical Society of Pennsylvania, 1935); John Fitch, *The Autobiography of John Fitch,* ed. Frank D. Prager (Philadelphia: American Philosophical Society, 1976). Valuable primary sources include the many petitions of inventors that are stored in the Patent Extension Files of the United States Archives and the running commentary and controversy in *Scientific American.*

74. Fitch, *Autobiography,* 170.

75. "Demonstrations by Means of Models," *Journal of the Franklin Institute* 14, 3rd ser. (1847): 44.

76. "Mechanics Institutes," *Scientific American* 2 (5 June 1847): 293.

77. Maria Edgeworth and R. L. Edgeworth, *Essays on Practical Education* 1 (London, 1815), 30–31.

78. Ibid.

79. "Review of J. R. Young, *The Elements of Mechanics,*" *Journal of the Franklin Institute* 24 (July 1834): 19.

80. Robert Brunton, *A Compendium of Mechanics or Text Book for Engineers, Mill-*

wrights, Machine Makers, Founders, Smiths, etc. . . . (New York: G. and C. and H. Carvill, 1830), 206–7.

81. Ibid., 228.

CHAPTER 3: THE HERITAGE OF NATURAL PHILOSOPHY, MATHEMATICS, AND PERSPECTIVE GEOMETRY

1. Things concerned with "sensible matter" were subsumed under natural philosophy, and the eight books of Aristotle's *Physics* were the primary subject matter. Their organization for instructional purposes was Aristotle's *libri naturalis*, a method of classification that distinguished natural philosophy from both mathematics and metaphysics (Quentin Skinner and Eckhard Kessler, eds., *Cambridge History of Renaissance Philosophy* [Cambridge: Cambridge University Press, 1988], 202).

2. *Library of Useful Knowledge* (London: Baldwin and Cradock, 1829), s.v. "natural philosophy," 14.

3. Gerald Holton, "The Thematic Imagination in Science," in *Science and Culture; A Study of Cohesive and Disjunctive Forces*, ed. Gerald Holton (Boston: Beacon Press, 1965), 104.

4. Gerald Holton, *Thematic Origins of Scientific Thought, Kepler to Einstein* (Cambridge: Harvard University Press, 1973), 53, 76; and Morris Kline, *Mathematics, The Loss of Certainty* (New York: Oxford University Press, 1980), 65.

5. Carl L. Becker, *The Heavenly City of the Eighteenth Century Philosophers* (New Haven: Yale University Press, 1932), 47, 53, 57, 64.

6. Graham Rees, "Mathematics and Francis Bacon's Natural Philosophy," *Revue Internationale de Philosophie* 159, no. 4 (1986): 404–5.

7. Ibid., 404.

8. Jerry Weinberger, *Science, Faith, and Politics: Francis Bacon and the Utopian Roots of the Modern Age* (Ithaca, N.Y.: Cornell University Press, 1985), 180.

9. Ibid., 181.

10. Benjamin Farrington, *Francis Bacon, Philosopher of Industrial Science* (New York: Henry Schuman, 1951), 44.

11. Anthony F. C. Wallace, *The Social Context of Innovation, Bureaucrats, Families, and Heroes in the Early Industrial Revolution, as Foreseen in Bacon's New Atlantis* (Princeton: Princeton University Press, 1982), 20–21.

12. Farrington, *Francis Bacon*, 45, 69, 94, 109.

13. Quoted in Farrington, *Francis Bacon*, 98–99.

14. Ibid., 122, 136.

15. Bacon saw mathematics as a branch of metaphysics rather than physics (Rees, "Mathematics," 402–7).

16. Rees, "Mathematics," 413.

17. Ibid., 115–17.

18. George H. Daniels, *American Science in the Age of Jackson* (New York: Columbia University Press, 1968), 51–55.

19. Ibid., 63–65.

20. Robert V. Bruce, *The Launching of Modern American Science, 1846–1876* (Ithaca, N.Y.: Cornell University Press, 1987), 68–69, 104.

21. Daniels, *American Science*, 69, 71, 76–77.

22. Bruce, *Modern American Science*, 120.

23. Daniels, *American Science*, 164–65, 167, 168.

24. Ibid., 168, 177, 183, 185.

25. Morris Kline, *Mathematics for the Nonmathematician* (New York: Dover, 1985), 336. See also Lloyd Motz and Jefferson Hane Weaver, *The Story of Physics* (New York: Plenum, 1989), 89.

26. Morris Kline, *Mathematics: The Loss of Certainty* (New York: Oxford University Press, 1980), 54.

27. Mathematics was more than a language for Newton; it was a conceptual representation (Kline, *Mathematics*, 57). Though his grand mechanical design was described mathematically, Newton had still anchored his system to a belief that "no hypothesis can be tolerated which is contrary to a single bit of evidence" and to " 'real' measurable quantities, such as space, time, force, and mass" (Kline, *Nonmathematician*, 338; Motz and Weaver, *Story of Physics*, 118).

28. A. Rupert Hall, *From Galileo to Newton* (New York: Dover, 1981), 101.

29. Max Jammer, *Concepts of Space, The History of Theories of Space in Physics*, 2nd ed. (Cambridge: Harvard University Press, 1969), 96–100. The difficulty of referring space, its attributes, and its relation to sense perception plagued mathematicians and physicists alike long before Newton. In Pythagorean geometry space has no "physical implications" apart from serving as the limiting agent between different bodies. For Aristotle space was a continuous quantity. The concept of absolute space was indispensable to Newton's system even though it could not be determined experimentally. To solve this dilemma Newton turned to the dynamics of motion, about which experimental evidence could be collected. He reasoned that if absolute space was a necessary condition to the existence of absolute motion, then from this identification of absolute motion the "identification of absolute space would follow" (9, 22, 47, 92–110 passim, 115, 122, 129).

30. Ibid., 96–97.

31. Kline, *Nonmathematician*, 253–54, 365–66, 388–89; Hall, *Galileo to Newton*, 110–11; L. W. B. Brockliss, "Aristotle, Descartes, and the New Science: Natural Philosophy at the University of Paris, 1600–1740," *Annals of Science* 38 (1981): 64; and Thomas L. Hankins, *Science and the Enlightenment* (Cambridge: Cambridge University Press, 1985), 14.

32. Hall, *Galileo to Newton*, 217; and Kline, *Mathematics*, 65.

33. President Thomas Clap of Yale College (1739–1756) taught a course in Newton's calculus, and Nehemiah Strong, a student and later professor at Yale, published a short work titled "Astronomy Improved, or a New Astronomy" (1781). Yale president Ezra Stiles lectured once a week on mathematics and natural philosophy and used his knowledge of the *Principia* to calculate the true place of sun and moon and the parallax of the moon. These famous examples aside, one should keep in mind that very few understood Newton's calculus (Frederick E. Brasch, "The Newtonian Epoch in the American Colonies [1680–1783]," Proceedings of the American Antiquarian Society, n.s., 49 [October 1939]: 319–21).

34. Motz and Weaver, *Story of Physics*, 94, 118.

35. Kline, *Mathematics*, 58.

36. As in Hankins, *Enlightenment*, 29.

37. Kline, *Mathematics*, 98, 153, 168–69.

38. Leonhard Euler made calculus a "formal theory of functions," no longer a convenient strategy for solving geometrical problems. The work of Lagrange further distanced

calculus from the "preconceptions of geometry, mechanics, or philosophy" (see Carl B. Boyer, *The History of the Calculus and Its Conceptual Development* [N.Y.: Dover, 1959], 192, 217, 221, 231–32, 243, 253). By the beginning of the nineteenth century Lacroix had made the concept of limit basic to calculus, and it was through the many editions of his *Traite elementaire* that the concept of limit became familiar. On the separation of geometry from calculus see Boyer, *History of Calculus*, 265, 272, 285, 294.

39. Quoted in Carl G. Hempel, "Geometry and Empirical Science," in *Our Mathematical Heritage; Essays on the Nature and Cultural Significance of Mathematics*, rev. ed., ed. William L. Schaaf (New York: Collier, 1963), 119, 122–25.

40. Alexandre Koyre, *Metaphysics and Measurement; Essays in Scientific Revolution* (Cambridge: Harvard University Press, 1968), 133.

41. Kline, *Mathematics*, 78.

42. Kline, *Nonmathematician*, 247.

43. Kline, *Mathematics*, 162.

44. William M. Ivins, Jr., *On the Rationalization of Sight, with an Examination of Three Renaissance Texts on Perspective*, paper no. 8 (New York: Metropolitan Museum of Art, 1938), 9. In his *Dioptics*, Descartes recognized the phenomena of size and shape constancy, theorizing that both could be accounted for by our "knowledge and opinion as to their distance" and "position of the various parts of the objects" (see Richard L. Gregory, *Eye and Brain: The Psychology of Seeing*, 4th ed. [Princeton: Princeton University Press, 1990], 160–61, 184).

45. Ivins, *Rationalization*, 9–10.

46. William M. Ivins, Jr., *Art and Geometry: A Study in Space Intuitions* (New York: Dover, 1964), 4–5.

47. Ibid., 32, 39.

48. Ivins, *Rationalization*, 8. For further discussion see Gisela M. A. Richter, "Perspective, Ancient, Medieval and Renaissance," *Scritti in onore Di Bartolomeo Nogara, Raccolt: in Occasione del Suo LXX Anno* [Vatican City, 1937], 381–88.

49. Kline, *Nonmathematician*, 242; and Kline, *Mathematics*, 162–63.

50. Ivins, *Rationalization*, 12.

CHAPTER 4: TEACHING NATURAL PHILOSOPHY

1. Crosbie Smith observed that Faraday's view "clearly implied the unity and conversion of the forces of nature, and *ipso facto* the unity of the subject matter of natural philosophy" (Crosbie Smith, "Mechanical Philosophy and the Emergence of Physics in Britain: 1800–1850," *Annals of Science* 33 [1976]: 6).

2. Hans Niels Jahnke and Michael Otte, "On 'Science as a Language,'" *Epistemological and Social Problems of the Sciences in the Early Nineteenth Century*, ed. Jahnke and Otte (Dordrecht, Netherlands: D. Reidel, 1981), 77, 79–85, 88.

3. Scottish natural philosophy focused on "dynamical" laws and employed the concept of force to unify the study of natural laws. Near the end of the eighteenth century John Robison, a leading Scottish philosopher and professor of natural philosophy at Edinburgh from 1774 to 1805, included natural history and natural philosophy in the study of physics. Robison included description, classification, and the scientific study of laws and causes under this term. He then refined the study of matter into that which could be observed in "sensible motion" and that which was "insensible," such as the "invisible particles of mat-

ter" in fluids, magnetism, electricity, and "luminous bodies." Chemistry and physiology dealt primarily with the "insensibles." Both mechanical philosophy and chemistry were part of physics, and their unifying characteristics were the study of motion itself(Smith, "Mechanical Philosophy," 3–9). Newton's laws of motion were taken to be axiomatic.

The tradition of Scottish natural philosophy was perpetuated through the work of John Playfair, Robison's successor at Edinburgh; William Meikleham, holder of the chair in natural philosophy at Glasgow; and William Thomson (Lord Kelvin), professor of mathematics at Glasgow and an important contributor to the study of thermodynamics. Natural philosophy gradually narrowed its scope to mechanical philosophy, which was classified separately from the study of chemistry. The concepts of motion and force remained central to mechanical philosophy, and the analytical mathematics of Lagrange and Laplace were introduced by Meikleham and Thomson (10–16).

At London University, Dionysius Lardner continued the Scottish tradition. There were variations in classification, but mechanical philosophy remained the focus. The division between mechanical and chemical philosophy remained, but mechanical philosophy continuously overlapped with chemistry. Under Thomas Young the emphasis on dynamics continued, but Young emphasized in his *Lectures on Natural Philosophy and the Mechanical Arts* (1807) the distinction between mathematical and experimental knowledge (20).

At Cambridge the influence of Newton was as pervasive as it was elsewhere. There, however, the emphasis was on a geometrical approach to mechanical philosophy. The study of natural philosophy was divided into those that were mathematized and those that were not. The unity of natural philosophy at Cambridge was less conceptual than methodological. Mathematics was its strong point (21–27).

4. Allan Ferguson, ed., *Natural Philosophy Through the Eighteenth Century and Allied Topics* (Totowa, N.J.: Rowman and Littlefield, 1972), 152–53.

5. Hyman Kuritz, "The Popularization of Science in Nineteenth-Century America," *History of Education Quarterly* 21, no. 3 (Fall 1981): 259–60.

6. Stanley M. Guralnick, *Science and the Ante-Bellum American College* (Philadelphia: American Philosophical Society, 1975), 117–23.

7. See Lee Soltow and Edward Stevens, *The Rise of Literacy and the Common School: A Socioeconomic Analysis to 1870* (Chicago: University of Chicago Press, 1981), 102. The sample includes Jacob Bigelow, *The Useful Arts Considered in Connexion with the Applications of Science*, vol. 1 (Boston, 1840); Robert Brunton, *A Compendium of Mechanics or Text Book for Engineers, Mill Wrights, Machine-Makers, Founders, Smiths* (New York, 1830); J. L. [John Lee] Comstock, *A System of Natural Philosophy* (New York, 1851); Oliver Evans, *The Young Mill-Wright and Miller's Guide*, 2nd ed. (Philadelphia, 1807); Thomas Fenwick, *Four Essays on Practical Mechanics* (Newcastle, Eng., 1801); Edward Hazen, *Popular Technology; or, Professions and Trades* (New York, 1842); Thomas Kelt, *The Mechanic's Text-Book and Engineer's Practical Guide* (Boston, 1854); Mrs. Marcet [Thomas P. Jones], *Conversations on Natural Philosophy* (Philadelphia, 1830); Peter Nicholson, *The Mechanic's Companion, or, the Elements and Practice of Carpentry, Joinery, Bricklaying, Masonry, Slating, Plastering, Painting, Smithing, and Turning* (Philadelphia, 1845); Denison Olmsted, *Compendium of Natural Philosophy: Adapted to the Use of the General Reader and of Schools and Academies* (New Haven, 1842); Denison Olmsted, *An Introduction to Natural Philosophy, Designed as a Text Book for the Use of the Students in Yale College* (New York, 1845); Almira Hart

Lincoln Philips, *Natural Philosophy, for Schools, Families, and Private Students* (New York, 1846); Alonzo Potter, *The Principles of Science Applied to the Domestic and Mechanic Arts and to Manufactures and Agriculture* (Boston, 1841).

8. Guralnick, *Science and the Ante-Bellum American College*, 63–64.

9. "Self Improvement for Adults," *American Journal of Education* 3 (1828): 34–35.

10. Hugh R. Slotten, "Science, Education, and Antebellum Reform: The Case of Alexander Dallas Bache," *History of Education Quarterly* 31, no. 3 (Fall 1991): 329, 336, 340.

11. The sample was taken from O. A. Roorbach, *Bibliotheca Americana, Catalogue of American Publications Including Reprints and Original Works from 1820 to 1852* (New York: Peter Smith, 1939).

12. "Elementary Works on Physical Science," *North American Review* 72, no. 151 (April 1851): 362–63, 365–68.

13. Ibid., 368–69.

14. "Bibliographical Note," *Journal of the Franklin Institute* 24, no. 1 (July 1834): 19–20.

15. George Gregory, *Lectures on Experimental Philosophy, Astronomy and Chemistry*, vol. 1 (London: Richard Phillips, 1808), 6–7.

16. A. H. Lincoln Phelps, *Natural Philosophy for Schools, Families, and Private Students*, new ed. (New York: Huntington and Savage, 1846), 98.

17. Ibid., 226–31.

18. Olmsted, *Compendium of Natural Philosophy*, 99.

19. Guralnick, *Science and the Ante-Bellum American College*, 66.

20. Richard Green Parker, *A School Compendium of Natural and Experimental Philosophy* (New York: A. S. Barnes and Burr, 1859), xiv–xvi.

21. "Self Improvement for Adults," *American Journal of Education* 3 (1828): 37; *Western School Journal* (October 1842): 27.

22. "Study of Natural History," *Common School Assistant* 1, no. 5 (May 1836): 40.

23. "Mechanics—No. 1," *Common School Assistant* 2, no. 12 (December 1837): 94–95; "Natural Philosophy—Balloons," *Common School Assistant* 3, no. 4 (April 1838): 29; and "Mechanics," *Common School Assistant* 3, no. 8 (August 1838): 62.

24. "Natural Philosophy," *Common School Assistant* 3, no. 1 (January 1838): 4; and "Natural Philosophy," *Common School Assistant* 3, no. 3 (March 1838): 22.

25. Richard G. Parker, *Juvenile Philosophy; or, Philosophy in Familiar Conversations, Designed to Teach Young Children to Think* (New York: A. S. Barnes and Co., 1857), 17, 57.

26. *Western School Journal* (October 1842): 27.

27. Ethel M. McAllister, *Amos Eaton, Scientist and Educator, 1776–1842* (Philadelphia: University of Pennsylvania Press, 1941), 184.

28. Maurice Daumas, *Scientific Instruments of the Seventeenth and Eighteenth Centuries*, trans. Mary Holbrook (New York: Praeger, 1972), 94, 102, 112–20, 135.

29. Ibid., 137.

30. "School Cabinets," *Common School Journal* 10, no. 16 (15 August 1848): 241–43.

31. "Apparatus for the Instruction of Children," *American Journal of Education* 4 (1829): 62–63.

32. Ibid., 64.

33. "Apparatus," *The Common School Journal* 3, no. 5 (1 March 1841): 77.

34. Walter R. Johnson, "On the Utility of Visible Illustrations," *American Annals of Education and Instruction* 3, no. 3 (March 1833): 103.

35. Ibid., 110.

36. Deborah Jean Warner, "Commodities for the Classroom: Apparatus for Science and Education in Antebellum America," *Annals of Science* 45 (1988): 387–88.

37. "Josiah Holbrook," *American Journal of Education* 8 (1860): 232–33, 254.

38. Warner, "Commodities for the Classroom," 393.

39. Charnel Anderson, *Technology in American Education, 1650–1900* (Washington, D.C.: Government Printing Office, 1962), 15.

40. Ibid, 15–16.

41. James G. Kelso, "The Lyceum and the Mechanics' Institutes: Pre-Civil War Ventures in Adult Education" (Ph.D. diss., Harvard University, 1953), 93.

42. Warner, "Commodities for the Classroom," 394.

43. Walter R. Johnson, "Address Introductory to a Course of Lectures on Mechanics and Natural Philosophy" (presented at the Franklin Institute, 19 November 1828) (Boston, 1829), 11.

44. Ibid., 9–10, 11.

45. Ibid., 14.

46. Ibid.

47. Abraham Rees, *The Cyclopedia; or Universal Dictionary of Arts, Sciences, and Literature*, vol. 22, 1st American ed. (Philadelphia: Samuel F. Bradford and Murray, Fairman, and Co., 1818).

48. Alonzo Potter, *The Principles of Science Applied to the Domestic and Mechanic Arts* (Boston: Marsh, Capen, Lyon, and Webb, 1841), 34.

49. Dionysius Lardner, *Popular Lectures on Science and Art*, vol. 1 (New York: Greeley and McElrath, 1846), 20.

50. Kelt, *Mechanic's Text-Book and Engineer's Practical Guide*, 78.

51. Ibid., 313.

52. Guralnick, *Science and the Ante-Bellum American College*, 65.

53. Gulian Verplanck, "Introductory Address," (presented to the Mechanics' Institute of the City of New York, 27 November 1833), *Mechanics Magazine and Register of Inventions and Improvements* 3, no. 1 (January 1834): 53–54.

54. "Science and Language," *Scientific American* 3, no. 23 (26 February 1848): 181.

55. *Scientific American* 4, no. 33 (5 May 1849): 261.

56. *Scientific American* 2, no. 48 (21 August 1847): 381; and "Scientific Knowledge," *Scientific American* 3, no. 24 (4 November 1848): 189.

57. *Scientific American* 3, no. 19 (29 January 1848): 149; and "Mechanics Awake," *New York State Mechanic* 1, no. 24 (7 May 1842): 189.

58. *American Railroad Journal and Advocate of Internal Improvements* 3, no. 4 (1 February 1834): 54–55; 6, no. 28 (5 July 1837): 435–37; 6, no. 34 (26 August 1837): 535–38.

59. *Apprentice's Companion* 1, no. 1 (April 1835): 12.

60. *Apprentice's Companion* 1, no. 2 (May 1835): 26–27.

61. *Scientific American* 2, no. 46 (7 August 1847): 365; 2, no. 47 (14 August 1847): 373; 2, no. 49 (28 August 1847): 389.

62. *Scientific American* 6, no. 18 (18 January 1851): 142.

63. *Scientific American* 6, no. 49 (23 August 1851): 389; 7, no. 46 (31 July 1852): 368, 363; 7, no. 45 (25 July 1852): 354.

64. Articles are from the *Journal of the Franklin Institute*. "General Rules for Proportioning the Length of Boilers for Stationary Engines," 3rd ser., 21, no. 3 (March 1851): 164–66; L. Turnbull, "A Series of Lectures on the Telegraph Delivered Before the Franklin Institute, 1850–1851," 3rd ser., 21, no. 3 (March 1851): 190–96; "Calculation by Ohm's Law," 3rd ser., 21, no. 6 (June 1851): 401–7; John Trautwine, "On the Field Practice of Laying Out Circular Curves for Railroads," 3rd ser., 26, no. 6 (June 1851): 361–79; "On Measuring the Length of Connecting Rods of Steam Engines," 3rd ser., 31, no. 2 (February 1856): 125–26; H. Howson, "Mechanical Engineering as Applied to Farm Implements," 3rd ser., 30, no. 6 (December 1855); 3rd ser., 31, no. 1 (January 1856): 42–43; 3rd ser., 31, no. 2 (February 1856): 138–40; John Richardson, "Trigonometrical Development, and Integration of Trigonometrical Functions," 3rd ser., 32, no. 6 (December 1856): 409–11; and "What Constitutes an Engineer," 3rd ser., 21, no. 1 (January 1851): 55–56.

65. *American Railroad Journal* 27, no. 957 (19 August 1854): 524; 12, no. 5 (2 February 1856): 65; n.s., 1 (1838): 33–35; 5, no. 37 (17 September 1836): 585; 3, no. 4 (1 February 1834): 54; 6, no. 22 (1 June 1850): 337; 4, no. 24 (20 June 1835): 206; and *American Polytechnic Journal* 2 (July–December 1853): 234; 3 (January–June 1854): 14, 85; 4 (July–December 1854): 62.

CHAPTER 5: MATHEMATICS INSTRUCTION

1. Quoted in National Council of Teachers of Mathematics, *A History of Mathematics Education in the United States and Canada* (Washington, D.C.: NCTM, 1970), 13–14.
2. Patricia Cline Cohen, *A Calculating People: The Spread of Numeracy in Early America* (Chicago: University of Chicago Press, 1982), 118.
3. Ibid., 120–21.
4. Secretary of the Board, *Sixth Annual Report of the Board of Education [of Massachusetts]* (1843), 55.
5. Cohen, *A Calculating People*, 26–27.
6. Ibid., 111.
7. Thomas T. Smiley, *The New Federal Calculator: or Scholar's Assistant* (Philadelphia, 1830), 63, 88, 103.
8. Thomas Dilworth, *The Schoolmaster's Assistant: Being a Compendium of Arithmetic Both Theoretical and Practical* (Air: J. and P. Wilson, 1800), 178.
9. *History of Mathematics Education*, 14–15. See, e.g., Nathan Daboll, *Schoolmaster's Assistant, Improved and Enlarged, Being a Plain Practical System of Arithmetic Adapted to the United States* (New London, 1823), 215, 241.
10. Ibid., 16.
11. Ibid., 17.
12. Cohen, *A Calculating People*, 26.
13. "Arithmetic and Geometry as Studies for Children," *American Journal of Education*, n.s., 42, no. 1 (January 1830): 24–25.
14. "Arithmetic," *American Annals of Education* 1 (June 1831): 262.
15. "Arithmetic and Geometry as Studies for Children," 25.
16. "Palmer's Prize Essay, Chapter 5," *Common School Journal* 2, no. 20 (15 October 1840): 317.
17. Warren Colburn, *An Introduction to Algebra upon the Inductive Method of Instruction* (Boston: Cummings, Hilliard, 1825), 32.

18. Daniel Adams, *Arithmetic, in Which the Principles of Operating by Numbers Are Analytically Explained, and Synthetically Applied* (Keene, N.H., 1840), preface.

19. Warren Colburn, *Intellectual Arithmetic upon the Inductive Method of Instruction* (Boston, 1829), vii–viii.

20. Joseph Ray, *The Little Arithmetic. Elementary Lessons in Intellectual Arithmetic, on the Analytic and Inductive Method of Instruction* (Cincinnati, 1834), 1.

21. See, e.g., the series in *Common School Journal* titled "How to Teach Elementary Arithmetic" 8, nos. 15–17 (1 August 1846): 230, (15 August 1846): 249, (1 September 1846): 262.

22. Secretary of the Board [Horace Mann], *Fifth Annual Report of the Board of Education [of Massachusetts]* (Boston, 1842), 55.

23. Secretary of the Board [Horace Mann], *Seventh Annual Report of the Board of Education [of Massachusetts]* (Boston, 1844), 56–57, 104–5.

24. Charles Davies, *Arithmetic, Designed for Academies and Schools* (New York, 1852), 9.

25. Ibid., 274.

26. Quoted in *History of Mathematics Education*, 26.

27. John F. Stoddard, *The American Intellectual Arithmetic* (New York, 1849), v.

28. A. Caswell, "Importance of the Mathematical Studies, Considered as a Branch of a Liberal Education," *Biblical Repository and Quarterly Observer* 21 (January 1836): 4–8.

29. Secretary of the Board of Education [Horace Mann], *Sixth Annual Report of the Board of Education [of Massachusetts]* (Boston, 1843), 55.

30. Charles Davies, *Elementary Algebra: Embracing the First Principles of the Science* (New York, 1851), 1.

31. Ibid., 81.

32. Ibid., 169.

33. Charles Davies, *Elements of Algebra: on the Basis of M. Bourdon* (New York, 1856), 272–73; 303–6.

34. S. F. Lacroix, *Elements of Algebra*, trans. John Farrar (Boston, 1831), 1.

35. *History of Mathematics Education*, 16.

36. Charles Davies, *Practical Mathematics with Drawing and Mensuration Applied to the Mechanic Arts* (New York, 1870), 215–33.

37. Addison Ballard, "Advantages, to the General Student, of the Study of Geometry," *American Journal of Education and College Review* 2, no. 8 (August 1856): 134–35.

38. Cohen, *A Calculating People*, 143.

39. A. M. Legendre, *Elements of Geometry and Trigonometry*, trans. David Brewster, ed. Charles Davies (Philadelphia: A. S. Barnes, 1834), iii.

40. A. M. Legendre, *Elements of Geometry*, trans. John Farrar (Boston, 1831).

41. W. E. Dean, *The Element of Geometry* (New York, 1836), 5.

42. "Mechanical Geometry, No. III, Theorem IV," *American Mechanics' Magazine* 1, no. 9 (2 April 1825): 143.

43. T. S. Davies, "Practical Geometry," *American Mechanics' Magazine* 2, no. 5 (5 March 1825): 70, 72, 74; "Measuring Circumferences," *American Mechanics' Magazine* 1, no. 7 (19 March 1825): 105; and "Problem IV," "Problem V," *American Mechanics' Magazine* 1, no. 8 (26 March 1825): 118–19, *American Mechanics' Magazine* 2, no. 1 (6 August 1825): 12.

44. "Problem for Millwrights," *American Mechanics' Magazine* 2, no. 5 (5 March 1825): 75.

45. Ellwood Morris, "Rules for Solid Mensuration," *Journal of the Franklin Institute*, 3rd ser., 23, no. 4 (April 1852): 240–41; J. M. Richardson, "Investigation of the Angle-Block of Houe's Truss," *Journal of the Franklin Institute*, 3rd ser., 29, no. 5 (May 1855): 306–7; and "Bibliographic Notice, *Journal of the Franklin Institute*, 3rd ser., 34, no. 5 (November 1857): 357–58.

46. H. Howson, "On Curves for Mechanical Draughtsmen," *Journal of the Franklin Institute*, 3rd ser., 36, no. 2 (August 1858): 78–80; J. K. Whilldin, "Construction of Arcs of Circles Having Large Radii, the Versed Sine Being Unknown," *Journal of the Franklin Institute*, 3rd ser., 43, no. 1 (January 1862): 56–58.

47. "Useful Problems," *Scientific American* 4, no. 29 (16 June 1849): 307; "To Cut Elbows and Stove Pipes by Rule and Compass," *Scientific American* 10 (7 October 1853): 50; "How to Cut a Piece of Leather Which Will Exactly Fit a Cone Drum," *Scientific American*, n.s., 13, no. 36 (15 May 1858): 286; "Rule for Cutting Bevels," *Scientific American*, n.s., 6, no. 3 (18 January 1862): 37.

48. *Apprentice's Companion* 1 (April 1835): 32; and *Apprentice's Companion* 1 (July 1835): 52.

49. T. S. Davies, "Practical Geometry," *American Mechanics Magazine* 2 (5 March 1825): 70.

50. Ibid., 1; *American Mechanics Magazine* 2 (26 February 1825): 53, (5 March 1825): 70, 72, 74, (19 March 1825): 106, (26 March 1825): 117–18, 120, (2 April 1825): 143, (16 April 1825): 171, (23 April 1825): 185, (20 June 1825): 315.

51. *Mechanics' Magazine and Register of Inventions and Improvements* 1 (May 1833): 217; *Mechanic's Magazine and Register of Inventions and Improvements* 3 (January 1834): 47.

CHAPTER 6: NEW EDUCATIONAL INSTITUTIONS FOR A NEW SOCIETY

1. Lee Soltow and Edward Stevens, *The Rise of Literacy and the Common School in the United States: A Socioeconomic Analysis to 1870* (Chicago: University of Chicago Press, 1981), 52–53, 155–61, 168, 178–80.

2. James G. Kelso, "The Lyceum and the Mechanics' Institutes, Pre-Civil War Ventures in Adult Education" (Ph.D. diss., Harvard University, 1953), 255–59.

3. Gary J. Kornblith, "From Artisans to Businessmen: Master Mechanics in New England, 1789–1850" (Ph.D. diss., Princeton University, 1983), 39.

4. Ibid., 16–17, 19, 22.

5. Ibid., 96–97, 100.

6. See "London Mechanics' Institute," *Mechanic's Magazine* 8 (18 October 1823): 114–18; and "Public Meeting for the Establishment of the London Mechanics' Institute, *Mechanic's Magazine* 12 (15 November 1823): 177–80. For a general account see James Hole, *An Essay on the History and Management of Literary, Scientific, and Mechanics' Institutions* (London: Longman, Brown, and Green, 1853; reprint, London: Frank Cass, 1970). Hole's assessment of the efficacy of mechanics' institutes was sobering. He disappointingly concluded that "Mechanics' Institutes have failed" because of the inadequate "early and sound intellectual and moral training for the mass of our operative population." And, he added, poor reading habits led operatives to spend their time on "amusing

books and lectures, rather than [on] technical instruction" (14, 16–17, 20, 24–25, 30–31).

7. George B. Emerson, "Mechanics Institutes," *American Journal of Education* 2 (1827): 273, quoted in Kelso, "The Lyceum and Mechanics' Institutes," 28; and Edward Everett, *Orations and Speeches* (Boston, 1850), quoted in Kelso, "The Lyceum and Mechanics' Institutes," 31.

8. Edward Everett, *Importance of Practical Education and Useful Knowledge, Being a Selection from His Orations and Other Discourses* (New York: Harper and Bros., 1840), 152.

9. Clarence Ray Aurner, *A History of Education in Iowa* (Iowa City, 1914), quoted in Kelso, "The Lyceum and Mechanics' Institutes," 61.

10. Walter R. Johnson, "Essay on Education," *Journal of the Franklin Institute*, n.s., 2 (July 1828): 56–57. See also Bruce Sinclair, *Philadelphia's Philosopher Mechanics: A History of the Franklin Institute, 1824–1865* (Baltimore: Johns Hopkins University Press, 1974), 108.

11. John Craig, "An Address Delivered at a Meeting of the Citizens of Cincinnati Convened for the Purpose of Forming a Mechanics' Institute" (Cincinnati, 1829), 1.

12. To offset the baleful effects of industrialization Craig adopted a position similar to that of such British reformers as Hannah More. He recommended that a "system of Sunday Schools be established at each [manufacturing establishment]." "Due attendance" was to be "exacted from every youth, who has not acquired sufficient education, before admission to the establishment" (Craig, "Address," 12–13).

13. Ibid., 15.

14. E. L. Magoon, "Oration, Delivered July 4, 1848, at the Laying of the Corner Stone of the Ohio Mechanics' Institute, Cincinnati" (Cincinnati, 1848), 5.

15. Ibid., 6–8, 14, 22.

16. Kornblith, "Artisans to Businessmen," 16. A list of delegates to the State Convention of Mechanics held in Utica, New York, in 1834 recorded the following occupations: tailor, cooper, silver plater, cordwainer, iron founder, plane maker, chair and cabinet maker, hatter, saddler, blacksmith, machinist, watchmaker, tanner, tin plate worker, stone cutter, carriage maker, brass founder, brush maker, printer and publisher, piano forte maker, locksmith, marble cutter, and carpenter (proceedings of the State Convention of Mechanics, 21–22 August 1834, Utica, N.Y.). Membership lists of other mechanics' associations indicate a similar broad use of the term.

17. Ibid., 132–33.

18. Kornblith, "Artisans to Businessmen," vi, 16, 169. See Edwin Freedley, *Philadelphia and Its Manufactures, A Hand Book Exhibiting the Development, Variety, and Statistics of the Manufacturing Industry of Philadelphia in 1857; Together with Sketches of Remarkable Manufactories; and a List of Articles Now Made in Philadelphia* (1858), 21.

19. Ibid., 94–95.

20. Sinclair, *Philosopher Mechanics*, 14–15.

21. Rex Burns, *Success in America: The Yeoman Dream and the Industrial Revolution* (Amherst: University of Massachusetts Press, 1976), 95, 101, 103.

22. "To Our Mechanics—'Come Let Us Reason Together,'" *Scientific American* 6 (17 May 1851): 277; and "Intelligent Mechanics," *Scientific American* 8 (25 December 1852): 117.

23. J. K. Mitchell, "A Lecture on Some of the Means of Elevating the Character of the

Working Classes" (Philadelphia, 1834), 3, 8, 10–12. This lecture was reprinted in J. K. Mitchell, "On Some of the Means of Elevating the Character of the Working Classes. A Lecture Delivered at the Close of the Winter Course, 1833–34, of the Franklin Institute of Philadelphia," *Mechanics Magazine and Register of Inventions and Improvements* 4, no. 2 (9 August 1834), 82–88.

24. Ibid., 8, 11. Emphasis in original.

25. Ibid., 12–13.

26. Walter R. Johnson, "Address Introductory to a Course of Lectures on Mechanics and Natural Philosophy" (Boston, 1829), 3.

27. Ibid., 4–5.

28. Ibid., 7–8.

29. Stephen Wright, "Historical Sketch of the Society" appended to General Society of Mechanics and Tradesmen of the City of New York, "Centennial Celebration of the General Society" (New York: The Society, 1885), 42. See also "Original Charter of the Society" in "The Charter and By-Laws of the General Society of Mechanics and Tradesmen of the City of New York" (New York: The Society, 1856), 27.

30. George Clinton, Jr., "An Oration Delivered on the Fourth of July, 1798, Before the General Society of Mechanics and Tradesmen, the Democratic Society, the Tammany Society or Columbian Society, and a Numerous Concourse of Other Citizens," 9–10.

31. Circular, "Mechanics' Institute of the City of New York," c. 1851.

32. Wright, "Historical Sketch," 42. The courses in drawing were immensely successful, judging by the enrollment records a decade later. From 1861 to 1865 enrollment varied from 312 to 396, with an average attendance of 215. Drawings produced by students were exhibited every evening. Naval architecture was introduced as a subspeciality during these years, and in 1864 mathematics and debating classes began. Those attending made up a diverse group that included carvers, painters, machinists, pattern makers, brass finishers, carpenters, shipwrights, ship carpenters, and clerks. Of the 396 pupils enrolled in 1863, the best represented were carvers and painters (24 percent), carpenters (15 percent), and machinists (14 percent) (*Reports of the Finance Committee of the General Society of Mechanics and Tradesmen of the City of New York* [3 February 1862, 8–9; 4 February 1863, 8–9; 3 February 1864, 7–8; 1 February 1865]. Hereafter cited as GSMT, New York.)

33. The situation was similar in England, where, say Stephens and Roderick, "it was the promotion of science as much as any other area of national life which gained from the philosophy of self-improvement (Michael Stephens and Gordon W. Roderick, "Science, Self-Improvement and the First Industrial Revolution," *Annals of Science* 31, no. 5 [1974]: 469). The modern teaching of science in England, asserts one author, "had its beginning in the Mechanics' Institutes of the early nineteenth century and spread from this into the schools" (Charles Foster, "One Hundred Years of Science Teaching in Great Britain," *Annals of Science* 2, no. 3 [15 July 1937]: 335, 337, 339–40).

34. Wright, "Historical Sketch," 43; and M. M. Noah, "An Address Delivered Before the General Society of Mechanics and Tradesmen of the City of New York on the Opening of the Mechanic Institution" (New York, 1822), 16–17.

35. "Second Report of the Board of Directors of the Mechanics' Institute of the City of New York," *Mechanics Magazine and Register of Inventions and Improvements* 2, no. 5 (November 1833): 284.

36. Wright, "Historical Sketch," 43.

37. Letter from L. S. Gale to J. K. Mitchell, 4 May 1835, *Franklin Institute and the Making of Industrial America* (1987), microfiche 202. Hereafter cited as F. I. microfiche.

38. Ibid.

39. Kelso, "The Lyceum and Mechanics' Institutes," 67.

40. *Annals of Massachusetts Charitable Mechanic Association*, comp. Joseph T. Buckingham (Boston, 1853), 174, 187. Massachusetts Charitable Mechanic Association Collection, Massachusetts Historical Society, Boston (hereafter cited as MCMA coll.); and Kornblith, "Artisans to Businessmen," 457.

41. Kornblith, "Artisans to Businessmen," 458–60.

42. Ibid., 459–60.

43. Kelso, *The Lyceum and Mechanics' Institutes*, 55.

44. Kornblith, "Artisans to Businessmen," 460–63.

45. Ibid., 527.

46. "Scrapbook," box 4, MCMA coll.; and Rollo G. Silver, "The Boston Lads were Undaunted," *Library Journal* (July 1949): 997.

47. Mechanic Apprentices' Library Association, Minutes, 2 November 1832, 3 September 1833, MCMA coll.

48. *Annals of the Massachusetts Charitable Mechanic Association*, 241.

49. Mechanic Apprentices' Library Association, Minutes, "Presidential Address," vol. 5, 4 March 1834, MCMA coll.

50. Mechanic Apprentices' Library Association, Minutes, 9 October 1832, 2 November 1832, 12 November 1833, 6 February 1835, MCMA coll.

51. MCMA *Proceedings and Transactions*, vols. 4 and 5, October 1832–February 1833, box 11, MCMA coll.

52. *Annals of MCMA*, 315–16, MCMA coll.

53. Ibid., 336.

54. *The Franklin Institute and the Making of Industrial America* (Bethesda, Md.: Academic Editions, 1987), Committee on Lectures, 3 June 1824, F. I. microfiche.

55. Minutes, 3 June 1824, February 1826, 8 December 1831, 12 January 1833, F. I. microfiche.

56. Mitchell, "Elevating the Character of the Working Classes," 16.

57. Ibid., 112–14.

58. *Saturday Evening Post*, 24 October 1829, quoted in Sinclair, *Philosopher Mechanics*, 114.

59. Committee on Instruction, Minutes, 5 March, 3 June, 4 August 1824; 6 October 1825, F. I. microfiche.

60. Sinclair, *Philosopher Mechanics*, 120–21; Committee on Instruction, Minutes, 5 March 1824, 10 December 1829, 12 January 1832, F. I. microfiche.

61. Committee on Instruction, 10 March 1831, 13 October 1831; and Sinclair, *Philosopher Mechanics*, 123.

62. W. R. Johnson, "Essays on Education," *Journal of the Franklin Institute*, n.s., 2 (August 1828): 109.

63. "Address of the Committee on Instruction of the Franklin Institute of Pennsylvania on the Subject of the High School Department Attached to that Institution," n.d. [1826]: 2. Before coming to Pennsylvania, Johnson taught at the Framingham Academy and in a small classical school in Salem. Johnson later accepted an appointment as professor of chemistry and natural philosophy in the medical department at Pennsylvania

College at Gettysburg. He promoted the study of agricultural chemistry and was "one of the first twenty who organized the American Association of Geologists at Philadelphia in 1840" ("Walter R. Johnson," *American Journal of Education*, 5 [Hartford, 1858]: 781–802).

64. Sinclair, *Philosopher Mechanics*, 65–68; 124; David F. Labaree, *The Making of an American High School: The Credentials Market and the Central High School of Philadelphia, 1838–1939* (New Haven: Yale University Press, 1988), 15–16.

65. "Address of the Committee of Instruction of the Franklin Institute of Pennsylvania on the Subject of the High School Department Attached to That Institution" (c. 1826), 2, 5, 8.

66. Committee on Instruction, Minutes, c. 1826, Franklin Institute microfiche.

67. "Walter R. Johnson," *American Journal of Education* 15 (December 1858): 799–802.

68. W. R. Johnson, "Essays on Education," *Journal of the Franklin Institute*, n.s., 2 (November 1828): 354.

69. Ibid.

70. Ibid.

71. Johnson, "Essay on Education" (December 1828): 367–69.

72. Johnson, "Essay on Education" (October 1828): 278.

73. Ibid.

74. Ibid.

75. Catalog of Committee on Models, 1824–35, F. I. microfiche.

76. Walter Johnson, "On Schools of the Arts" (speech presented at the American Institute of Instruction, August 1835, Boston); "Memorial of the Committee Appointed at the Town Meeting of the Citizens of the City and County of Philadelphia Praying for the Establishment of a School of Arts," 4 January 1838 (Harrisburg, 1838), 3, 8; and "For the Establishment of a School of Arts, Memorial of the Franklin Institute of the State of Pennsylvania, for the Promotion of the Mechanic Arts to the Legislature of Pennsylvania" (Philadelphia, 1837), 6.

77. Johnson, "On Schools of the Arts," 3–7, 9–11, 14.

78. Ibid., 17, 20.

79. "Memorial for School of the Arts," 1838, 4.

80. "Memorial for School of the Arts," 1837, 7, 9.

81. Ibid., 7–8.

82. Ibid., 10.

83. Ibid., 11. See also Sinclair, *Philosopher Mechanics*, 134.

84. Theodore Lyman, Jr., "Address at the Founding of the Apprentice Library Association in Boston," 22 February 1820, 3; Kornblith, "Artisans to Businessmen," 523; and Silver, "Boston Lads Were Undaunted," 995. Lyman gives the figure of fifteen hundred books, and Silver gives the figure as five hundred.

85. Lyman, "Address," 20 February 1820, 5.

86. "Report of the Vice President, 4 September 1832," *Proceedings and Transactions of the Apprentices' Library Association with Records and Other Documents*, September 1832–March 1834, vol. 4, box 11, MCMA coll. *Proceedings and Minutes of Apprentice Library*, 6 February 1835, vol. 5, box 11, MCMA coll.; "Report of the Committee on the Library in Relation to the Mechanics' Apprentice Library Association" (Boston, 1859), box 4, MCMA coll.

87. *Proceedings and Transactions of Apprentices' Library Association*, 1 March 1834, vol. 4, box 11, MCMA coll.

88. Wright, "Historical Sketch," 43; M. M. Noah, "An Address Delivered Before the General Society of Mechanics and Tradesmen of the City of New York on the Opening of the Mechanic Institution" (New York, 1822).

89. *Reports of the Finance Committee*, 3 February 1864, 12; 1 February 1865, 11; 6 February 1867, 11; 5 February 1868, 13; 3 February 1869, 17.

90. *Catalogue of the Books in the Apprentices' Library, April 1839* (New York, 1839), vi–vii.

91. *Catalog of the Apprentices and De Milt Libraries, New York, July 1, 1855* (New York, 1855).

92. "Ohio Mechanics' Institute," OMI archives, Cincinnati Historical Society; "Constitution and By-Laws of the Apprentices Library," vol. 173, OMI archives.

93. "Report on the State of the Ohio Mechanics' Institute," 11 December 1843, box 4, file 3, OMI archives.

94. Ohio Mechanics' Institute Library Catalogs, 1840, 1849.

95. Library Register, 1834–1840, vol. 80, OMI archives.

96. Library Record, 1836–1838, OMI archives.

97. Report of the Committee on Library and Reading Room, 2 March 1848, box 4, file 9, OMI archives.

98. Ladies Department, Library Register, 1842–1856, OMI archives.

99. American Institute, Circular, New York, 4 July 1833, F. I. microfiche.

100. William Grierson, "Observations on Competitions Among Working Tradesmen," *Journal of the Franklin Institute* 12 (September 1833): 203–4.

101. Sinclair, *Philosopher Mechanics*, 86–89.

102. Kornblith, "Artisans to Businessmen," 463–66.

103. Exhibition and Fair of the Massachusetts Charitable Mechanic Association, Boston, 1837, MCMA coll.; Kornblith, "Artisans to Businessmen," 467.

104. Circular, "Mechanics' Institute Rooms" [New York], F. I. microfiche.

105. *Scientific American* 8 (13 November 1852): 69.

106. Ibid., 67.

107. *Scientific American* 9 (17 September 1853): 13.

CHAPTER 7: SCIENCE FOR WOMEN

1. Emma Willard was born to Lydia and Samuel Hart in 1787 near Berlin, Connecticut. One of her ancestors was Stephen Hart, the founder of Hartford. See Alma Lutz, *Emma Willard: Pioneer Educator of American Women* (Westport, Conn.: Greenwood Press, 1983); and Thomas Woody, *A History of Women's Education in the United States*, 2 vols. (New York: Science Press, 1929; reprint, New York: Octagon Books, 1966).

2. Lutz, *Emma Willard*, 8–16.

3. Ibid., 20–24.

4. Ibid., 27–38.

5. Ibid., 35–39.

6. David F. Allmendinger, Jr., "Mount Holyoke Students Encounter the Need for Life-Planning, 1837–1850," *History of Education Quarterly* 19 (Spring 1979): 27–46.

7. Patricia Cline Cohen, *A Calculating People: The Spread of Numeracy in Early America* (Chicago: University of Chicago Press, 1982), 144.

8. Deborah Jean Warner, "Science Education for Women in Antebellum America," *Isis* 69 (1978): 58–63. See also Deborah Jean Warner and Nathan Reingold, "Definitions and Speculations: The Professionalization of Science in America in the Nineteenth Century," in Alexandra Oleson and Sanborn Brown, eds., *The Pursuit of Knowledge in the Early American Republic* (Baltimore: Johns Hopkins University Press, 1976).

9. Barbara Solomon, *In the Company of Educated Women: A History of Women and Higher Education in America* (New Haven: Yale University Press, 1985), 27; and Anne Fiore Scott, "The Ever-Widening Circle: The Diffusion of Feminist Values from the Troy Female Seminary, 1822–1872," *History of Education Quarterly* 19 (Spring 1979): 3–25.

10. Mrs. Townshend Stith, *Thoughts on Female Education* (Philadelphia, 1831), 9.

11. Quoted in Carole B. Shmurak and Bonnie S. Handler, "'Castle of Science': Mount Holyoke College and the Preparation of Women in Chemistry, 1837–1941," *History of Education Quarterly* 32 (Fall 1992): 315; and Catherine McKeen, "Mental Education of Woman," *American Journal of Education* 1 (1856): 571, 576 (emphasis in original).

12. Emma Willard, *An Address to the Public; Particularly to the Members of the Legislature of New York Proposing a Plan for Improving Female Education* (Middlebury, Vt., 1819). I worked from a typescript copy; the page references listed here refer to a reprint of The Plan in John Lord, *The Life of Emma Willard* (New York: D. Appleton, 1873).

13. Ibid., 65–67.

14. Ibid., 67–68.

15. Nancy Beadie, "Emma Willard's Idea Put to the Test: The Consequences of State Support of Female Education in New York, 1819–67," *History of Education Quarterly* 33 (Winter 1993): 559.

16. The Plan, 69–70.

17. Beadie, "Emma Willard's Idea Put to the Test," 545. See Linda K. Kerber, *Women of the Republic: Intellect and Ideology in Revolutionary America* (Chapel Hill: University of North Carolina Press, 1980). For changes in the "model of American womanhood" in the early nineteenth century see Glenda Riley, *Inventing the American Woman: A Perspective on Women's History, 1607–1877* (Arlington Heights, Ill.: Harlan Davidson, 1986), 63–87.

18. Riley, *Inventing the American Woman*, 70. On the role of women see also Carl F. Kaestle, *Pillars of the Republic: Common Schools and American Society, 1780–1860* (New York: Hill and Wang, 1983), 84.

19. Riley, *Inventing the American Woman*, 74–75. See also David Tyack and Elisabeth Hansot, *Learning Together: A History of Coeducation in American Schools* (New Haven: Yale University Press, 1990), 34–35.

20. Trustees of the Troy Female Seminary, Annual Reports to the University of the State of New York, [1822], 1839–52, box 1, special collections, Emma Willard School, Troy, New York. Hereafter cited as EWS coll. Calculation of average ages was based on a sample of every tenth student listed in the Annual Reports.

21. Ibid.

22. "Additional Remarks," Report of the Trustees of the Troy Female Seminary to the New York State Regents, January 1841, EWS coll.

23. Ibid.

24. Letter from Emma Clark to Master Grosvenor Clark, 7 December 1823, Student Correspondence, box 1, EWS coll.

25. "Additional Remarks."

26. Ibid.

27. Ibid.

28. "Notes on Plan for Female Education," typescript, p. 1, EWS coll.

29. "Additional Remarks," EWS coll.

30. Margaret W. Rossiter, *Women Scientists in America: Struggles and Strategies to 1940* (Baltimore: Johns Hopkins University Press, 1982), 4.

31. Emma Willard, *Journals and Letters from France and Great Britain* (Troy, N.Y.: N. Tuttle, 1833), 16–17.

32. Ibid., 18–19, 33.

33. Ibid., 337.

34. Daniel H. Calhoun, "Eyes for the Jacksonian World: William C. Woodbridge and Emma Willard," *Journal of the Early Republic* 4 (Spring 1984): 7, 13–14, 19–20.

35. Diary [and Letters] of Caroline Eliza Wills, Troy Female Seminary, 1839–40, 22 January, 9 May, 22 June 1840, EWS coll.

36. Sarah Dennis, Copybooks, 1845, 27, EWS coll.

37. Eaton was also mentor to Mary Lyon at Amherst, where she attended his lectures on chemistry and natural history so that she "might be prepared to illustrate by experiments the science of chemistry" (Ethel M. McAllister, *Amos Eaton, Scientist and Educator, 1776–1842* [Philadelphia: University of Pennsylvania Press, 1941], 354).

38. Ibid., 485.

39. Ibid., 204, 207. See also Letter from Julie Bacon to Mrs. Martha Bacon, 7 June 1821; Anonymous Letter in Kennedy Philips Letters, 19 June 1822; and Letter from Louise Russell to Sister Susan, 1 March 1823, all in Student Letter Collection, EWS coll.

40. McAllister, *Amos Eaton*, 488, 352.

41. Emma Lydia Bolzau, "Almira Hart Lincoln Phelps, Her Life and Work" (Ph.D. diss., University of Pennsylvania, 1936), 76, 78.

42. Ibid., 210–11.

43. Ibid., 212–14.

44. Ibid., 215–16.

45. Quoted in Bolzau, 216–17.

46. Ibid., 217 (emphasis in original).

47. Ibid., 218.

CHAPTER 8: A PRECEDENT FOR TECHNOLOGICAL EDUCATION

1. Amos Eaton was born in 1776 to Azubah and Abel Eaton in New Concord parish in Chatham, New York. See Ethel M. McAllister, *Amos Eaton, Scientist and Educator, 1776–1842* (Philadelphia: University of Pennsylvania Press, 1941).

2. McAllister, *Amos Eaton*, 71, 132, 155.

3. Ibid., 14–17.

4. Ibid., 172–74.

5. Ibid., 184. Silliman drew large audiences at the Lowell Institute in the early 1840s.

Rossiter notes that he "made it a point to visit many industrial works and to include practical items, but his main interest remained in describing the elements and their chemical compounds" (Margaret W. Rossiter, "Benjamin Silliman and the Lowell Institute: The Popularization of Science in Nineteenth-Century America," *New England Quarterly* 44 [December 1971]: 620).

6. Deborah Jean Warner, "Commodities for the Classroom: Apparatus for Science and Education in Antebellum America," *Annals of Science* 45, no. 4 (1988): 387–97; and Rossiter, "Benjamin Silliman and the Lowell Institute," 602–16.

7. McAllister, *Amos Eaton*, 212–13, 219.

8. Ibid., 264, 273, 289, 299.

9. McAllister, *Amos Eaton*, 346–47, 351. See also H. S. Van Klooster, *Amos Eaton as a Chemist* (Troy: Rensselaer Polytechnic Institute, n.d.).

10. McAllister, *Amos Eaton*, 357–58.

11. Ibid., 364–68; emphasis in original. A valuable summary of the state of engineering education in the United States before the Morrill Act of 1862 is found in Terry S. Reynolds, "The Education of Engineers in America before the Morrill Act of 1862," *History of Education Quarterly* 32, no. 4 (Winter 1992): 459–82. Reynolds argues that American colleges were not averse to practical education despite their reputation as bastions of classicism (459). He notes that the Rensselaer experiment in its first four years was not an engineering school and had more in common with mechanics' institutes and lyceums in its mission to diffuse useful knowledge (466).

12. Letter from Stephen Van Rensselaer to the Rev. Dr. Blatchford, Constitution and By-Laws of Rensselaer School in Troy, New York, 1825, 6–7, Archives and Special Collections, Rensselaer Polytechnic Institute. Hereafter cited as RPI coll.

13. Ibid., 8.

14. Ibid., 9; and Constitution and By-Laws, p. 18, RPI coll. Laboratory instruction in chemistry had several precedents in Europe, though Eaton may have known little of them. M. V. Lomonosov, who was a professor of chemistry at the Academy of Sciences of St. Petersburg gave lectures on physical chemistry from 1752 to 1756. After having heard the lectures, students worked in a laboratory studying the physical properties of substances. Practical chemistry was taught at Schemnitz in Hungary in 1770. At the Ecole du Genie Militaire and the Ecole Polytechnique, courses in practical chemistry were offered. At the latter, applied chemistry made great gains under A. F. Fourneroy and Bertahallet. Students carried out projects and received first-hand experience with a glassworks, pottery furnace, and lead chamber plant operated by the college. Regular visits were made to factories (W. A. Smeaton, "The Early History of Laboratory Instruction in Chemistry at the Ecole Polytechnique, Paris, and Elsewhere," *Annals of Science* 10, no. 3 (September 1954): 224–33.

15. Constitution and By-Laws, pp. 9, 15–16, RPI coll.

16. Constitution and By-Laws, p. 17, RPI coll.

17. "Rensselaer School Exercises, in the Fall, Winter, and Spring Terms, Including Those of the Preparation and District Branches," 1827, pp. 35–36, RPI coll.

18. The details of the critique are related in a "report" of the officer of the day, 27 August 1828. At 9:30, the officer of the day lectured before the special assistant and other students. This was followed by student critiques of the student lecture. Following this, the students broke into small groups. In these small groups, the students in one section

lectured to the officer of the day; in another, to the Senior Professor. The designation "officer of the day" can probably be traced to Eaton's experience while teaching at West Point. (McAllister, *Amos Eaton*, 389–90).

19. Constitution and By-Laws, Notices for the Ninth Annual Course, 1832 and 1833, pp. 15–16 RPI coll.

20. McAllister, *Amos Eaton*, 415.

21. Samuel Rezneck, *Education for a Technological Society: A Sesquicentennial History of Rensselaer Polytechnic Institute* (Troy, N.Y.: Rensselaer Polytechnic Institute, 1968), 43–44.

22. "Subjects Constituting the Course on Civil Engineering," Catalog of Rennselaer Institute, 1841–42, pp. 4–5.

23. McAllister, *Amos Eaton*, 418.

24. Rezneck, *Education for a Technological Society*, 78.

25. Benjamin Franklin Greene, "The Rensselaer Polytechnic Institute," *The True Idea of a Polytechnic Institute, Reprint for the 125th Anniversary of Rensselaer Polytechnic Institute* (Troy, 1949), 42–44.

26. "Programme, Etc., of the Rensselaer Institute; Polytechnic Institution at the City of Troy," February 1851, 5.

27. Robert McManus, Papers, 1827–31, 6 October 1828, RPI coll.

28. Ibid.

29. Ibid., 10.

30. George H. Cook, "Outlines of a Course of Lectures on Chemistry in Rensselaer Institute, Winter, 1844–45," Papers, 1838–44, RPI coll.

31. George H. Cook, "Diary," RPI coll.

32. Cook, "Diary"; Rezneck, *Education for a Technological Society*, 67.

33. Minutes of Meeting of Trustees, 1835, RPI coll.

34. Minutes of Meeting of Trustees, 1842, RPI coll.

35. Letter from Edward Augustine Holyoke Allen, 16 December 1849, Papers, 1847–54, RPI coll.

36. Ibid.

37. Dascom Greene, "Materials Used in Construction," Papers, 1852, RPI coll.

38. Ibid.

39. Theodore Cooper, Notebook, c. 1858, RPI coll.

40. Charles Downe, Lecture Notebook, 1859, RPI coll.

41. Thaddeus Sanford Smith, Papers, 1858–61, RPI coll.

42. Thaddeus Sanford Smith, "Course for Shades and Shadows," Papers, 1858–61, RPI coll.

43. McAllister, *Amos Eaton*, 181.

44. Emma Lydia Bolzau, "Almira Hart Lincoln Phelps, Her Life and Work" (Ph.D. diss., University of Pennsylvania, 1936, 74).

45. McAllister, *Amos Eaton*, 429.

46. Ibid., 484.

47. Ibid., 488–89.

48. Ibid., 489.

49. Ibid., 490.

50. Ibid.

51. Rezneck, *Education for a Technological Society*, 112.

INDEX

Abbott, Jacob, 25
*Abortion of the Young Steam Engineer's
  Guide* (1805), 13. *See* Evans, Oliver
Academies, female, 135
Adams, Daniel, 91
Adams' New Arithmetic (Adams) (1890),
  91
Advancement of Learning, 53. *See*
  Bacon, Francis
Algebra, 58, 59, 63; teaching of, 94–96,
  104
*American Annals of Education and
  Instruction*, 37, 39, 91
American Association for the Advance-
  ment of Science, 160
American Institute, 129
American Intellectual Arithmetic, The
  (Stoddard), 94
American Journal of Education, 38, 39,
  42, 64, 90
American Journal of Science, 64
American Mechanics' Magazine, 101
American Polytechnic Journal, The, 38,
  85
American Railway Journal, 80, 83, 85
American system, 23, 181n61. *See*
  Interchangeable parts
Analytic Mechanics (Lagrange) (1788),
  57

Apparatus, 47, 66, 73, 75, 76, 79, 85,
  117, 123, 171, 172; in colleges, 75, 140
*Applications of the Science of Mechan-
  ics to Practical Purposes* (Renwick)
  (1840), 80. *See* Renwick, James
Apprentice, 24, 25, 30, 83, 101, 117;
  moral advice to, 24, 109
Apprentice's Companion, The (New
  York), 80, 83, 101
Apprentices' Library (Cincinnati), 127
Archimedean screw, 68
Aristotle, 51, 53, 54, 187n1
Arithmetic, 38; teaching of, 87–94, 119
*Arithmetic, Designed for Academies
  and Schools* (1852), 93, 96. *See*
  Davies, Charles
*Arithmetical Dictionary, or Book of
  Reference* (W. Young) (1847), 90
Armories, 19, 22; and John H. Hall,
  22; at Springfield, Mass., 22; Eli
  Whitney's, 22
*Art Without Science; or the Art of Sur-
  veying . . .* (Eaton) 148. *See* Eaton,
  Amos
Artisans (craftsmen), 26, 64, 107, 110

Bacon, Francis, 51, 54, 55, 61, 74, 104,
  172; empiricism of, 3; philosophy of
  induction, 52; utopia of, 53